JACOB B

ESSENTIAL READINGS

Robin Waterfield

has been a student of Boehme for over 50 years, and study of his writings and his life has led to a fascination for the Western form of the universal Hermetic Tradition. This proved invaluable for his 15 years' work as a Christian missionary in Iran and his training as a Jungian counsellor. His previous books for Crucible— *The Esoteric Path* (which he translated and expanded) and *René Guénon*—both stemmed from his respect for Boehme, whom he considers to be a seminal figure for the Aquarian Age.

Frontispiece: From *Works of Jacob Behmen, Vol I*, 1764 (courtesy of The Bodleian Library, Oxford : Shelfmark Vet A5.d1133).

JACOB BOEHME

ESSENTIAL READINGS

Edited and introduced by
ROBIN WATERFIELD

First published 1989

Selection and Introduction © **Robin Waterfield**

All rights reserved. No part of this book
may be reproduced or utilized in any form
or by any means, electronic or mechanical,
including photocopying, recording,
or by any information storage and
retrieval system, without permission
in writing from the Publisher.

British Library
Cataloguing in Publication Data

Boehme, Jacob, *1575–1624*
Jacob Boehme : essential readings.
1. Christian theology
I. Title   II. Waterfield, Robin
230

ISBN 1-85274-041-8

Crucible is an imprint of
The Aquarian Press,
part of the Thorsons Publishing Group,
Wellingborough, Northamptonshire, NN8 2RQ,
England

Photoset by
Rowland Phototypesetting Limited,
Bury St Edmunds, Suffolk

Printed and bound in Great Britain by
Woolnough Bookbinding, Irthlingborough, Northants

1 3 5 7 9 10 8 6 4 2

ESSENTIAL READINGS

The *Essential Readings* series is designed as an introduction to the thought and work of major figures in the history of ideas, particularly in the realm of metaphysics. An anthology of Boehme's writings is a particularly welcome addition to this series because his is, perhaps, one of the most interesting minds in the history of European mystical thought. As such Boehme has held an appeal for such distinguished minds as Milton and Blake; Angelus Silesius and William Law; Hegel and Schopenhauer. Though he himself was a relatively uneducated man, often lamenting his inability to express his ideas more clearly, Boehme has had an influence upon many of our intellectual giants. There is no doubt that their indebtedness to his thought is far greater and more pervasive than the few references to him would suggest.

In his writing, Boehme, sometimes called the 'Teutonic Theosopher', treats of things beyond everyday experience. His works, therefore, are not always easy to understand. His language can be obscure, his imagery hard to interpret. One of the difficulties is that his language is not always consistent; sense and meaning shift, images change, really demanding new definitions. Modern readers may be thrown by his cosmology and the references to alchemical and cabbalistic imagery and symbolism which Boehme borrowed from his knowledge of Paracelsus. Robin Waterfield's guidance on Boehme's language in the chapter 'The World of Boehme's Writings' is an important and useful aspect of this anthology.

NICHOLAS GOODRICK-CLARKE
June 1988

Dedicated to the memory of
Herr & Fräulein von Kersting and Frau Hasenklever of
Langewehe who first spoke to me of Boehme in 1931–2.

CONTENTS

'. . . insistence on personal first-hand experience and practice of the Christ-Life, as the ground of true religion, is the fundamental feature of Boehme's Christianity. He travels as we shall see through immense heights and deeps. Like Dante . . . he saw the eternal realities of heaven and hell and the world between and he told as well as he could what he *saw*, but his practical message which runs like a thread through all his writings is always simple—almost childlike in its simplicity—"Thou must thyself be the way. The spiritual understanding must be born in thee". "A Christian is a new creature in the ground of the heart." "The Kingdom of God, is not from without, but it is a new man, who lives in love, in patience, in hope, in faith and in the Cross of Jesus Christ." "Life," he once said, "is a strange bath of thorns and thistles" and he himself experienced that "bath", but he went through the world hearing everywhere a divine music and "having a joy in his heart which made his whole being tremble and his soul triumph as if it were in God".'

R.M. JONES
Spiritual Reformers of the 16th and 17th Centuries (1914) p.171

Joannes Sparrow.

Amator τῆς. { Θεοσοφίας και Φιλοσοφίας. } IACOBI Boehme.

Teutonici.

I. S. natus: 1615. 12. II. May

D. Loggan delin. et sculp. 1659.

From *Mysterium Magnum*, 1656.

PART ONE

THE BACKGROUND

1

INTRODUCTION

JACOB BOEHME, born in Germany in the last quarter of the
sixteenth century, was born at a time and place of peculiar
significance. Luther had been dead nearly thirty years and the
Reformation he inaugurated had passed through its original stage
of ardent revolt, confusion, and intense opposition to Rome.
The situation in many places was somewhat similar to that in
Revolutionary Russia in the Stalinist era. The reformers like the
revolutionaries had settled down to consolidate their gains. This
they did by propagating a hardline orthodoxy with all the
bigotry and intolerance of their predecessors against whom they
had rebelled.

But then, as now, Orthodoxy was not entirely successful.
Minority groups of dissidents persisted and proliferated. The
Reformation was international and dissidents could find refuge
in other places; an advantage not available in Stalin's Russia. The
imposition of uniformity was not possible. Shortly before
Boehme's birth the Counter-Reformation inaugurated by The
Council of Trent (1546–63) had restored some of the initiative
for Reform to the Roman Church. But dissidents equally sus-
picious of both orthodoxies remained active and carried on their
subversive activities with varying success. Görlitz, Boehme's
birthplace, was a place of refuge for members of many such
groups.

From Boehme's point of view the most influential of these
groups was that which stemmed from the life and teachings of
Caspar Schwenkfeld (1489–1561), a Silesian nobleman who was

persecuted by both Protestants and Catholics.

Schwenkfeld had once been a pupil of Luther but later became one of his most dedicated opponents, accusing him of having betrayed the cause of Reform and of having done no more than perpetuate Popery under a new guise. As time went by Schwenkfeld became more and more convinced that the visible institutional dogmatic church, no matter what it called itself, was a work of man and so tainted with human sin and ignorance that it could never provide the individual seeker with any sure foundation. For him the only church was the *Kirche ohne Mauer*, the invisible church, whose members were freely united in bonds of mutual tolerance. A place where, as Boehme says in one of his letters, 'all grows there in friendly companionship, all rejoice to have the one mother and the branches of the tree mutually exchange their sap and their strength in mutual support'. (Letter 46). The mother be it noted was not the church but Sophia, the Divine Wisdom. It is worth noting that though Boehme was greatly influenced by Schwenkfeld's ideas and many of his patrons were Schwenkfeldians, he always maintained his status as a practising Lutheran and criticized some of Schwenkfeld's more extreme theological positions.

Schwenkfeld was expelled from Silesia in 1529 and lived in exile in Strasburg. But he left behind a small body of adherents, chiefly among the landed gentry, from which class he himself had come. This group remained and even flourished in spite of periodic harassment by the ecclesiastical authorities, and survived into the nineteenth century. In 1826 some of Schwenkfeld's followers established themselves in the United States, where they still exist to this day.

Besides the followers of Schwenkfeld, Silesia gave refuge to many other such groups, including Anabaptists, Moravian Brothers, Crypto-Calvinists and Hussites, against all of whom the established church had to contend.

But the religious ferment was only one aspect of a more comprehensive stirring in the human mind of the time. It was a time when men and women seemed to be waking from a long sleep and beginning to look in a new way at the world around them. The mediaeval dream was over and the closed universe of

Ptolemy had gone with it. Copernicus (1473–1543) had begun
the new way of looking at the world and there is evidence that
Boehme knew of his theories. Paracelsus (1493–1541), sometimes called the Luther of Medicine, also led the long return to an
experimental method of understanding the world which had
been neglected for a thousand years.

Many others contributed to this new way of looking at the
world but I have chosen these two men because they are supreme
examples of the fact that in Boehme's day men still retained a
holistic view of nature. Theology and the scientific method were
still complementary, with theology remaining Queen of the
Sciences. Copernicus and many others could still pay serious
attention to astrological teachings, and Paracelsus still believed in
sympathetic magic, something akin to what we today might call
holistic medicine. Both astrology and alchemy were part of the
intellectual furniture of every thinking man at this time and
Boehme was no exception.

The time, like our own, was a hinge period when old
certainties were destroyed and thinking people felt inclined to
face two ways; striving to save something from the past and yet
fascinated and exhilarated by the prospects of new forms of
living held out to them by the future.

One other source of influence which moulded Boehme's way
of seeing things was undoubtedly the movement known as
Rosicrucianism. Boehme, and many others, felt that Luther's
reformation had not gone far enough and that a *Reformatio Nova*
was called for which would establish Christ's reign in men's
hearts and sweep away Babel. Babel was the word Boehme used
for all the worldly wrangling and power-seeking and enmity
which he saw both amongst religious people and in the secular
world of politics and diplomacy.

The Rosicrucian ideas had long been abroad and the publication of a strange pamphlet in 1614 only brought them into
the open. In Cassel, a north German town, there appeared a
pamphlet with the strange title 'Allgemeine und General
Reformation der ganzen weiten Welt der Fama Fraternitatis dess
Loblichen Ordens des Rosenkreutzes . . . *Cassel* 1614'. Other
similar pamphlets appeared all over Europe and aroused great

curiosity and the expectation that some new and startling revelation was about to be made. The tone of the pamphlets was satirical but their readers felt that they had some deeper meaning and significance.

The original pamphlet is now widely considered to have been from the hand of Johann Valentin Andrae (1586–1654). The long and very obscure history of Rosicrucianism is unnecessary here. It is sufficient for our understanding of its influence on Boehme to say that it represented an age-old secret tradition linking the West with the East, sometimes called the Hermetic Tradition. The movement is also sometimes called Pansophism, by which is meant the search for a universal wisdom uniting and explaining all things, a means of reconciling the ways of God to man and of penetrating the mystery of nature by finding its underlying unity. Andrae was a Lutheran pastor and one of a distinguished band of Lutherans who sought a more personal, and some would say spiritual, religion than that evolved in the mainstream Lutheran churches. Two names are important in this respect, Sebastian Franck and Valentin Weigel, whose influence was enormous and was undoubtedly felt by Boehme who called Weigel 'the high master'.

The Hermetic Tradition also included such sacred sciences as Astrology, Alchemy, the Cabala and its related numerology, all of which will be considered separately.

It would therefore be wrong to see Boehme as an isolated eccentric or as psychologically ill because he entertained such ideas. He was obviously extremely well-versed in this Hermetic Knowledge, knowledge which has always had a precarious and semi-concealed place in the history of the Christian church in the West and can be ranged alongside the more openly heretical ideas of Gnostics, the Albigensians, and the Templars. In addition, one may point to certain similar tendencies within the monastic orders often associated with the name of Joachim da Fiore and in a more general way with Dante's *Divine Comedy* and his *Convitio*.

Such, in a very compressed form, is the background against which Boehme's writings have to be understood. We do not claim that he was aware of all the sources of the Hermetic Tradition. But he was obviously conversant with many of the subjects we have mentioned and had many personal friends who would have introduced him to such ideas, and we know that he was an avid reader.

In addition to these intellectual and personal influences we should not neglect the importance of the geographical situation of Görlitz. Lusatia, a province of Silesia, is far to the East on the border where Germans and Slavs meet. The name Boehme suggests that his family may have been of Slav origin.

Lusatia was a poor province compared with its neighbours, having neither the mineral wealth of Saxony nor the trade brought to Silesia by the river Oder. The province enjoyed a degree of religious freedom and toleration unknown to its neighbour Saxony, where in 1555 the Elector Palatine had instituted a very strict political and confessional regime.

Görlitz in Boehme's day was by no means a provincial backwater. It had 10,000 inhabitants, about the same number as Munich and nearly half as many again as Heidelberg. It was an important trading post between East and West and had a prosperous trade in leather and textiles.

At this time also Görlitz was an important centre of humanist thought and tolerance after the example of Erasmus. This was largely due to the activities of one of its municipal councillors Bartholomaeus Scultetus (Schultze). He was keenly interested in the natural sciences and was a friend of Tycho Brahe who was at that time astronomer to the Danish court. In 1607 Schultze was visited by no less a celebrity than Johannes Kepler. Schultze himself had written a book on astronomy and had attempted to reform the Gregorian calendar.

Both Boehme and his milieu are important, and an appreciation of them will help us to see his writings not as the eccentric outpourings of a religious maniac or an unbalanced visionary but rather as the flowering of a long and noble religious and philosophical inheritance under the genius of a religious and philosophical giant whose influence has spread throughout the Western world and whose writings still contain a lot for us to learn today.

2

LIFE AND TIMES

JACOB BOEHME was born in 1575 in the village of Alt Seidenberg near the larger town of Görlitz in Upper Lusatia. The exact date of his birth is not known but we know that he was the fourth son of a prosperous yeoman farmer whose family had long been settled in the area. He attended the school in Alt Seidenberg where the headmaster Dr Leder had the reputation of being a learned man. Besides being well-grounded in the basic subjects and in religion Boehme may well have picked up at least a smattering of Latin. During his school-days he would have helped on the farm. Very early on it seems he had unusual experiences as when he and some of his school friends discovered a hole in the mountainside and a cave full of money which they could never find again.

When he left school at the age of fourteen he was deemed not to be sufficiently physically strong for the life of a farmer so he was apprenticed to a shoemaker in Görlitz. His apprenticeship would have lasted five years, after which he would be a journeyman entitled to work anywhere. He does not appear to have found life as an apprentice easy. He is reported to have complained about the bad language used in the workshop and his master said he did not want a prophet in his house. From 1594 to 1599 it seems probable that Boehme did what many journeymen did at that time, travelled. We know nothing about these *wanderjahre* but we find him back in Görlitz in 1599. In April he was admitted into the Guild of Shoemakers as a master-craftsman and became a citizen of Görlitz. He set up on his own in a shop in the square known as the Untermarkt and in May of the same year he married Katherina Huntschmann, daughter of a butcher. In August they bought a house near the Niesse Gate on Topferberg Hill.

So by the turn of the century Boehme seemed, in spite of the turbulence of the times, to be set to lead a happy pious family life. His first son was born on 29 January 1600 and christened Jacob. Six more children followed between then and 1613. In 1610 he bought a larger house and in 1612 between New Year and Whit Sunday he composed his first book *Morgenrote im Anfang oder Aurora*. He states that he had no intention of publishing it, having written it solely as an *aide memoire* for himself.

How did it come about then that a humble shoemaker should write such a work? The popular notion of an illiterate cobbler must at once be discarded. Boehme had obviously attracted the attention of some of the better educated people in the town. We know for instance that when Martin Moller became Primarius of Görlitz in 1600 he set about organizing a study group in the parish which he called the 'Conventicle of God's Real Servants' and Boehme joined it. Moller was a learned man and the author of numerous works of a mystical nature which owed much to the Fathers of the Church, notably St Augustine, and to a very wide range of later mystical writers, both French and German. We also know that in 1610 Boehme had an inner vision alerting him to the fact that God had given him a special revelation and calling. This was the sequel to an earlier vision when he saw the sun shining on a pewter jug and felt an inward illumination that revealed to him the secrets of hidden nature.

But his life was not all plain sailing; in 1604 he found himself in trouble with the Tanners' Corporation for tanning hides without their consent. For the next eight years there was a running battle between the Shoemakers and the Tanners, Boehme particularly upsetting the latter by buying hides in bulk. Eventually the Shoemakers emerged the victors. There is a document in the Town Archives in what looks very like Boehme's handwriting recording the fact and praising God for victory.

These disputes and the fact that he had begun to write and

acquire a certain following among some enquiring spirits in the town are probably the reason why in 1613 he sold his shop.

As we have already suggested Görlitz was a centre of heterodox teaching and the town and surrounding countryside had known a succession of wandering preachers who spread heresies of various kinds and who gave the authorities great cause for alarm. When Martin Moller left Görlitz he was replaced by Gregor Richter, a man of a very different stamp. He was coarse and harsh and, if Boehme himself is to be believed, addicted to alcohol. His language was typical of the earthy crude vulgarity of the day, his ecclesiastical stance was that of unbending Lutheran orthodoxy.

Boehme's troubles began when Carl von Ender, who was of a noble family and had been a member with Boehme of Moller's Conventicle, took the manuscript of Boehme's book and had it copied and circulated. A copy came into the hands of Richter who was appalled that a shoemaker should issue such a book. On 26 July 1613 Boehme was arrested on the orders of the Town Council and spent some days in prison. Bartholomaeus Schultze's diary for this period has survived and under this date we read: 'Jacob Boehme a shoemaker was summoned to the Town Hall and at the same time his book a quarto manuscript was brought by Oswald the town policeman, after which he was released from prison and commanded to refrain from such activities'.

Boehme agreed to this and did not publish anything more for a long time. But Richter vindictively pursued him, preached against him in the church, and turned the townspeople against him. Richter went so far as to issue a number of pamphlets against 'the illiterate and smelly' shoemaker. This must surely indicate that Boehme had some standing amongst those liable to be interested in mystical writings which were in Richter's eyes bound therefore to be heretical.

Among Boehme's friends we know were included a number of Schwenkfeldians and Balthasar Walter. Walter was a very unusual man, he had travelled widely in Europe and the Middle East. He was greatly interested in Paracelsus and wrote a number of books of a mystical or occult kind. Later he took up a post in Dresden and finally became physician to the Prince of Anhalt. He was so impressed by Boehme that he actually spent several months living in his house in Görlitz. Other friends who no doubt influenced Boehme were Johann Huser, the editor of an edition of Paracelsus, and the doctor Tobias Kober who attended him in his last illness.

As a result of giving up his shop Boehme and his family suffered some hardship. They received help from some of his wealthy patrons, but he had to travel a lot buying and selling in order to make a living. Matters were not made easier by the outbreak of the Thirty Years War in 1618 and the general disruption of normal life in the area which this event caused.

In 1619 Boehme was in Prague on business and witnessed the triumphal entry of Frederick the Fifth, the Elector Palatine, and his English wife Elizabeth, daughter of King James the First. It is interesting to recall that at this time the young René Descartes, then aged 25, was a volunteer in the Bavarian army which overwhelmed Bohemia and ended the reign of Frederick.

Boehme's letters show that he had a hard time but was able to do some business supplying the various armies as the war spread into Lusatia, Silesia, and other parts of Germany. In 1620 Bautzen, only forty kilometres from Görlitz, was besieged and Boehme in a letter to Balthasar Walter describes the state of the city and of the unfortunate soldiers who took part in the siege, using the eye witness accounts of refugees whom he had met.

During all this period Boehme was intensely active travelling on business; visiting friends and writing them long letters; and engaging in meetings and semi-public discussions of his ideas. It was also during these five years 1619–24 that he wrote the vast majority of his books, which when one recalls that his collected works extend to eleven volumes totalling over a quarter of a million words, to say nothing of the mass of unpublished material collected and edited by Werner Buddecke in two large quarto volumes, one can only be amazed at his industry.

The last year of Boehme's life, 1624, was crowded with incident. In January a Dresden nobleman, Johann Siegismund von Schweinichen, had Boehme's devotional treatise *Der Weg zu Christo* printed by Johann Rhamba in Görlitz. This was his first appearance in print. This outrageous behaviour incensed Pastor

Richter who attacked Boehme from the pulpit and issued more virulent printed attacks on him, including a Latin poem of great coarseness.

In March the following extract is found in the Memorials of the Town of Görlitz: '26.3.1624 Jochem Boehme shoemaker the enthusiast or confused phantast . . . was invited to pitch his tent elsewhere', i.e. he and his family were forcibly compelled to leave the town.

In May he received an invitation through his patron to the Court of the Elector of Saxony in Dresden. He went but was disappointed in only having several unofficial conversations with Court officials but not the interview with the Elector and the proposed formal debate on his works which he had hoped for.

He returned home disappointed and dispirited to find his family undergoing persecution and the schoolmaster refusing to teach his children. One slight relief occurred when on 24 August his great enemy Paster Richter died, only to be replaced by another hard-liner, Pastor Nikolaus Thomas. In September and October Boehme made a last round of visits to his friends in various parts of Silesia. He arrived back on 7 November accompanied by his friend and doctor Tobias Kober. He was ill and worn out physically, though not spiritually; even under these conditions he had to undergo a doctrinal inquisition from Pastor Thomas before he was allowed to receive communion. He died on 17 November at his house in Görlitz. Pastor Thomas at first refused to take the burial service but Doctor Kober persuaded the Town Council to compel him to do so. A few days later a rabble from the town desecrated his grave and smashed the stone cross which his friends had erected on it. Many people have seen a certain parallelism between the fate of the servant and that of his Master.

3

THE WORLD OF BOEHME'S WRITINGS

MANY have spoken of the poetic supralogical nature of Boehme's thought as expressed in his writings. As Alexander Koyré says: 'Words and speech are not for Boehme, a means of recording conceptual thought; but are the living expression of living reality which takes shape and definition in the process of expression, this is why all the constituent elements of the spoken discourse contribute to and are an integral part of the actual expression' (l.c. p xv).

So any schematic or logical analysis of Boehme's thought would provide us with a skeleton only. Boehme more than most writers puts all of himself into his writing. An authentic living person is present in everything he wrote, with a voice, a vocabulary, and a way of saying things which is entirely his own and unlike any other. We, if we are to understand him, have to put as much of ourselves into the reading of him as he has put into the writing of what we are reading. The truths he propounds have to be lived to be understood. For as Koyré wrote, Boehme 'does not present the reader with ready made ideas, he does not wish to instil his reader with *his* ideas but rather to suggest and stimulate acts and mental attitudes which will encourage the dawning light of truth in the individual soul'. Hegel, who devoted a eulogistic chapter of his *History of Philosophy* to Boehme, said that he should be read by one free of all prior assumptions and *idées reçues*, allowing the words to take charge of us rather than our attempting to dominate and explain them. He called Boehme's language *Natur-sprache*, natural speech, communicating freely and personally through the heart and the emotions, or rather through that deeper fusion of them with reason and the will, which constitutes the whole person. This his words do by means of their mysterious sonority and the power of resonating in us which that gives them; they can truly strike a chord in any human heart ready to receive them.

The question of language is all important for Boehme, and we may well sympathize with L. C. de St Martin and wish to emulate him when late in life he taught himself German in order to read Boehme's works in their original language. However, the early English translations, mainly the work of John Sparrow a translator of genius, were made within half a century of the translations of the Authorized Version of the Bible and share with it much of the richness and beauty of its language, for which it is so justly famous. It is in the main Sparrow's translations which I have used in this volume. Given that Boehme's writings are an entire microcosm, reflecting through one individual the whole of God's creation, including His self-creation, it is obviously impossible to provide the new reader with a simple guide. Every reader will find his own way in the writings as he lives with them and will take from them what he personally finds of value.

I will highlight certain recurring themes or concepts and, as far as space permits, reveal the nature of certain sources of his language and imagery with which the non-specialist reader is unlikely to be familiar, namely, Alchemy (mainly as understood by Paracelsus), the Cabala (particularly as it was interpreted by Christians), and Mediaeval Astrology.

One of the dominant themes in Boehme's writings is the utter transcendence of God: His existence outside time and space, inaccessible to all human thought, ineffable by any human tongue.

What then is left which we can conceive of? Nothing is left, a nothing which Boehme calls the *Ungrund*, often translated into English by the word Abyss, a depth which has no end, a bottomless empty nothingness. Such a concept is difficult for

Western minds to conceive but is quite familiar to Eastern thought.

What then is this Void? It is not absolutely 'nothingness'. It is the alogical to which no categories drawn from the world of name and form apply . . . A Vedantist would say that Being or Is-ness [German: Istigkeit] is applicable to it even in the case of the Void . . . but it is nothing known to finite experience in form and therefore for those who have no other experience, it is nothing (Woodroffe in the introduction to Evans Wentz, *Tibetan Book of the Dead*, xxxvii).

This *Ungrund* can only be imagined and is the primal image of the unknowable entity who in traditional wisdom is not to be given a name but can only be announced as 'I AM'.

With the introduction of the personal pronoun, imagination has taken a great leap of faith. For Boehme this Void, this dark abyss, is not sterile and passive but is active and fertile, possessed by a motivating energy and Desire (Trieb). This Desire is for self-knowledge and moves both the knower and the known. Even though they are but One, in them the first division appears. For the essential nature of the undetermined Divinity is freedom. Therefore in the *Ungrund* there is infinite potentiality as regards all that lies within it: not static perfection but dynamic ever-increasing perfection, always becoming, not being, but still in perfectly harmonious balance. For Boehme the *Ungrund* is also *'die ewige Stille'*, eternal Rest.

Once this movement has been revealed to our imagination we can then, by the same faculty, trace its development. This Boehme does in considerable detail. From our present standpoint · we may say, as did Schleiermacher, that Boehme's writings are in fact 'esoteric psychology' or, the psychology of the depths. When Boehme describes the birth of God, we may prefer to say that he is describing the birth of God in the individual human soul. God's desire and man's desire are one, each mutually engendering the other. Boehme indicates that this desire is to be seen in all creation; all is moved by the same urge to perfection —consummation. This divine impulse, God's fiat, is for Boehme the *Mysterium Magnum*, a desire existing in the Heart or Centre of God which has to be given form and substance. We will return to the subject of creation later when we consider the Cabala and its doctrine of *Tsim-Tsum*.

Boehme's imagery is always very close to our natural physical experience. He chose the fundamental concept of fire and his theology has been described as a theology of fire, fire in its dual aspect of the giver of heat and light, and of destroyer and transformer.

This desire Boehme compares to a burning sensation, which produces anxiety and pain as we are confronted with the impenetrability of the *Mysterium Magnum*. Boehme in one of his letters says: 'The more man reaches out to God, groans and struggles to reach Him, the more he departs from his aim and must start again at the beginning'. He likens the struggle to the pangs of a woman giving birth, since the birth of the new man—the birth of God in us—is always accompanied by terror and anguish.

For Boehme the activity within the *Ungrund* and the emergence of a contrary will to that which maintained the eternal rest may be imaginatively compared to Light and Dark, since movement could only occur as there are opposites by which differences can be made manifest. So Light can never be known without Darkness.

Boehme describes what occurs eternally as the Divine manifests itself continually in seven stages or Forms of Nature. The first Form Boehme calls **Harshness** or Obduracy. It is the principle which maintains the status of all and resists changes. It is a turning in on the Self, it is darkness, obscurity, concentration, solidification (hardening), and may occur spiritually in us. It is the inertia that refuses to be convicted of sin, or to submit to God's will or to be loving and open towards others; it is Darkness. Once the process of Manifestation has begun it is irreversible, but the primal Will still wills the original state of unity and light to be maintained, so it gives rise to the second Form of Nature, **Attraction**.

This is the contrary motion or reaction to the first Form and is the means whereby unity can be restored, by seeking to draw things into combinations and relationships. Attraction is active whereas Harshness is passive. It is the desire which drives us ever

onward and is thus insatiable. It is the tension between these two
Forms which gives rise to the third Form of Nature which
Boehme calls **Bitterness**, the feeling of tension or what G. W.
Allen calls strain, of being pulled two ways, of having an
incurable wound caused by the division. A tension which may
lead us to repentance and hope or to defiance and despair.

Out of this tension or friction rises the fourth Form, **Fire**. It is
at this point, when the first triad, comparable to the philosophical notion of thesis, antithesis, and synthesis, has been manifested, that human self-consciousness arises and so also the
possibility of choice. This possibility is reflected in the ambivalent nature of Fire.

It is difficult for us today with our central heating and
electricity to easily recall the part that fire played in the everyday
life of Boehme's time. Fire was produced from hard flintstone
and the spark or *Funkelein* was an image of the Divine Life from
Eckhart onwards. It is also, as we shall see, one of the prime
features of Alchemy. Boehme had obviously seen fire used to
heat and work on metals and uses this imagery frequently. When
a metal bar is heated it does not immediately glow red hot, there
is a period of dark heat when it can be painful and wounding.
This is the first stage in the evolution. The strain and friction
increases and fire eventually reaches its light-giving glow, but
before it reaches this final stage there is the intermediate stage of
being red hot when there is some element of light as well as heat,
but the light is weak and low and only reveals things dimly. This
is the half light by which unregenerate man sees things and is full
of greed, wrath, and pride.

But the process can continue until the iron glows white-hot
giving rise to the fifth Form, **Light**—the true light and the light
of truth. As this light arises the angry fire sinks down into a calm
and pleasant warmth, its anger having been turned into light.

In this Light the first three Forms change their contentious
character and become calm, gentle, and harmonious. They are
reconciled to their interdependence and the role they *all* have to
play in the 'great work'. 'It is the change', says Allen, 'which
could be called the passing from self-consciousness to cosmic
consciousness', i.e. when, instead of thinking that the universe

was made for us, we realize that we were made for the universal whole to serve a greater purpose than self-gratification.

The sixth Form of Nature Boehme calls **Sound** (Ton). The idea of sound was connected in the mediaeval mind with two concepts: that of the fiat of God who *spake* and it was done and also of the notion of harmony, the harmony of the spheres, the heavenly music in which all conflicting individual sounds were harmoniously united in perfect concord.

These six Forms of Nature are in numerical agreement with the six days of creation, six being as St Augustine said the perfect number representing the six possible extensions in time and space. St Clement of Alexandria said of God: 'He is Alpha and Omega, in him are completed the six infinite extensions of time and from them they extend towards the infinite and herein lies the secret of the number seven'.

In Boehme's sequence the seventh and final Form of Nature is **Figure**, the total realization or ideal expression or configuration of the whole which is greater than the sum of its parts. All the parts of the whole are seen as signs of the whole, each individual part pointing to the whole and endueing it with its *sign*-ificance or meaning.

I hope that enough has been said to enable the reader to set out with some confidence on his own voyage of discovery.

Numbers for Boehme, as for all his contemporaries, were imbued with a significance far beyond that of elementary mathematics. They pointed towards an otherwise unattainable reality. It is not surprising therefore that for Boehme, believing Christian as he was, the number three should have a special significance. Boehme's Three Principles are in fact a reworking of his exposition of the seven Forms on a ternary basis.

The Three Principles

We have included in the text Boehme's own exposition of the Three Principles. I think we shall find that Boehme's exposition is a little uneasy in that he has attempted to impose a trinitarian form on his seven Forms of Nature. The first Principle corresponds to the Father, the second to the Son, and the third to the Holy Ghost. The first three forms together with the fourth as a hinge or bridge uniting the first and second Principles leaves the last in an ambivalent situation. Most frequently it represents man in his created and manifest state and is the locus of the action of the Holy Spirit. Boehme never completely reconciled the wrath of God of which he was intensely conscious with the notion of the all-loving God of conventional Christianity.

But we can see Boehme's writings not as the final word on the absolutely insoluble question of the Nature of God and the origin of evil, but as the wrestling of an intensely serious human soul, seeking the way to Christ, and in seeking finding the Way which is Christ himself. For over and above Boehme's speculations in the earlier sense of the word, there remains his absolute conviction of the indwelling of the Trinity in us if we so desire. All his writings, as his letters show, are designed to bring this to pass in his readers. The tragedy of Lucifer, the fallen angel, is potentially the tragedy that can befall each one of us. Over and over again the nowness, the presentness, the presence of Salvation are brought home with a wealth of imagery.

Where does the soul go after death? Boehme replies: 'It has no need to go; it has heaven and hell within itself. The Kingdom of God is within you—Heaven and Hell are within one another and are to one another as a nothing'.

Again and again he rebuts the prevailing emphasis on the transcendence of God which located Him far away in Heaven and in need of a whole hierarchy of ecclesiastical mediators before we can reach Him, and a whole school of theologians to explain Him to us by dogmas and doctrines.

This call to immediacy and a personal relationship with the Christ within us has always been that which above all else draws men to Him. May those who read this book and are led to study Boehme achieve this relationship in and through him.

4

THE SACRED SCIENCES

THE title of this chapter may cause some puzzlement to many of its readers. The association of the two words seems somehow to be wrong. Science has to do with material things and as such is not to be confused with the spiritual, the religious, or the sacred. Has not the West spent the last 500 years emancipating science from the restraining shackles of religion? It is true this is what we have done and in so doing have unlocked the secrets of the material world and harnessed it to the satisfaction of our material ambitions. But in so doing we have lost a whole dimension. By divorcing the sacred from the scientific we have discovered a great deal but we have lost even more. We have lost our tripartite nature and reduced ourselves to a Cartesian dualism of body and mind and nothing else.

But in Boehme's time this reduction had not occurred. All knowledge (science) was sacred and the sacred was as accessible to us as are the secrets of Nature. Hence Boehme's fearless tackling of the deepest and most abtruse problems concerning the origin and nature of God, the point of difference being the means whereby such knowledge could become available to us.

For material science, man's reasoning powers applied to his observations of nature were sufficient; for the sacred sciences, man's ability to respond as a spiritual being to God's word given through nature and received directly in the heart. In Nature everything was a sign, by means of which, under the guidance of the Holy Spirit, we could interpret the *Liber Mundi*, the Book of the World in which the Heavens declare the glory of God and the

Earth shows forth His handiwork. The Venerable Bede, for instance, had no hesitation in compiling a list of rules for divination from thunder.

The sacred sciences by and large are concerned with the same objects as material science but they look at them differently, they ask different questions about them. Essentially they seek to learn what message they have for us from our common originator, God. Boehme devoted a whole book which he called *De Signatura Rerum* to this sacred science and not surprisingly it is one of the most difficult for moderns to understand.

Today the words 'sacred sciences' seem to include a contradiction. We tend to think of individual sacred sciences such as alchemy and astrology as pre-scientific guesses at the true sciences we now call chemistry and astronomy. Other sacred sciences, such as that concerned with the siting and orientation of buildings, that concerned with divination, geomancy and sacred geometry, the arts connected with the Cabala, and the various means of interpreting sacred texts, all seem to us, as we might say, mere superstitions. And notions such as the macrocosm and the microcosm and the ancient idea of correspondences enshrined in the gnomic saying 'as above so below' are all virtually meaningless to us.

But if we are to come to grips with Boehme we have also in some measure to come to grips with this neglected knowledge and to relate it wherever we can to our fumbling efforts to recover it, whether it be by means of the range of alternative medicine, depth psychology, or certain scientific speculations such as Neils Bohr's principle of complementarity or Jung's concept of synchronicity. Others will find it easier to understand Boehme if they have some familiarity with Hindu, Buddhist, or Taoist teachings.

Some development of these ideas seems necessary to understand Boehme and his particular use of these ways of looking at Nature and God.

Modern science has achieved its success by analysis, by discriminating between one thing and another, by isolating chemical substances from one another, by discovering the *how* of everything. For a long time this materialistic, mechanical model seemed to fit all the facts—and still does for all practical purposes. Only with the advent of quantum mechanics has this model proved to be inadequate. Now we are once again at a hinge point, when synthesis seems as important as analysis, where a field theory uniting previously unrelated phenomena is now worth seeking for, where a holistic approach to man as a tripartite entity consisting of body, mind, and spirit is a valid way forward.

Alchemy

If we first take as an example the ancient science of alchemy, it may help us to understand. Many people are surprised to hear that Sir Isaac Newton, founder of modern science, had an almost lifelong interest in alchemy. Even as late as the eighteenth century some vestiges of the sacred sciences still had a hold on the minds of thinking people, and Newton's alchemy, as the research of Ms Dobbs has shown, 'is a crucial link between Renaissance Hermeticism and rational chemistry'. By Newton's time the sacred nature of alchemy had been almost entirely forgotten. The sacred nature of alchemy means two things: first, that the aims and objectives of all alchemical work were subsumed under one ultimate objective, the achievement of which was known as 'The Great Work'. This was expressed in various ways: as the discovery of the Elixir Vitae, the finding of The Philosopher's Stone, or the Transmutation of Base Metals into the highest and purest metal, Gold. It does not need much insight to see that all these objectives had a transcendental aspect and symbolized a spiritual objective. The attainment of the physical success was only a symbolic confirmation of the ultimate objective which was spiritual. For this reason the attitude of mind and spiritual intention of the alchemist were of paramount importance. Equally, the correct planetary disposition according to the doctrine of correspondences was also of the utmost importance. This was based on the deepest conviction that all things were related. The macrocosm and the microcosm and all that lay in between in nature were linked in an interdependent whole in which action in or on any one part would affect all the rest.

One of the many difficulties which confront us in alchemy is the constant substitution of terms between alchemy and astrology, the seven planets being the equivalent of seven metals, and so on (see page 207). This was more logical than it seemed since everyone up to and including Newton believed that all matter was generated by fermentation and condensation from some common material (*Prima Materia*) and that the spiritual and the material were interchangeable. For some this *prima materia* was in some sense God Himself. Few in Boehme's time would have considered creation *ex nihilo* to be possible. The deliberate mystifications practised by alchemists, the enormous variety of interpretation, and the various levels at which they may be understood make alchemy a subject which few have been able to tackle with any degree of confidence.

Boehme's alchemical knowledge and his use of alchemical terms was derived from Paracelsus, who in turn derived much of his terminology and conceptual framework from earlier, mainly Arabic, writers. Taking man as the norm, minerals could by analogy be classified as bodies, i.e. solids, or spirit, i.e. volatile matter or gases. No clear distinction was made between matter in a gaseous state and the word spirit used in what we now call a religious way. Rhazes, the Arab physician, included some solids in his category of spirits, including sulphur and mercury. This classification was adopted by Paracelsus who taught that all metals are composed of Mercury, Sulphur, and Salt, Mercury being Spirit (cf. the name quicksilver, quick here meaning alive), Sulphur the soul, and Salt the body. As Crosland says: 'Such comparisons provided mystical writers with a rich store of verbal inspiration as is found for example in the works of Jacob Boehme' (l.c. 14).

For Boehme alchemy was spiritual alchemy and he uses its terminology in an entirely spiritual sense. For instance, the alchemical concept of tincture is frequently used by Boehme. By this he usually means the spirit which indwells and gives us the peculiar characteristics of that spirit, the colour of that spirit. Colour was understood as a quality *per se* which could be added to or subtracted from things, an idea which Boehme often uses as a metaphor for the work of the Holy Spirit in the soul.

Before leaving the subject of alchemy one more point should

be mentioned. It was believed in Boehme's time that metals grew in the earth in a way comparable to plant growth and that alchemy should aim at the reproduction in the laboratory of the various stages of this growth. This notion of universal growth and transformation was central to Boehme's thought. As Alexander Koyré says:

For [Boehme] to *be* means to realize one's potentialities actively, dynamically, and realization means manifestation, uncovering one's essential nature and deploying all inherent possibilities. The perfect being is the one in whom this self-realization is most complete. Essential nature becomes conscious of itself within us in order to be revealed. Being as personal is thus the highest form of being because it achieves self-realization and self-revelation. Only by defining itself and manifesting itself is self-realization and self-revelation fully achieved.

This dynamic vitalistic approach to life as growth and the capacity to change and be changed is the Great Work of Transformation on which all spiritual alchemists are engaged and is indeed the work of God Himself.

Astrology

As with all the other sacred sciences, astrology is based on the doctrine of the macrocosm and the microcosm, as above so below. Over the centuries the earlier interpretations of the nature of the influence exercised by the planets on human life has changed and new planets have been discovered. The church's attitude has always been ambivalent, cautious lest prediction should seem to deny free will. But true traditional wisdom in this respect says that the situation caused by the conjunction of the planets in any given human situation will be responded to by different people in different ways. Nevertheless, Christians did frequently accept the main astrological contention that the position of the stars at any given moment is reflected in what happens to individuals and to Nature at that moment, that is to say, the cosmos is an interrelated whole.

Another concept was the idea of the Great Year, the period of time which must elapse before the planets return to the position which they held at the moment of their creation. Such an expectation was one of the underlying supports of much millen-

arian and apocalyptic speculations, i.e. that time must have a
stop. In the Appendix I have given a list of planetary equivalents
which in some cases Boehme used, though quite often he seems
to have used his own unique interpretation.

The Cabala

I do not think that I can do better than quote Gershom Scholem's
account of the origin of evil according to the Jewish Zohar since it
corresponds very closely indeed to Boehme's own ideas, indeed,
it is almost certainly the origin of them.

Scholem writes:

The totality of divine potencies form a harmonious whole, and as long
as each stays in relation to all others, it is sacred and good. This is true
also of the quality of strict justice, rigor and judgement in and by God,
which is the fundamental cause of evil. The wrath of God is symbolized
by His left hand while the quality of mercy and love, with which it is
intimately bound up, is called His right hand. The one cannot manifest
itself without involving the other. Thus the quality of stern judgement
represents the great fire of wrath which burns in God but is always
tempered by his mercy. When it ceases to be tempered . . . it tears itself
loose from the quality of mercy, then it breaks away from God
altogether and is transformed into the radically evil, into Gehenna and
the dark work of Satan (l.c. 237).

Whether Boehme discovered anew this Cabalistic doctrine or
whether he learnt it from his friends in Görlitz is immaterial.
What is true is that the eighteenth century German Cabalist,
Koppel Hecht, told an enquirer that Boehme was the best
introduction to Cabalist thought that he knew. A later reader of
Boehme was so impressed by his affinity with Cabalism that he
was converted to Judaism. Other aspects of Cabalistic teaching
of which Boehme was obviously aware are the teachings on the
interpretation of words.

These methods are three in number: *Gematria*, the calculation
of the numerical value of words and their connection with other
words of the same numerical value; *Notarikon*, the interpretation
of the letters of words as the abbreviation of sentences; and finally
Temurah, or the interchange of letters according to fixed rules.
Boehme had a considerable interest in playing with words,

something which Coleridge found ridiculous and which led a rather solemn Freudian psychologist to describe this interest as 'an obsessional neurosis', and a modern sociologist to call Boehme 'a paranoid mystic'.

One other Cabalistic doctrine which is important for understanding Boehme's writings on creation is the doctrine of *Tsim-Tsum* which Scholem rightly calls 'one of the most amazing and far-reaching conceptions ever put forward in the whole history of Cabalism'. The word means concentration or contraction, and more specifically in Cabalistic terms it means withdrawal or making space within God. The first act of creation of *En-Sof*, the Primordial Being, is not an outward act but an inward one of withdrawal; in the divine breathing, inhale preceded exhale. Space was made for the subsequent emanation which gave rise to the manifest world. This reveals to us that cosmic process is inevitably and invariably two-fold.

Those who wish to discover more about the Cabala and Jewish mysticism should refer to Gershom Scholem's excellent book *Major Trends in Jewish Mysticism*, 1955, which will greatly assist in understanding much that would otherwise be incomprehensible in Boehme's writings.

5

THE SPREAD OF BOEHME'S WRITINGS AND HIS INFLUENCE AFTER HIS DEATH

The spread in Europe

EVEN before his death Boehme had achieved considerable fame in his native Silesia, a fact which was noted by his great adversary Gregorius Richter and which increased his opposition to all that he believed Boehme stood for. Boehme was a supreme representative of the many heterodox and separatist groups who posed such a serious threat to the newly-founded Lutheran Church. Small groups of followers of Boehme were scattered all over Saxony, Lusatia, and Silesia and even in Bohemia, and presented a continual threat to the peace of mind of the established church.

Many of his earliest adherents were drawn from country gentlemen, members of the learned professions, doctors, scientists, and the wide range of intelligent tradespeople, all of whom resented the dictatorial attitude of the Lutheran church almost as much as they had resented the ultramontane discipline of the Church of Rome. In company with many others, touched by the new spirit of independence and revolt against blind obedience to authority, Boehme's admirers wanted to be left alone to work things out for themselves and not to be subjected to any new tyranny in place of the old. For them the *Reformatio Nova* was an urgent priority and they were determined to go far beyond the narrow reforms inaugurated by Luther.

Utopian and millenarian aspirations were abroad, it was the age of the prophet, the age of the Aurora or Dawn, as Boehme indicated in choosing this as the title of his first book. Very early on Boehme became known as the Philosophus or Theosophus Teutonicus. Thanks to his friend and first biographer, Abraham von Frankenberg, Boehme became known in other parts of Germany and in the Low Countries, the refuge and centre for many who had to flee their own homes because of their heterodox views. Frankenberg introduced Boehme's writings to that strange figure Johannes Scheffler, better known as Angelus Silesius (1624–77), who first read Boehme's works in Holland and at once became a lifelong admirer. Naturally he wrote one of his quatrains about him:

> The fish lives in water and plants in the earth
> Birds in the air and the sun in the sky
> In fire the salamander lives alone
> As for Jacob Boehme, God's heart is his home.

Amongst the many exiles in Amsterdam in the middle of the seventeenth century, one figure in the history of the dissemination of Behmenist ideas stands out, Georg Gichtel (1638–1710). He was a native of Ratisbon, a free town with a long, historic past. During the Reformation its position in the north of catholic Bavaria and only a few miles distant from the Protestant Palatinates ensured that it was a centre of religious activity and controversy, as well as being a place of refuge for Lutherans fleeing from Austria.

Gichtel was born into a noble family, his father holding an important position in the town as *Steuerherr*, or director of fiscal policy. Unfortunately, the elder Gichtel's loyalty to the Emperor and the Duke of Sachsen-Weimar brought financial ruin on the family and the young Georg was hard put to it to find the means to complete his legal studies. He studied at the University of Strasburg and two of his teachers influenced him greatly: Heinrich Bockler, the noted historian who subsequently became historiographer-royal to Queen Christina of Sweden, and

Philipp Jacob Spener (1635–1705), the founder of German pietism and a powerful advocate of greater lay participation in church affairs. Gichtel's career in the law did not prosper and from 1664 onwards he became increasingly involved in religious activities of an anti-establishment nature. He was soon playing quite a prominent part in that great anti-established church movement inaugurated by Schwenkfeld, Sebastian Franck, and Valentin Weigel. Other activists in this movement in Gichtel's own lifetime were J. V. Andrae (1586–1654), author of the Rosicrucian pamphlets and a long utopian work, *Christianopolis*, and Johann Amos Komensky, known in England as Comenius, the friend of Milton and author of *The Labyrinth of The World*.

All these men, whether Catholic or Protestant, were deeply opposed to any union between church and state. The movement they represented was very widespread and was often referred to as the Spiritualist Movement, and its adherents known as Spirituals.

Gichtel was introduced to the Spirituals by a Hungarian nobleman, Baron Justinian Ernest von Welz, whom it is said he met in a bookshop in Ratisbon. They formed an immediate friendship and planned to start a lay missionary movement to be called *Die Jesus-liebende Gesellschaft*. This lay initiative met with great clerical opposition and Welz was accused of being an Anabaptist. Welz and Gichtel were soon joined by another powerful character, Friedrich Breckling (1629–1711), who was well acquainted with most of the anti-establishment pietistic movements of the time. He was also the guide and mentor of Quirinus Kuhlmann, who later became an ardent student of Boehme. He met Welz and Gichtel on their first visit to the Low Countries in 1664.

On his return home from this visit Gichtel continued his anti-establishment agitation so fiercely that the following year a sentence of banishment *ad vitam eternam* was passed on him. After many difficulties he eventually reached Amsterdam in 1668. During his years of wandering Breckling was his mentor and, at least in part, his financial supporter. Gradually Gichtel's sensitive nature and his prolonged contacts with a leader of the Spirituals wrought a great change in his outlook and aspirations. He withdrew into himself and renounced all worldly ambitions and it seems virtually certain that during the years 1664–68 he made the acquaintance of Boehme's writings which had appeared in Holland spasmodically both in Dutch and German. The earliest publication was in 1635 in Dutch in a volume published by Abraham von Beyerland; by 1665 over thirty of Boehme's works had been published.

Gichtel was to spend the rest of his life in Amsterdam living very modestly with the help of an increasing number of friends and admirers who helped in providing for his very modest needs, so much so that towards the end of his life he could remark that for thirty-four years he had never lacked anything.

Like Boehme before him Gichtel had his groups of followers but they were dispersed and can in no way be described as an organized group or community. He had two special admirers, Alhart de Raedt, professor of theology at Harderwijk, who lost his post for defending the wandering preacher Johann Roth, the friend of the English Fifth Monarchy men. The other important follower was a German from Frankfurt, J. W. Ueberfeld. The two admirers did not get on well together and quarrelled over an edition of Boehme's works which Gichtel wished to publish. Eventually Gichtel and Ueberfeld completed the work which was published between 1682 and 1730. This edition was standard up to the present time when the research of Werner Buddecke brought much new material to light.

Gichtel was helped in his editing by people such as Heinrich Prunius and von Frankenberg who had known Boehme personally and helped with the collection of manuscripts from the Enders von Sercha family and others. Gichtel himself wrote a very influential work under Boehme's influence, the *Theosophia Practica*, a massive work in seven volumes. His voluminous correspondence was also published by Ueberfeld and Gottfried Arnold.

One strange way in which Boehme's works were spread abroad was through the agency of Quirinus Kuhlmann who was, as we have noted, helped by Gichtel's mentor Breckling. Kuhlmann (1651–89) was a very different character from the shy introspective Gichtel. He was born in Breslau and after a serious illness as a young man, he had a very profound religious experience and believed himself to be in direct unbroken communication with God.

Being of a restless turn of mind he set out on his travels and eventually turned up in Amsterdam where he met both Gichtel and Johann Roth. From Gichtel he learnt of Boehme, whose doctrines were very congenial to him. In 1679 he stayed in London and two of his works were translated into English. Prior to his visit to England he had been to Constantinople and the following year he and a friend Conrad Nordermann went to Moscow to win over the Russians to his views, which were by now largely Behmenist. Eventually the activities of the two young men attracted the attention of the authorities and in 1689 on the orders of Czar Peter the Great he was executed as a heretic and subversive.

Less flamboyant than Kuhlmann but more influential in the dissemination of Behmenist ideas was another German refugee, Pierre Poiret, a former Calvinist minister from Metz who fled from the war and came under the influence of the French Quietist writers Antoinette Bourignon and Madame Guyon, whose works Poiret was later to edit. All of these writers were greatly influenced by Boehme, especially by his teaching on the divine indwelling and his trinitarian speculations. Antoinette Bourignon also firmly believed in the androgynous nature of Adam.

Boehme in England

We know that manuscripts of Boehme's writings were circulating in England possibly as early as 1630. By 1644 he must have been sufficiently well known to make it worthwhile publishing Richard Whittaker's short biography of him. From then on, under the patronage of King Charles I, his works began to appear in considerable numbers. Their three main translators were John Sparrow, Humphrey Blunden, and John Ellistone, all of whom succeeded in the very difficult task of producing readable and reasonably fair translations of very difficult originals.

In 1646 a young Cambridge graduate named Charles Hotham delivered a Latin oration entitled *Ad Philosophiam Teutonicam manuductio sive determinatio de origine animae Humanae*. Two years later this work was translated into English by the author's brother, Durant Hotham, who subsequently wrote a life of Boehme. Charles Hotham's oration was preceded by some Latin verses addressed to his friend Henry More, the Platonist who also wrote on Boehme in a somewhat critical manner. More, a scholarly shy academic was not likely to approve whole-heartedly of the passionate theosophist. But his correspondence printed in *The Conway Letters* shows he had a good opinion of Boehme at least in comparison with Henry Nicklaes, founder of the Familists, an extreme sect of the time (l.c. 297). Later in the same correspondence he says: 'Honest Jacob is wholesome at bottom, though a philospher but at randome' (306). We also know that during More's long stay at Ragley with Lady Anne Conway in 1667 Boehme was the chief topic of conversation.

Much has been written about the probability that Sir Isaac Newton was influenced by Boehme. Various writers from William Law onwards have claimed that Newton derived his theory of attraction and repulsion from Boehme. But the recent release of all Newton's hitherto unexamined papers fails to yield any extracts from Boehme or mention of his ideas. Newton's great interest in alchemy was purely scientific; he shows very little interest in alchemy as a spiritual exercise.

But with regard to Milton, Newton's older contemporary, we are on very different ground. Through his contacts with Comenius, Samuel Hartlib, and John Dury, he must have become aware of the mystical Hermetic Tradition in which they were all well versed and of which Boehme was a recent expositor. Boehme's ideas were very much in the air in England while Milton was writing *Paradise Lost*. Miss M. L. Baily in her thesis *Milton and Jakob Boehme*, New York, 1914, gives an excellent summary of the significant resemblances between the two sets of ideas.

So far we have discussed Boehme's influence on individuals in England. But there were also groups devoted to his teaching and the term 'Behmenist' was often used in much the same way as the term 'Puseyite' was used of other groups in the nineteenth century, that is to say, very imprecisely and usually pejoratively.

The group most clearly and unequivocally connected with

Boehme was *The Philadelphian Society* and its predecessor The Family of Love, whose members were known as Familists and to whose founder Nicklaes (Nicholas) we have already referred.

Henry Nicklaes (1502–80) was known in England as Henry Nicholas or by his initials H.N., which were also taken to stand for Homo Novus. He spent some years in the mid-sixteenth century in England, where his ideas were eagerly accepted and groups were started in many parts of the country. His adherents were chiefly artisans and small tradespeople. A hundred years later the Familists were still active in England though they had disappeared on the Continent. Henry More's correspondence with Lady Anne Conway in the 1660s proves they were still a source of considerable curiosity and were often associated with Behmenist groups. In 1645 a certain John Pordage, curate in charge of St Laurence Church in Reading, was noted as an expounder of Familist ideas. On his appointment to the rectory of Bradfield in 1647 he founded a little community on Familist lines and was visited there by many of the more radical independent preachers and itinerant evangelists, such as the Ranter Abiezer Coppe, John Everard, the translator of *The Poimandres* of Hermes Trismegistus, and many other anti-establishment figures. In 1654 Pordage was ejected from his parish, regained it at the Restoration, but in 1662 was again ejected.

He was the spiritual father of a remarkable visionary, Jane Leade. Both were united in their devotion to Boehme and together they founded *The Philadelphian Society*, so called because they saw themselves as the remnant of true believers, as did the members of the Church of Philadelphia mentioned in the Book of Revelation. Meetings were held at various locations in the City of London and attracted a good deal of attention. Mrs Leade was a mystic and a visionary and a copious author of works closely inspired by Boehme's writings. Amongst those who were connected with *The Philadelphian Society* was Francis Lee, a learned orientalist known as Rabbi Lee. Lee had read one of Jane Leade's books when he was in Holland where she had a considerable following and was so impressed that he came to London to meet her. He eventually became her amanuensis when her sight began to fail and married her daughter. Lee eventually lost his enthusiasm and returned to a more conventional form of Anglicanism. One cannot help being reminded of the influence of the charismatic movement of our own day, a movement which shares many of the characteristics of such extreme groups as *The Philadelphian Society*.

It is worth notking that *The Philadelphian Society* attracted the attention of numerous well educated and aristocratic people. The Duke of Buckingham is claimed to have tried to interest King Charles II in Boehme's writings and employed Dr Pordage's son, Samuel, in his entourage. Dr Pordage wrote two long and important treatises on Boehme. In 1691 a book was published, *Jacob Boehme's Theosophick Philosophy Unfolded* by an Englishman Edward Taylor who had lived for a long while in Dublin, where interest in Boehme's works persisted for a very long time. This interest surfaced again in the 18th century in the person of Henry Brooke (1703–83), author and playwright, who corresponded with Law and Wesley and the Swedenborgian missionary, Ralph Mather, whose detailed notes of people he met form a fascinating insight into how widespread Boehme's ideas were at that time.

We have mentioned William Law (1686–1761) as one of Henry Brooke's correspondents. Law was undoubtedly the greatest and most influential of all Boehme's admirers. He inherited the papers of Francis Lee and was a great admirer of Dionysius Freher, a neglected Behmenist worthy of brief notice at least. Freher (1649–1728) was born in Nuremberg but settled in England during the reign of William and Mary, as did many other Germans. Before coming to England he had spent some years in Holland where he knew both Gichtel and Poiret.

In England he soon gathered around him a group of Behmenists, including the mathematician Charles Hayes, and a future Master of the Clockmakers' Company, John Berry. He also attracted two respected London clergymen, John Heylin, already a well known Behmenist who was rector of St Mary le Strand from 1724 to 1759, and Edward Waple, Rector of St Sepulchre's in the City of London.

Law read and studied Freher's commentaries and studied Boehme's writings over a number of years and came to believe that Boehme was one of the greatest mystics of all time. His work and Boehme's influence on him have been studied by Stephen Hobhouse in his edition of the Danish Bishop Martensen's book on Boehme and in his edition of Law's selected writings.

One interesting aspect of Law's interest in Boehme not mentioned by Hobhouse is Law's interest in scientific matters, particularly electricity. He read all the current books on the subject such as those by Lovett, 1756, Hoadley and Wilson, 1756, Jones, 1762, and Symes, 1771, and actually corresponded with John Freke (1688–1756) who was curator of the Museum at St Bartholomew's Hospital and whose *Treatise on the Nature and Property of Fire*, 1752, Law felt confirmed Boehme's writings. Law's influence has finally waned, but over two centuries his calm and deep understanding of Boehme's ideas gave a depth and resonance to his writings after 1735 when the influence of Boehme became dominant and justified Evelyn Underhill's claim that Law was 'the only spiritual thinker of the first rank among the English mystics of the Post-Reformation Church' (quoted by Hobhouse, *Selected Mystical Writings of William Law*, viii).

We have spoken of Boehme in England and in Ireland. In Wales in the seventeenth century he had one devoted admirer, the great Welsh poet Morgan Llwyd (1619–59). Llwyd was one of the early Welsh puritan radicals. He was a true Welshman from Gwynedd 'the heartland of traditional Welsh values', and from a family of great breadth of cultural and religious views. His kinsman Huw Llwyd (1533–1620) spent years as a soldier of fortune on the Continent. He also was a poet and tradition has it that he was well versed in occult and mystical arts.

Morgan Llwyd himself was converted to the Puritan cause by Walter Cradock who had been dismissed from his curacy in Cardiff for his radical views and had settled in Wrexham; it was here that Llwyd heard him preach. On the outbreak of the Civil War, Llwyd and Cradock took refuge in Bristol, then a stronghold of Parliamentarianism. Here Llwyd met many enthusiasts, including Peter Sterry, later to become Cromwell's chaplain and a friend of the Cambridge Platonists. Sterry was also a student of Boehme as the numerous quotations from him in his commonplace books confirm.

Llwyd eventually returned to Wrexham where he gathered a small congregation around him. Like Boehme, Llwyd felt he was living in a sunrise period of history and that the millennium was close at hand, views which he soon began to express in print. In 1653 he published his long poem *Llyfr Y Tri Aderyn* (The Book of The Three Birds) and in 1657 he published two prose works in Welsh based on Boehme's *Dialogue concerning the Supersensual Life* and his *Treatise on True Resignation*. *The Book of the Three Birds* is truly Behmenist in character based as it is on the symbolism of the three birds: the Eagle, the Raven, and the Dove. It draws freely on Boehme's *Mysterium Magnum*.

A connection undoubtedly exists of the early Quakers with Behmenist ideas, as a comparison of their ideas will show, notably in their rejection of outer forms and ceremonies and in the concept of the indwelling of Christ in every individual believer.

The eighteenth century saw a general decline in sectarianism. The millenarian excitement generated by the Civil War in the shape of the Ranters, Fifth Monarchy Men and their kind, had exhausted ordinary people. Such interest in Boehme as remained was marginalized and survived in a diffused way in such sects as the Muggletonians and the followers of Joanna Southcott and Richard Brothers.

The rise of science as a branch of knowledge quite separate from theology and the increasingly material emphasis drove all such mystical and spiritual speculations underground. Desirée Hirst in her excellent book on the influence of the Hermetic Tradition and Boehme on William Blake is right to call it *The Hidden Stream*.

Blake stands out as the one eighteenth-century figure of note who was undoubtedly much influenced by Boehme whom he had read and many of whose ideas he incorporated in his own way into The Prophetic Books.

Blake was one of the first signs of the change in sensibility which was to come to fruition in the Romantic Movement, both in England and on the Continent. Boehme's influence on the German Romantic Movement, both in literature and philosophy, has been well documented as a glance at the bibliography

will show. But his influence in England, particularly on Coleridge, is not quite so well known. Coleridge records that he first
became interested in Boehme when he was still a schoolboy.
Later in 1805 when he was in Germany he met Ludwig Tieck and
discussed Boehme with him. In 1808 his friend De Quincy gave
him the so-called Law edition of Boehme's works in four large
quarto volumes which Coleridge, as was his custom, annotated
copiously over the years. He was obviously very drawn to
Boehme's ideas and in 1810 wrote a long letter to Lady Beaumont
about Boehme and about the possibility of a new edition of his
writings. Some of Coleridge's notes are as incomprehensible as
anything Boehme ever wrote but perhaps Coleridge's judgement on Boehme may also be applied to him. In an early note he
speaks of Boehme contemplating

Truth and the forms of Nature thro' a luminous mist, the vaporous
darkness rising from his Ignorance and accidental peculiarities of fancy
and sensation, but the Light streaming into it from his inmost soul.
What wonder then if in some places the Mist condenses into a thick
smoke . . . the true wonder is that in so many places it thins away
almost into a transparent Medium and Jacob Behmen the philosopher
surprises us in proportion as Behmen the visionary has astounded us.

Coleridge's annotations made over many years are full of
illuminating comments revealing the evolution of Coleridge's
thought and his interpretation of Boehme. They merit close
attention. The Behmenist interest continued through J. P.
Greaves, Francis Barham the Alist, and above all, Christopher
Walton (1809–77) whose devotion ensured that an enormous
amount of material both manuscript and printed on Boehme,
Freher and Law was preserved and is now available in the Dr
Williams Library in London. This chain of interest is virtually
unbroken. Walton died in 1877 just about the time that the
modern Theosophical Movement was taking root in England.
This attracted the attention of many of those interested in
Boehme, notably Mrs Anne Judith Penny (1825–93) and her
husband Edward Burton Penny, who studied Boehme and to
that end translated L. C. de Saint Martin's correspondence with
Baron Kirchberger in the late eighteenth century which throws a

great deal of light on the diffusion of Behmenist ideas in Europe at that time. Another keen Boehme student was the Revd G. W. Allen, vicar of Bretby near Burton on Trent and author of the valuable article on Boehme in Hastings' *Encyclopaedia of Religion and Ethics* and editor of a Behmenist periodical *The Seeker*.

The stream still flows in England and America where Rufus Jones, Howard Brinton, and C. A. Muses have all made valuable contributions. The latter also edited a short-lived but valuable periodical, the Journal of the Jacob Boehme Society.

Boehme in Russia

We have already mentioned the early plantation of Behmenist ideas in Russia by Quirinus Kuhlmann. His most recent Russian admirer is the noted Russian philosopher and theologian Nicholas Berdyaev (1874–1948) who edited an edition of the *Mysterium Magnum* in French and contributed two very valuable essays on Boehme and frequently refers to him in many of his books. In Boehme's concept of the *Ungrund* Berdyaev finds validation of his concept of absolute freedom on which so much of his thought is based.

Engraving of Boehme's Tombstone.

PART TWO

SELECTIONS

PREFACE

ATTEMPTS to condense Boehme's writings have been made in the past, notably by Franz Hartmann and W. Scott Palmer. These works do not lack value, but by presenting a number of very short quotations strung together according to subject, they deprive the reader of any real experience of Boehme's rich poetical style and of the way in which he developed his thought.

I have limited my selection to fairly lengthy extracts, not readily available elsewhere, in which Boehme grapples with his main themes: the birth of God and the vindication of His goodness—in technical terms, his insights into theogony and theodicy.

These also serve the useful purpose of demonstrating Schleiermacher's contention that Boehme's theology was essentially immanentist and psychological. His frequent attacks on formal external argumentative sectarian religion have as much value today as ever they did in his own time. Recent events in the Church of England have confirmed this.

The more strictly devotional writings, such as *The Way to Christ* are available and every student of Boehme should read them in conjunction with this work—and remember that Boehme warned his readers that his works required humble study under the guidance of the Holy Spirit.

The letters which have been unavailable in English for a hundred years demonstrate Boehme's loving concern for his disciples that they should understand and grow in holiness through his writings. They also give us some insight into the man himself and his setting in the world of his time.

I would hope that the reader will accept the book in the spirit of the quotation which follows this preface, and will thereby acquire a longing to penetrate more deeply into Boehme's thought, which has been a beacon to many in the two and a half centuries since his death and which still has a vital and extremely relevant message for us today.

Boehme's Advice to his Readers

God-loving reader! If it is your earnest and serious will and desire to devote yourself to that which is divine and eternal, the reading of this book will be very useful to you; but if you are not fully determined to enter the way of holiness, it would be better for you to let alone the sacred names of God, wherein His supreme sanctity is invoked, because the wrath of God may become ignited in your soul. This book is written only for those who desire to be sanctified and united with the Supreme Power from which they have originated. Such persons will understand the true meaning of the words contained therein and they will also recognize the source from which these thoughts have come.

FOREWORD: HOW WE MAY UNDERSTAND

How that all whatever is spoken of God without the knowledge of the Signature is dumb and without understanding; and that in the mind of Man the Signature lies very exactly composed according to the Essence of all essences.

ALL whatever is spoken, written, or taught of God, without the knowledge of the signature is dumb and void of understanding; for it proceeds only from an historical conjecture, from the mouth of another, wherein the spirit without knowledge is dumb; but if the spirit opens to him the *signature*, then he understands how the spirit has manifested and revealed itself (out of the essence through the principle) in the sound of the voice. For though I seek one to speak, teach, preach, and write of God, and though I hear and read the same, yet this is not sufficient for me to understand him; but if his sound and spirit out of his signature and similitude enter into my own similitude, and imprint his similitude into mine, then I may understand him really and fundamentally, be it either spoken or written, if he has the hammer that can strike my bell.

By this we know, that all human properties proceed from one; that they all have but one root and mother; otherwise one man could not understand another in the sound, for which the sound or speech the form notes and imprints itself into the similitude of another; a like tone or sound catches and moves another, and in the sound the spirit imprints its own similitude, which it has conceived in the essence, and brought to form in the principle.

So that in the word may be understood in what the spirit has conceived, either in good or evil; and with this signature he enters into another man's form, and awakens also the other such a form in the signature; so that both forms mutually assimilate together in one form, and then there is one comprehension, one will, one spirit, and also one understanding.

And then secondly we understand, that the signature or form is no spirit, but the receptacle, container, or cabinet of the spirit, wherein it lies; for the signature stands in the essence, and is a lute that liest still, and is indeed a dumb thing that is neither heard nor understood, but if it be played upon, then its form is understood, in what form and tune it stands, and according to what note it is set. Thus likewise the signature of nature in its form is a dumb essence; it is as a prepared instrument of music, upon which the will's spirit plays; what strings he touches, they sound according to their property.

In the human mind the signature lies most artificially composed, according to the essence of all essences; and man wants nothing but the wise master that can strike his instrument, which is the true spirit of the high might of eternity; if that be quickened in man, that it stirs and acts in the centre of the mind, then it plays on the instrument of the human form, and even then the form is uttered with the sound of the word: As his instrument was set in the time of his incarnation, so it sounds, and so is his knowledge; the inward manifests itself in the sound of the word, for that is the mind's natural knowledge of itself.

Man has indeed all the forms of the three worlds lying in him; for his is a complete image of God, or of the Being of all beings; only the order placed in him at his incarnation; for there are three work-masters in him which prepare his form [or signature], viz. the threefold fiat, according to the three worlds; and they are in contest about the form, and the form is figured according to the contest; which of the masters holds the predominant rule, and obtains it in the essence, according to that his instrument is tuned, and the other lie hid, and come behind with their sound, as it plainly shews itself.

So soon as man is born into this world, his spirit plays upon his instrument, so that his innate genuine form [or signature] in good or evil is seen by his words and conversation; for as his instrument sounds, accordingly the senses and thoughts proceed from the essence of the mind, and so the external spirit of the will is carried in its behaviour, as is to be seen both in men and beasts; that there is a great difference in the procreation, that one brother and sister does not as the other.

Further we are to know, that though one fiat thus keeps the upper hand, and figures the form according to itself, that yet the other two give their sound, if their instrument be but played upon; as it is seen that many a man, and also many a beast, though it is very much inclined either to good to evil, yet it is moved either to evil or good by a contrary tune, and often lets its inbred signature [or figure] fall, when the contrary tune is played upon his hidden lute or form: As we see then an evil man is often moved by a good man to repent of and cease from his iniquity, when the good man touches and strikes his hidden instrument with his meek and loving spirit.

And thus also it happens to the good man, that when the wicked man strikes his hidden instrument with the spirit of his wrath, that then the form of anger is stirred up also in the good man, and the one is set against the other, that so one might be the cure and the healer of the other. For as the vital signature, that is, as the form of life is figured in the time of the fiat at the conception, even so is its natural spirit; for it takes its rise out of the essence of all the three principles, and such a will it acts and manifests out of its property.

But now the will may be broken; for when a stronger comes, and raises his inward signature with his introduced sound and will's spirit, then its upper dominion loses the power, right, and authority; when we see in the powerful influence of the sun, how that by its strength it qualifies a bitter and sour fruit, turning it into a sweetness and pleasantness; in like manner how a good man corrupts among evil company, and also how that a good herb cannot sufficiently shew its real genuine virtue in a bad soil; for in the good man the hidden evil instrument is awakened, and in the herb a contrary essence is received from the earth; so that often the good is changed into an evil, and the evil into a good.

And now observe, as it stands in the power and predominance of the quality, so it is signed and marked externally in its outward form, signature, or figure; man in his speech, will, and behaviour, also with the form of the members which he has, and must use to that signature, his inward form is noted in the form of his face; and thus also is a beast, an herb, and the trees; everything as it is inwardly [in its innate virtue and quality] so it is outwardly signed; and though it falls out, that often a thing is changed from evil into good, and from good into evil, yet it has its external character, that the good or evil [that is, the change] may be known.

For man is known herein by his daily practice, also by his course and discourse; for the upper instrument, which is most strongly drawn, is always played upon: thus also it is with a beast that is wild, but when it is overawed and tamed, and brought to another property, it does not easily shew its first innate form, unless it be stirred up, and then it breaks forth and appears above all other forms.

Thus it is likewise with the herbs of the earth; if a herb be transplanted out of a bad soil into a good, then it soon gets a stronger body, and a more pleasant smell and power, and shews the inward essence externally; and there is nothing that is created or born in nature, but it also manifests its internal form externally, for the internal continually labours or works itself forth to manifestation. As we know it in the power and form of this world, how the one only essence has manifested itself with the external birth in the desire of the similitude, how it has manifested itself in so many forms and shapes, which we see and know in the stars and elements, likewise in the living creatures, and also in the trees and herbs.

Therefore the greatest understanding lies in the signature, wherein man (viz. the image of the greatest virtue) may not only learn to know himself, but therein also he may learn to know the essence of all essences; for by the external form of all creatures, by their instigation, inclination, and desire, also by their sound, voice, and speech which they utter, the hidden spirit is known;

for nature has given to everything its language according to its essence and form, for out of the essence the language or sound arises, and the fiat of that essence forms the quality of the essence in the voice or virtue which it sends forth, to the animals in the sound, and to the essentials in smell, virtue, and form.

Everything has its mouth to manifestation; and thus is the language of nature, whence everything speaks out of its property, and continually manifests, declares, and sets forth itself for what it is good or profitable; for each thing manifests its mother, which thus gives the essence and the will to the form.

1

A LETTER TO AN ENQUIRER

A letter to Caspar Lindner, Customs' Officer at Beuten. Wherein is described the plain and simple way which the author took for the attainment of his High Knowledge: also, his censure, judgment, and answer, concerning divers authors of different opinions, tending to lead Christians into the excellent and desired way of Love and Union.

MAY the open fountain in the heart of Jesus Christ refresh us, and lead us to Himself that we may live in His power, and rejoice in Him; that so we may love and understand one another, and enter into one only will.

Much respected and discreet sir, my most worthy friend in the love and humanity of Jesus Christ; my hearty desires from God in our *Immanuel* for prosperity upon soul and body premised; I give you, Sir, to understand that I have received your letter, and therein perceive that you are a seeker and great lover of the mystery or of the knowledge of God; and do diligently take care everywhere to pick up some divine crumbs, bearing likewise a great desire and hunger after them.

Which on my part doth highly rejoice me, that God doth thus draw and lead His children; as it is written, Those who are driven by the spirit of God be the children of God; and as one branch of the tree doth rejoice in the other, and mutually minister sap, and assistance one to another; so likewise do the children of God in *their tree, Jesus Christ:* And at this, my simple person doth exceedingly rejoice, that God in the fountain of His heart doth draw us (as simply children of our mother) to Himself; even to the right breast and bosom of our mother, that so we should long after Him, as children after their mother.

And whereas (my beloved sir, and brother in the love of Christ) I see and perceive that you do thirst after the open well-spring of Christ, and likewise do enjoy the same accordingly to the will of God, yet you do inquire after the enjoyment of your brethren, and desire (as a branch on the tree) mutually to recreate, refresh, and satiate yourself in them; and it is also acceptable to me to impart my sap and my spirit (*in my knowledge which God hath given me*) unto my brethren and members (being my fellow-branches of the *tree, Jesus Christ*) and so to rejoice in them; namely, in their sap, power, and spirit; for it is the pleasant food of my soul, to perceive that my fellow-branches, and members do flourish in the Paradise of God.

But I will not conceal from you the simple child-like way which I walk in Christ Jesus; for I can write nothing of myself; but as of a child, which neither knoweth nor understandeth anything: neither hath ever been learned, but only that which the Lord vouchsafeth to know in me; according to the measure, as He manifests Himself in me.

For I never desired to know anything of the Divine Mystery, much less understood I the way how to seek or find it; I knew nothing of it, as it is the condition of poor laymen in their simplicity, I sought only after the heart of Jesus Christ, that I might hide myself therein from the wrathful anger of God, and the violent assaults of the devil; and I besought the Lord earnestly for His holy spirit, and His grace, that He would be pleased to bless and guide me in Him; and take that away from me, which did turn me away from Him, and I resigned myself wholly to Him, that I might not live to my own will, but to His; and that He only might lead and direct me: to the end, that I might be His child in His Son Jesus Christ..

In this my earnest Christian seeking and desire (wherein I suffered many a shrewd repulse, but at last being resolved rather to put my life to utmost hazard, than to give over and leave off) the gate was opened unto me, that in one quarter of an hour I saw and knew more than if I had been many years together at a University; at which I did exceedingly admire, and I knew not how it happened to me; and thereupon I turned my heart to praise God for it.

For I saw and knew the Being of all Beings, the Byss (the ground or original foundation), and Abyss (that which is without ground, or bottomless and fathomless); also the birth or eternal generation of the holy Trinity; the descent, and original of this world, and of all creatures, through the divine wisdom; I knew and saw in myself all the three worlds; namely, the divine, angelical, and paradisical world and then the dark world; being the original of nature to the fire: And then thirdly, the external, and visible world, being a procreation, or extern birth; or as a substance expressed, or spoken forth, from both the internal and spiritual worlds; and I saw, and knew the whole Being in the evil, and in the good; and the mutual original, and existence of each of them; and likewise how the pregnant mother (genetrix or fruitful bearing womb of eternity) brought forth, so that I did not only greatly wonder at it, but did also exceedingly rejoice.

And presently it came powerfully to my mind to set the same down in writing, for a memorial to myself; albeit I could very hardly apprehend the same in my external man, and express it with the pen; yet however I must begin to labour in these great Mysteries as a child that goeth to school: I saw it (as in a great deep) in the internal, for I had a thorough view of the universe as in a CHAOS, wherein all things are couched and wrapt up, but it was impossible for me to explicate and unfold the same.

Yet it opened itself in me from time to time, as in a young plant: albeit the same was with me for the space of twelve years, and I was as it were pregnant (or breeding of it) with all, and found a powerful driving and instigation within me, before I could bring it forth into external form of writing; which afterward fell upon me as a sudden shower, which hitteth whatsoever it lighteth upon; just so it happened to me, whatsoever I could apprehend, and bring into the external principle of my mind the same I wrote down.

However, afterward the sun did shine on me a good while,

but not in a continual constant manner; for when the same did
hide itself, I scarce knew, or well understood my own labour or
writings so that, man must acknowledge that his knowledge is
not his own, or from himself, but God's and from God; and that
God manifests the ideas of his wisdom in the soul of man after
what manner and measure He pleaseth.

I intended to keep this my writing by me, all the days of my
life, and not to deliver it into the hands of any; but it fell out
according to the providence of the Most High that I entrusted a
certain person with some of it; by means whereof it was published, and made known without my knowledge and consent,
and the first book (called *Aurora*) was thereby taken from me (by
Gregory Richter, Lord Primate of Gorlitz); and because many
wonderful things were revealed therein (which the mind of man
was not presently capable to comprehend) I was fain to suffer
much from *reason*.

I saw this first book no more in three years; I supposed that it
was dead and gone, till certain learned men sent me some copies
of it, who exhorted me to proceed, and manifest my talent, to
which the *outward reason* would by no means agree, because it had
suffered so much already for it; moreover, the spirit of *reason* was
very weak and timorous, for my high light was for a good while
also withdrawn from me, and it did glow in me as a hidden fire;
so that I felt nothing but anguish and perplexity within me; outwardly I found contempt, and inwardly fiery instigation; yet I was
not able to comprehend that light till the inspiration of the Most
High did help me to it again, and awakened new life in me, and
then I obtained a better style in writing, also deeper and more
grounded knowledge: I could bring everything better into the
outward expression; which the book, treating of the threefold life
through (or according to) the three principles, doth demonstrate;
and the godly reader, whose heart is opened, shall see that it is so.

Thus now I have written, not from the instruction of knowledge received from men, not from the learning or reading of
books; but I have written out of my own book which was opened
in me, being the noble similitude of God, the book of the noble
and precious image (understand God's own similitude or likeness) was bestowed upon me to read; and therein I have studied as

a child in the house of its mother, which beholdeth what the father doth, and in his child-like play doth imitate his father; I have no need of any other book.

My book hath only three leaves, the same are the three principles of eternity, wherein I can find all whatsoever Moses and the prophets, Christ and his apostles have taught and spoken; I can find therein the foundation of the world and all mysteries; yet not I, but the spirit of God, doth it according to the measure, as He pleaseth.

For I have besought, and begged of Him many hundred times, that if my knowledge did not make for His glory, and conduce to the amending and instructing (bettering or benefit) of my brethren, He would be pleased to take it from me, and preserve me only in His love; yet I found that by my praying and earnest desiring I did only enkindle the fire more strongly in me; and in such inflammation, knowledge, and manifestation I made my writings.

Yet I did not intend to make myself known with them among such persons, as now I see is come to pass; I still thought I wrote for myself only, albeit the spirit of God, in the mystery of God, in my spirit, did sufficiently show me to what end it was; yet outward reason was always opposite, save only sometimes when the morning star did arise, and even then reason was also thereby enkindled, and did dance along, as if it had comprehended the pearl, yet it was far from it.

God dwelleth in the noble image, but not in the spirit of the stars and elements; He possesseth nothing, save Himself only, in His own likeness; and albeit He doth possess something (as, indeed, He possesseth all things), yet nothing comprehends Him, but what doth originally arise and spring from Him; as, namely, the soul in the similitude of God.

Besides, all my writings are like unto a young scholar's that is going to school; God hath, according to His will, brought my soul into a wonderful school; and in truth I cannot ascribe or arrogate anything unto myself, as if my selfhood were, or understood, anything.

No man must conceive higher of me than he seeth; for the work in my studying, or writing, is none of mine; I have it only according to the measure as the Lord is pleased to give it me; I am nothing but His instrument, whereby He effecteth what He willeth. This I relate unto you, my beloved friends, for an instruction and information, lest any should esteem me otherwise than I am, namely, as if I were a man of high art and deep understanding and reason, for I live in weakness and infirmity, in the childhood and simplicity of Christ; and my sport and pastime is in that child-like work which He hath allotted to me; yea, I have my delight therein, as in a garden of pleasure, where many noble flowers grow; and in the meantime I will joy and recreate myself therewith, till I shall again obtain the flower of Paradise in the new man.

But because, dear sir, and beloved friend, I see and perceive that you are a seeking in this way; therefore I write unto you with diligence my child-like course, for I understand that you make use of divers authors and writings, concerning which you desire my judgment, the which I shall impart unto you as my fellow-member, so far as God has given me to know, and that only in a brief and short comprisal: in my book of *the threefold life* you shall find it at large, according to all circumstances.

And this is the *answer* I give unto to you, viz.—That *self-reason* (which being void of God's spirit, is only taught and instructed from the bare letter,) doth cavil, taunt, deride, and despise whatsoever doth not punctually agree and conform to the canons and institutions of the Universities and high schools, which I do not wonder at, for it is from without, and God's spirit is from within; it is good and evil, it is like the wind, which is moved and driven to and fro; it highly prizeth man's judgment, and according as the high and great ones who have the respect and authority of the world do judge and censure, just so it gives its credit and verdict; it knoweth not the mind of the Lord because the same is not in it; its understanding is from the stars, and 'tis nothing else be a counterfeit shadow of fancy in comparison of the divine wisdom.

How can he judge of divine matters in whom the spirit of the Lord is not? The spirit of the Lord doth alone try, prove, and judge all things, for to him only all things are known and manifest; but reason judgeth outwardly, and one reason doth always square its judgment and opinion according to another; the inferior judgeth and censureth as his grand superior, the layman as the doctor, and yet none of them doth apprehend the sense, mind, and truth of the Lord without the spirit of God which judgeth in man and respects no man's person: the layman and the doctor are both one to Him.

Now whereas the children of God have divers and manifold gifts in writing, speaking, and judging; and they have not all one manner of expression, phrase, and style; whereupon self-reason afterward doth by artificial conclusions draw out of them what maketh for its own turn, and frameth a Babel to itself; whence such a multitude and wearisome heap of opinions are risen; so that men out of their writings have forged and invented divers conjectures and ways unto God, and men must be forced to go in those ways, whereby such controversies and unchristian contentions are arisen; that men for the present look only upon the strife of words, and disputes about the letter, and those which, according to their reason and principles, do overcome by verbal jangling, and exchanging Scripture for Scripture, are applauded; but this is nothing but Babel, a mother of spiritual whoredom, where reason entereth not in at the door of Christ through Christ's spirit; but presseth in of itself and climbeth up by its own might, strength, and pride, being yet a stranger, or unregenerated, and would always fain be the fairest child in the house; men must honour and adore it.

The children of God have a diversity of gifts, according to the rule of the apostle; God giveth an expression to every one as He pleaseth; the gifts and endowments of men fall out according to the unsearcheable will of God, and spring altogether out of one root; the which is the mother of the Three Principles; and as the spirit of every soul is constellated in the eternal mother, even so is its revelation, apprehension, and knowledge.

For God bringeth not a new or strange spirit into us; but He openeth with His spirit our spirit; namely the mystery of God's wisdom which lieth in every man according to the measure, manner, and condition of his internal hidden constellation; for Christ said, *My father worketh and I also work.* Now the Father worketh in the essence of the soul's property, and the son in the essence of God's own image, that is in the divine similitude, or harmony.

The property of the soul belongeth to the Father, for Christ said, *Father, the men are Thine, and Thou has given them Me, and I give unto them eternal life.* Seeing then the property of the soul is from eternity, of and from the Father; therefore He had wrought in it from eternity, and still worketh in that same image to eternity, light and darkness, to either of which the *will* of the soul's property doth incline and give up itself.

Seeing, then, the Father's property or wisdom is unmeasurable and infinite, and that He being the wisdom itself worketh, and yet through His wisdom all things do arise; thereupon the souls of men are diversely constellated; indeed they arise and originally proceed out of one only essence, yet the operation is diverse and manifold; all according to God's wisdom: Now the spirit of Christ openeth the property of every soul, so that each speaketh from its own property of the wonders in the wisdom of God.

For the spirit of God maketh no new thing in man, or it infuseth no strange spirit in him; but He speaketh of the wonders in the wisdom of God through man, and that not from the eternal constellation only, but likewise from the eternal constellation; that is, through the spirit of the external world, He openeth in man the internal constellation of the soul; that he must prophesy and foretell what the external heaven worketh and produceth; also, he is driven to speak through the *Turba Magna*, as the prophets have many times spoken, and denounced unto the people their punishment which by God's permission through the *Turba Magna* should come upon them for their violence and sinfulness and their bitter imprecations, wicked contentions, and wrathful indignation in their envious will, one against another, do awaken the sword of anger in the *Turba Magna*.

Now the spirit of God speaketh in His children diverse manner of ways; sometimes in one it speaketh by the internal, and eternal constellation of the soul, of eternal punishment, or reward; of God's curse or blessing; and in another, it telleth through the external constellation, of the fortune or misfortune, of the prosperity or adversity of this world; also, of the rising and advancement of powers and authorities; and then likewise of the ruin and destruction of countries and cities, and also of strange and wonderful alterations in the world.

And though it happeneth oftentimes that the spirit of the outward world doth make its sport with its representations of fancy in man, and from its own might and strong influence doth insinuate itself into the spirit of man, and showeth diverse, strange, and marvellous figures, which only finds place among those who run on in their own reason only, in proud self-will, whence often false prophets arise; yet I say that every one speaketh from his own constellation; the one through the manifestation of God's spirit, really and sincerely; and the other through the manifestations of the external *astral* spirit uncertainly by conjecture and guess, yet from the same constellation; but he that speaketh from the mouth of another, and in like manner judgeth of the *mystery*, without a peculiar knowledge, he is in *Babel*, and entangled in opinion, wilfully amusing himself in those things which the heart finds not experimentally whether they be true or not but he *pins his faith* upon the sayings of other men.

And I say further, that all those precious men, who have been illuminated of God (some of whose writings you may have at hand), have spoken from their manifestation and revelation, each according to his apprehension or the model of his capacity; yet the centre is the soul, and the light is God; the revelation is wrought, and brought to pass by the opening or manifestation of God's spirit, through the constellation of the soul.

All the prophets, from the beginning of the world, have prophesied of Christ in different forms, one thus, and another so; they have not all concurred in one style, phrase, and form; but each according as the spirit of God hath revealed to him in the eternal constellation of the soul, yet they have all spoken out of one centre and ground. And even so it is nowadays, the children of God speak all from the revelation of Christ's spirit, which is God's; and every one according to his capacity, or that idea of wisdom which is formed in his mind; and therefore I put you in mind as a friend, and exhort you not to hearken after the vain babbling and prating of reason, or to be moved at the proud censure and judgement of the same, so as thereby to condemn or despise the gifts of any man, for he that doth so, contemneth the spirit of God.

These authors which you mention and others besides (concerning which you desire my judgment, whom I have not read all, but in part) I desire not to judge or despise them, God forbid; let that be far from me, albeit they have not all written in one style and form of expression; for the knowledge is diverse and manifold; yet it behoveth me to try (according to my gifts) their heart and will; but seeing I find that their heart and spirit doth flow and spring from one and the same centre, namely, from the spirit of Christ; therefore I must rest myself contented on the centre, and commend the expression to the *highest tongue*, viz. to the spirit of God's wisdom, which through the wisdom doth open and reveal to every one according to the measure and manner as He pleaseth.

I judge none, and to condemn any is a false and idle arrogancy, and vain prating; the spirit of God Himself judgeth all things; if that be in us, what need we care for prating, I much rather rejoice at the gifts of my brethren; if they have had other manner of gifts to hold forth than I, should I therefore judge them?

Doth any herb, flower, or tree say until the other, thou are sour and dark, I will not stand by thee? Have they not all one mother whence they grow? Even so all souls proceed from one, and all men from one; why then do we boast and glory to be the children of God, notwithstanding that we are more unwise than the flowers and herbs of the field; is it not so with us? Doth not God impart and reveal His wisdom to us diversely? As He bringeth forth and manifesteth the *tincture* of the *mystery* in the earth, through the *earth* with fair plants, even so *in us men*; we should rather congratulate and heartily love one another, that God revealeth His wisdom so variously *in us*; but he that judgeth, condemneth, and condemneth in a wicked way, he only runneth on in pride to show himself, and to be seen; and is the *oppressor in Babel*, a perverse stickler, that stirreth up contention and strife.

The true trial of God's children is this, which we may securely and safely follow, namely, a humble heart, that neither seeketh

nor honoureth itself, but continually seeketh the good of his
brother in love; that seeks not after its own profit, pleasure, and
applause, but after righteousness and the fear of God. The plain
and single way to come until God is this (so far as is made known
to me), viz. that man depart from his sinful courses, and make
with himself an earnest, constant purpose never to go on any
more in those sins which he hath committed, and in his forsaking
and turning away from them not to despair and doubt of God's
grace.

And albeit that reason suggesteth doubts (whereby a sinner is
terrified, and stands amazed and astonished at the anger of God),
yet let the will only in all simplicity and unfeigned sincerity
directly cast itself into the mercy of God, and wholly lie down
and shroud itself in the suffering and death of Christ, and
surrender itself to God through Christ, as a child that betakes
itself into the lap of the mother, which willeth to do only that
which is the will of the mother—it doth only cry and call unto the
mother, it always hopes to receive its refreshment from the
mother, and it only longs after the breasts of the mother;—even
so must our desire be wholly and only turned and directed to our
first mother, from whom we in *Adam* departed and went into
self-will.

Therefore Christ saith, *Unless you be converted and become as
children, you cannot see the kingdom of God.* Also, you must be born
again (that is, we must wholly disclaim and depart from our own
reason, and come again into resignation and self-denial into the
bosom of our mother, and give over all disputings, and, as it
were, stupify or mortify our reason), that the spirit of the
mother, viz. of the eternal Word of God, may get a form in us,
and blow up or enkindle the divine life in us, that so we may find
ourselves in the spirit of the mother in the cradle—if we desire to
be taught and driven by God.

And if we will be taught and driven by God, then we must
arise again from the cradle, and wholly submit and give up
ourselves unto Him, that so God's spirit may be in us *wholly, both
the will and the deed*—that we may acknowledge the knowledge to
be His, and not ours—that He only may be our *knowing*.

We must take no thought or solicitous care what we are to

know, and how we will know, but we must merely enter into the incarnation and birth of Jesus Christ, and into His suffering and death, and continually, with all willingness, *tread in his footsteps* and follow Him, and think that we are here only upon our pilgrim's path, where we must walk through a dangerous way, and enter again in Christ on the narrow way, into our native country, whence *Adam* had led us astray. In this way only lieth the *pearl of the mysterium magnum* or the jewel of the Great Mystery-all studying, book-reading, seeking, searching, and grounding besides, and, without this way, are but dead means, and obtain not the *virgin's crown* but gather together heaps of thistles and thorns, which sting and gall the children of God.

Therefore, dear sir, seeing you have desired my knowledge and judgment, I have no better counsel and advice to impart unto you than to show you the way which I myself walk in, and upon which way the *gate* was opened to me, so that I am learned without learning aforehand; for all *arts* and *sciences* come from God: He findeth all things in, and for man.

I have no controversy with the children of God, by reason of the variety and diversity of their gifts. I can reconcile them all in myself. I only bring them to the centre, and there I have the proof and touchstone of all things. Now, then, if you will imitate and follow me, then you shall find it so by experience, and afterwards, perhaps, better understand what I have written.

A real true Christian hath no controversy or contention with anybody; for, in the resignation in Christ, he dieth from all controversy and strife; he asketh no more after the way of God, but wholly surrenders himself to the mother, namely, unto the spirit of Christ; and whatsoever it doth with him it is all one to him; be it prosperity or adversity in this world—life or death—it is all alike to him; no adversity or calamity reacheth the *new man*, but only the old man of this world. With the same the world may do what it pleaseth: it belongeth unto the world; but the new man belongeth to God.

This is my way, my dear friend, in which I walk, and in which I must know without my foreknowledge. I do not purpose, premeditate, and muse aforehand what I am to write or speak, but I submit and resign myself to the knowledge of God.

He may know in me what he pleaseth; and in such a way as this I have obtained a pearl, which I esteem of greater worth than the whole eternal world.

And though it fall out many times that the children of God are contrary to one another in their knowledge, yet it proceeds only from the *turba* of the eternal reason which is in all men; and God permitteth it that man might be proved and exercised, and by praying and pressing unto God he might more earnestly and fervently enkindle his spirit; and then the spirit of God ariseth in the mystery of the *humanity*, like a burning and shining fire, and all must serve for the best to the children of God.

But concerning some persons of your *neighbourhood*, of whom you make relation, which *make money* of all they have, and run to the *supposed Zion*, I should rather think it better advice for them to stay at home; for *Zion* must be begotten and born *in us*. When they shall come to that place, it will be with them as formerly; and they must, however, live under the yoke of Christ.

God is in heaven, and the *heaven is in man*; and if man desireth to be in heaven, then must heaven be manifest, and revealed in him; and this must be wrought and brought to pass by *earnest, serious repentance and hearty resignation, or unfeigned self-denial*; and this they may do as well at *home* in their own places. That which they think to run from, they are like to run into. It would be more acceptable to God to walk at home in a godly, divine way, that others might take example by them.

There be among them arrogant, proud, scornful, deriding *people*, which do nothing but condemn and despise, and in many of them it is only a received *form* and custom; and a spiritual pride, or selfish pharisaical devotion, as I myself can speak by experience; for I in a Christian, brotherly, and friendly manner, besought and admonished one of them, by reason of a book which he put forth, wherein I found some points of great importance against God and the ground of truth; and I hoped that he would become seeing, but he answered in a proud, contemptuous, and slanderous manner, and gave forth such an answer, wherein there was no characters or prints of God's spirit to be seen; their *Confession of Faith* is rather an *opinion* than a true and sincere earnestness, for all of them are not that which they boast and glory to be; there may be many honest hearts among them; but many of them are so in name only, and desire only to show themselves, and to be *applauded*, as I myself had experience of one of the chiefest among them; they may learn at home to despise other men without their running to an *outward* supposed *Zion*.

So it is the way of the children of God's kingdom, and moreover their way is *Revoca*, be separated, and this they themselves make show of, but privately they are as they were before. I would to God it were in earnest with them, as they pretend and give forth, and then I would commend the same also; but to slander, condemn, and despise others is nothing else but *Babel*, the world is already full of such people, after such I run not.

Concerning Hans Weyrauch, so far as I can see by these his writings, he may be one that walketh in the love of God; if this his way be held in the real sincerity of the heart, but that he taunteth and dispraiseth others, by reason of the knowledge of the light of nature, it showeth that he hath no knowledge therein, and his gifts reach not thither; and because he hath no such gift, we must pass it over, and yet for all this esteem of him as a true and honest brother; for God produceth His gifts not only in simplicity but in many in a high strain or in a deep grounded understanding or magical meaning: for He only is high, and ordereth and directeth all His works as He pleaseth.

In like manner I answer the rest of the authors which you mention, some whereof were indued with high gifts, but they were not sufficiently capable to comprehend all; yet for *their time* they have done *enough*, but because this present time hath need of another *medicine*; therefore at this time also there are found other skilful, understanding knowers and showers of the *disease*, and all according to God's loving providential care, who will not that any should *perish*, but that all men should be *helped and cured*.

If the same authors were alive at this present, it may be they might have written in some points more clearly, and in another form; albeit for their time they have done enough, and they are in no wise to be despised and rejected, although some points might be amended. But their doctrine concerning the *Union of the Deity and Humanity is very clear*: and we may see how God's spirit hath been in them, but reason turns all things to the worst, and by its false expositions and logical glosses, wresteth them to a perverse sense.

Schwenckfeld stumbleth at this point, in that he holdeth Christ to be no creature; he hath not as yet comprehended the principles, and therefore it is impossible for him to distinguish how and in what He is no creature, for in respect of the Deity He is no creature, but in respect of the heavenly essence (concerning which He said, *That he was come from Heaven, and was also in Heaven*) He is in the humanity creatural, and outside the humanity uncreatural.

We, human as we are, live in the four elements and we ourselves consist of the properties of the four elements. In us these elements are present in a figurative manner: but outside us they exist in a nonfigurative manner, but these elements are one and the same; and so it is with the person of Christ.

The whole angelical world (which is the second principle) is His bodily being or personal essence, and as to the heavenly essentiality in the person of the humanity it is creatural, and without the person uncreatural, for He is the *Father's Heart and Word*, and the heart is everywhere in the *Father*; so that where His heart is, there is also heaven, and the divine essentiality environed with the complete fulness of wisdom.

Concerning His soul, which he commended into His Father's hands, and of the which He said upon the Mount of Olives, *That it was afflicted and heavy, even unto death*; the same is also of the property of our soul; for it was for the soul's sake that God became man, that He might bring the same again into Himself, and draw our will until Him again out of the earthliness; this same is a creature.

And the third principle (which is the external kingdom of this world, which God through His wisdom hath brought forth out of eternity) is also creatural in Him; for the whole Deity hath manifested itself in the man Christ: viz. That as God is all in the spirit, so likewise He is all in this man; we men are likewise even so, if we be born again in God; and this point (which doth exercise and trouble almost all others) may be easily amended and rectified if it were well considered, there would not be so much condemning and contending; the spirit of God careth not for any controversy; He judgeth all things in Himself.

Also *Weigelius* writeth, that *Mary* is not the daughter of *Joachim* and of *Annah*, and that Christ assumed nothing from us, but that she is an eternal virgin; and this indeed is true in respect of the mark or sign of the covenant, according to the virgin of the divine wisdom. But what should this avail me? What should become of my soul and my heavenly essentiality which disappeared in *Adam* (which is the paradisical image) if Christ had not assumed on Him the essence of our soul, and begotten again to life the disappeared image; the which in my book of *The Threefold Life* is set forth at large.

Except this, *Weigelius* writeth also of the new birth and of the union of the humanity of Christ very well with us, the which to speak of here I omit, because I have written clearly and punctually thereof, and I neither condemn nor despise his writings, nor those that read them.

Doth not a bee gather honey out of divers flowers? and though one flower is better than another, yet she sticks not at that, but taketh what serveth her turn; and if the sap and virtue of the flower doth not like her, should she therefore thrust her sting into it? As the despiser and mocker useth to do: Men contend and controvert much about the shell or outside of knowledge and religion but regard not the precious sap of love and faith which serveth and availeth to life.

What good doth knowledge do me, if I live not in and according to the same? The knowing, and also the will and real performance of the same must be in me. The mantle of Christ's suffering and satisfaction which men do now usually put about them shall become unto many a snare and hellish fire; in that they will only tickle and flatter themselves with the merits and satisfaction of Christ, and still keep their cunning hypocrisy and wickedness.

It is said: *You must be born again, else you shall not see the kingdom of God. You must become like children if you will see the kingdom of God.* Not only to contend and dispute about knowledge and opinions, but you must become a new creature which liveth in God in righteousness and holiness. The wicked one must be cast out, and Christ must be put on. And then we are buried in His death—in and with Him—and do arise again with Him, and live eternally with Him. What need I then to contend and wrangle about that which I myself am (which I have essentially in me, and of which no man can deprive me)?

I am at variance with none, but only against the wicked, and him the spirit rebuketh to his face. This I desire to let you know, and my intent is sincere and upright towards you.

As for my books, you may easily get them (I suppose) if you have a mind to them; for the Customs' Officer at *Zagan*, doth certify me that he hath lent two of them (namely, the book of *The Threefold Life*, which is the *chiefest in teaching*, and then *The Forty Questions Concerning the Soul*) to *your butler's brother*. If you make him acquainted with it he will not deny you, but if not, then I will help you to them in another way. You may also have them of Mr Christian Bernhart, if you desire them of him; and you cannot get them nearer at hand. I will write unto him that he shall lend them unto you, for I have mine seldom at home. Yet, in case you get them not, I will, as soon as I can get them home, lend them you one after another.

The several books, and the titles of them, are these:—The first book, called *Aurora*, climbeth up out of infancy, and shows you the creation of all beings, yet very mysteriously and not sufficiently explained; of much and deep magical, cabalistical, or parabolical understanding or meaning, for there may be many mysteries therein that shall yet come to pass.

The second is a great book of a hundred sheets. It treateth of *The Three Principles of the Divine Essence*, and of the Being of all beings. The same is a key and an alphabet for all those who desire to understand my writings. It treateth of the creation, also of the eternal birth or generation of the Deity, of repentance, of the justification of man, of his Paradisical life; also of the fall, and then of the new birth, and of the testaments of Christ, and of the total salvation of man. Very profitable to be read, for it is an eye to know the wonders in the mystery of God.

Thirdly, a book of *The Threefold Life*. The same hath sixty sheets. It is a key for above and below to all mysteries, to whatsoever the mind is able to think upon, or whithersoever the

heart is able to turn and move itself. It showeth the whole ground
of the Three Principles. It serveth every one according to his
property (constellation, inclination, disposition, complexion,
profession, and condition). He may therein sound the depth and
the resolve of all questions, whatsoever reason is able to devise
and propound. It is the most necessary to serve your turn. You
would be soon weary of all contentious books, if you entertain
and get that into your mind.

Fourthly, *The Forty Questions about the Soul*. It hath twenty-
eight sheets; it treateth of all things which are necessary for a man
to know.

The fifth book hath three parts; the first part is concerning the
Incarnation of Christ; the second part is very deep and profound,
treating of *Christ's Passion, Suffering, and Death*, and how we
must enter into Christ's death, and both die and arise again in and
with Him, and why Christ was to die, wholly brought forth,
enlarged and confirmed out of the centre, through the Three
Principles, very deep. The third part is the *Tree of Christian Faith*,
also demonstrated through the Three Principles, very profitable
to be read.

The sixth book, or part of these writings, are *the six points*
treating of the greatest depths and secrets: viz. how the Three
Principles do mutually beget, bring forth, and bear each other, so
that in the eternity there is no strife betwixt them, and yet each
principle is in itself as it is in its own property, as if it were only
one, and alone; and they show whence strife and disunity do
arise, and whence good and evil have their original wholly
induced out of the ground (that is, out of nothing into something), and all in the ground and centre of nature; this sixth book
is such a mystery (however in plainness and simplicity it is
brought to light) that no reason can sound, fathom, or understand the same without the light of God; it is the *key* to all.

Seventhly, a small book *For the Melancholy*, being written for
the tempted and afflicted in spirit, showing whence sadness and
dejectedness of soul cometh, and how the same may be resisted
and remedied.

Eighthly, a very deep book, *De Signatura Rerum*, concerning
the signature of all things, and of the signification of the several

forms and shapes in the creation; and it showeth what the beginning, ruin, and cure of everything is; this entereth wholly into the eternal, and then into the temporal, inchoative, and external nature, and its form.

These are my books, besides some small treatises which I have given here and there, and have kept no copy of them; for I have no need of them for myself; I have enough in *my three leaves*.

If my occasion permit me (for I must oftentimes take journeys, by reason of my affairs), then I myself will call upon you so soon as I come that way; it was my full intent to have seen you at Weichau after *Easter*, but God disposed it otherwise; by His providence I light upon another man, who led me out of that intended way to one who had need of me; so that afterward I understood that my way was from the Lord.

Mr Balthasar Walter stayed the last winter and spring with the *Prince Augustus of Anhalt at Plessa*; and hath written unto me from thence. Now he is with the *Earl of Gleichen*, three miles from *Erfurt*; he is his physician, and is to stay with him a whole year.

Ezekiel Meth is also at the same court, yet they be not both of one mind, as the letter of *Balthasar* showeth, which I received three weeks since. If you have a desire to write, and there goeth no messenger this way, be pleased to send to *Christian Bernhart, Receiver of Sagan*; to him I can have opportunity to send weekly; he is a pious Christian companion.

If you find anything that is too hard and dark to be understood in my writings, I pray you set it down, and let me know it, and I will make it plainer unto you, that you may understand it; for the wise and full taught, who are high, and advance themselves in their own knowledge, who can go alone, and are rich aforehand, I have written nothing; but only for the babes and sucklings, who suck on their mothers' breasts, and would fain learn.

He that can understand it, let him understand it; but he that cannot, let him not censure and cavil at it, for such cavillers and deriders I have written nothing; I have written for myself.

But if a brother thirsteth, and asketh water of me, to him I give to drink; he shall experimentally find and feel what I have given him, if the Lord vouchsafe him the drinking; and I commend myself to your favour, and us all into the pleasant and gracious love of Jesus Christ.

Dated at Gorlitz, on the day of
Mary's Ascension, 1621.
JACOB BEME
The name of the Lord is a strong tower,
the righteous goeth thither,
and is exalted.

2

GOD AND CREATION

Of the first principle of the divine essence

SEEING we are now to speak of God, what he is, and where he is, we must say, that God himself is the essence of all essences; for all is generated or born, created and proceeded from him, and all things take their first beginning out of God; as the Scripture witnesseth, saying, *Through him, and in him are all things*. Also, *The heaven and the heaven of heavens are not able to contain him*: Also, *Heaven is my throne, and the earth is my footstool*; And in *Our Father* is mentioned, *Thine is the kingdom and the power*; understand all power.

But there is yet this difference to be observed, that evil neither is, nor is called God; this is understood in the first Principle, where it is the earnest fountain of the wrathfulness, according to which, God calleth himself an angry, wrathful, and zealous God. For the original of life, and of all mobility, consisteth in the wrathfulness; yet if the tartness be kindled with the light of God, it is then no more tartness, but the severe wrathfulness is changed into great joy.

Now when God was to create the world, and all things, he had no other matter to make it of, but his own being, out of himself. But now, God is a spirit that is incomprehensible, which hath neither beginning nor end, and his greatness and depth is all. Yet a spirit doth nothing but ascend, flow, move, and continually generate itself, and in itself hath chiefly a threefold manner of form in its generating or birth, viz. Bitterness, Harshness, and

Heat, and these three manners of forms are none of them the first, second, nor third; for all these three are but one, and each of them generateth the second and the third. For between harshness [attraction] and bitterness [repulsion] fire is generated: and the wrath of the fire is the bitterness or sting itself, and the harshness is the stock or father of both these, and yet is generated of them both; for a spirit is like a will, sense or thought, which riseth up, and in its rising beholdeth, perfecteth, and generateth itself.

Now this cannot be expressed or described, nor brought to the understanding by the tongue of man; for God hath no beginning. But I will set it down as if he had a beginning, that it might be understood what is in the first Principle, whereby the difference between the first and second Principles may be understood, and what God or spirit is. Indeed there is no difference in God, only when it is enquired from whence evil and good proceed, it is to be known, what is the first and original fountain of anger, and also of love, since they both proceed from one and the same original, out of one mother, and are one thing. Thus we must speak after a creaturely manner, as if it had a beginning, that it might be brought to be understood.

For it cannot be said that fire, bitterness, or harshness, is in God, much less that air, water, or earth is in him; only it is plain that all things have proceeded out of that original. Neither can it be said, that death, hell-fire, or sorrowfulness is in God, but it is known that these things have come out of that original. For God hath made no devil out of himself, but angels to live in joy, to their comfort and rejoicing; yet it is seen that devils came to be, and that they became God's enemies. Therefore the source or fountain of the cause must be sought, viz. What is the *prima materia*, or first matter of evil, and that in the originalness of God as well as in the creatures; for it is all but one only thing in originalness: All is out of God, made out of his essence, according to the Trinity, as he is one in essence and threefold in Persons.

Behold, there are especially three things in the originalness, out of which all things are, both spirit and life, motion and comprehensibility, viz. *Sulphur, Mercurius*, and *Sal*. But you will say that these are in nature, and not in God; which indeed is so, but nature hath its ground in God, according to the first Principle of the Father, for God calleth himself also an angry zealous God; which is not so to be understood, that God is angry in himself, but in the spirit of the creation or creature which kindleth itself; and then God burneth in the first Principle therein, and the spirit of the creation or creature suffereth pain, and not God.

Now to speak in a creaturely way, *Sulphur, Mercurius,* and *Sal,* are understood to be thus. S UL is the soul or the spirit that is risen up, or in a similitude it is God: PH UR is the *prima materia,* or first matter out of which the spirit is generated, but especially the harshness; *Mercurius* hath a fourfold form in it, viz. harshness, bitterness, fire, and water: *Sal* is the child that is generated from these four, and is harsh, eager, and a cause of the comprehensibility.

This is as was mentioned before; the harshness is the *prima materia,* or first matter, which is strong, and very eagerly and earnestly attractive, that is *Sal:* The bitterness is in the strong attracting, for the spirit sharpeneth itself in the strong attracting, so that it becometh wholly aching [anxious or vexed]. For example, in man, when he is enraged, how his spirit attracteth itself, which maketh him bitter [or sour] and trembling; and if it be not suddenly withstood and quenched, we see that the fire of anger kindleth in him so, that he burneth in malice, and then presently a substance or whole essence cometh to be in the spirit and mind, to be revenged.

Which is a similitude of that which is in the original of the generating of nature: Yet it must be set down more intelligibly [and plainly]. Mark what *Mercurius* is, it is harshness, bitterness, fire, and brimstone-water, the most horrible substance; yet you must understand hereby no *materia,* matter, or comprehensible thing; but all no other than spirit, and the source of the original nature. Harshness is the first essence, which attracteth itself; but it being a hard cold virtue or power, the spirit is altogether prickly, stinging and sharp. Now the sting and sharpness cannot endure attracting, but moveth and resisteth or opposeth and is a contrary will, an enemy to the harshness, and from that stirring cometh the first mobility, which is the third form. Thus the harshness continually attracteth harder and harder, and so it becometh strong or fierce, so that the virtue or power is as hard as the hardest stone, which the bitterness, that is, the harshness' own sting or prickle, cannot endure; and then there is great anguish in it, like the horrible brimstone spirit, and the sting of the bitterness, which rubbeth itself so hard, that in the anguish there cometh to be a twinkling flash, which flieth up terribly, and breaketh the harshness: But it finding no rest, and being so continually generated from beneath, it is as a turning wheel, which turneth anxiously and terribly with the twinkling flash furiously, and so the flash is changed into a pricking [stinging] fire, which yet is no burning fire, but like the spark struck from a stone.

But seeing there is no rest there, and that the turning wheel runneth as fast as a swift thought, for the prickle driveth it so fast, the prickle kindleth itself so much, that the flash (which is generated between the astringency and bitterness) becometh horribly fiery, and flieth up like a horrible fire, from whence the whole *materia* or matter is terrified, and falleth back as dead, or overcome, and doth not attract so strongly to itself any more, but each yieldeth itself to go out one from another, and so it becometh thin. For the fire-flash is now predominant, and the *materia*, or matter, which was so very harsh or attracting in the originalness, is now feeble, and as it were dead, and the fire-flash henceforth getteth strength therein, for it is its mother; and the bitterness goeth forth up in the flash together with the harshness, and kindleth the flash; for it is the father of the flash, or fire, and the turning wheel henceforth standeth in the fire-flash, and the harshness remaineth overcome and feeble, which is now the water-spirit; and the *materia*, or matter, of the harshness, henceforth is like the brimstone-spirit, very thin, raw, aching, vanquished, and the sting in it is trembling; and it drieth and sharpeneth itself in the flash; and being so very dry in the flash, it becometh continually more horrible and fiery, whereby the harshness or astringency is still more overcome, and the water-spirit continually greater. And so it continually refresheth itself in the water-spirit, and continually bringeth more matter to the fire-flash, whereby it is the more kindled; for (in a similitude) that is the fuel of the flash or fire-spirit.

Understand aright the manner of the existence of this *Mercurius*. The word M E R, is first the strong, tart, harsh attraction; for in that word (or syllable *Mer*) expressed by the tongue, you understand that it jarreth proceeding from the harshness, and you understand also, that the bitter sting or prickle is in it; for the word M E R is harsh and trembling, and every syllable is formed or framed from its power or virtue and expresseth whatsoever the power or virtue doth or suffereth. You [may] understand that the syllable C U signifieth the rubbing or unquietness of the sting or prickle, which maketh that the harshness is not at peace, but boileth and riseth up; for that syllable thrusteth itself forth with the breath from the heart, out of the mouth. It is done thus also in the virtue or power of the *prima materia* in the spirit, but the syllable C U having so strong a pressure from the heart, and yet is so presently snatched up by the syllable RI, and the whole sense or meaning is changed into it; this signifieth and is the bitter prickly wheel in the generating, which vexeth and whirleth itself as swiftly as a thought. The syllable US signifieth the swift fire-flash, that the *materia*, or matter, kindleth in the fierce whirling between the harshness and the bitterness in the swift wheel; where you may very plainly understand in the word, how the harshness is terrified, and how the power or virtue in the word sinketh down, or falleth back again upon the heart, and becometh very feeble and thin: Yet the sting or prickle with the whirling wheel, continueth in the flash, and goeth forth through the teeth out of the mouth; where then the spirit hisseth like a fire akindling, and returning back again strengtheneth itself in word.

These four forms are in the originalness of nature, and from thence the mobility doth exist, as also the life in the seed, and in all the creatures, hath its original from thence; and there is no comprehensibility in the originalness, but such a virtue or power and spirit. For it is a poisonous or venomous, hostile or inimical thing: And it must be so, or else there would be no mobility, but all would be as nothing, and the source of wrath or anger is the first original of nature.

Yet here I do not altogether [mean or] understand the *Mercurius* [mercury or quicksilver] which is in the third Principle of this created world, which the apothecaries use (although that hath the same virtue or power, and is of the same essence), but I speak of that in the first Principle, viz. of the originalness of the essence of all essences, of God, and of the eternal beginningless nature, from whence the nature of this world is generated. Although in the originalness of both of them there is no separation; but only the outward and third Principle, the sidereal and elementary kingdom is generated out of the first Principle by the Word and spirit of God out of the eternal Father, out of the holy heaven.

Of the first and second Principles, what God and the Divine Nature are; wherein is set down a further description of the Sulphur and Mercurius.

Because there belongeth a divine light to the knowledge and apprehension of this, and that without the divine light there is no comprehensibility at all of the divine essence, therefore I will a little represent the high hidden secret in a creaturely manner, that thereby the Reader may come into the depth. For the divine essence cannot be wholly expressed by the tongue; the *spiraculum vitae*, that is, the spirit of the soul which looketh into the light, only comprehendeth it. For every creature seeth and understandeth no further nor deeper than its mother is, out of which it is come originally.

The soul which hath its original out of God's first Principle, and was breathed from God into man, in the third Principle, (that is, into the sidereal and elementary birth) that seeth further into the first Principle of God, out of, in and from, the essence and property of which it is proceeded. And this is not marvellous, for it doth but behold itself only in the rising of its birth; and thus it seeth the whole depth of the Father in the first Principle.

This the devils also see and know; for they also are out of the first Principle of God, which is the source of God's original nature. They wish also that they might not see nor feel it; but it is their own fault that the second Principle is shut up to them, which is called and is God, one in essence, and threefold in personal distinction, as shall be mentioned hereafter.

But the soul of man, which is enlightened with the Holy Spirit of God, (which in the second Principle proceedeth from the Father and the Son in the holy heaven, that is, in the true divine nature which is called God), this soul seeth even into the light of God, into the same second Principle of the holy divine birth, into the heavenly essence: But the sidereal spirit wherewith the soul is clothed, and also the elementary [spirit] which ruleth the source, or springing and impulsion of the blood, they see no further than into their mother, whence they are, and wherein they live.

Therefore if I should speak and write that which is purely heavenly, and altogether of the clear Deity, I should be as dumb to the reader, who hath not the knowledge and the gift to understand it. Ye I will so write in a divine and also in a creaturely way, that I might stir up any one to desire and long after the consideration of the high things: And if any shall perceive that they cannot do it, that at least they might seek and knock in their desire, and pray to God for his Holy Spirit, that the door of the second Principle might be opened to them; for Christ biddeth us to pray, seek, and knock, and then it shall be opened unto us. For he saith, All that you shall ask the Father in my name, he will give it you: Ask and you shall receive; seek, and you shall find; knock, and it shall be opened unto you.

Seeing then that my knowledge hath been received by seeking and knocking, I therefore write it down for a Memorial, that I might occasion a desire in any to seek after them, and thereby my talent might be profitable, and not be hidden in the earth. But I have not written this for those that are wise aforehand, that know all things, and yet know and comprehend nothing, for they are fully satisfied already, and rich; but I have written it for the simple, as I am, that I may be refreshed with those that are like myself.

FURTHER OF THE SULPHUR, MERCURIUS, AND SAL

The syllable SUL, signifieth and is the soul of a thing; for in the word it is the oil or light that is generated out of the syllable PHUR; and it is the beauty or the value of a thing, that which is lovely and dearest in it: In a creature it is the light by which the creature seeth; and therein reason and the senses consist, and it is the spirit which is generated out of the PHUR. The syllable

PHUR, is the *prima materia*, or first matter, and containeth in itself in the third Principle the *macrocosm*, from which the elementary dominion, or region, or essence is generated: But in the first Principle it is the essence of the most inward birth, out of which God generateth or begetteth his Son from eternity, and thereout the Holy Ghost proceedeth; understand out of the SUL and out of the PHUR. And in man also it is the light which is generated out of the sidereal spirit, in the second centre of the *microcosm*; but in the *spiraculum* and spirit of the soul, in the most inward centre, it is the light of God, which that soul only hath which is in the love of God, for it is only kindled and blown up from the Holy Ghost.

Observe now the depth of the divine birth; there is no Sulphur in God, but it is generated from him, and there is such a virtue or power in him. For the syllable PHUR signifieth the most inward virtue or power of the original source or spring of the anger of the fierce tartness, or of the mobility, as is mentioned in the first chapter.

THE GATES OF GOD

Behold now, when the bitterness, or the bitter sting [or prickle] (which in the original was so very bitter, raging and tearing, when it took its original in the harshness) attaineth this clear light, and tasteth now the sweetness in the harshness, which is its mother, then it is so joyful, and cannot rise or swell so any more, but it trembleth and rejoiceth in its mother that bare it, and triumpheth like a joyful wheel in the birth. And in this triumph the birth attaineth the fifth form, and then the fifth source springeth us, viz. the friendly love; and so when the bitter spirit tasteth the sweet water, it rejoiceth in its mother, the sour tart harshness, and so refresheth and strengtheneth itself therein, and maketh its mother stirring in great joy; where then there springeth up in the sweet water-spirit a very sweet pleasant source or fountain: For the fire-spirit (which is the root of the light, which was a strong fierce rumbling cry, crack, or terror in the beginning) that now riseth up very lovely, pleasantly, and joyfully.

And here is nothing but the kiss of love, and wooing, and here the bridegroom embraceth his beloved bride, and is not otherwise than when the pleasing life is born or generated in the sour, tart, or harsh death; and the birth of life is thus, in a creature. For from this stirring, moving, or wheeling of the bitterness in the essence of the harsh astringent tartness of the water-spirit, the birth attaineth the sixth form, viz. the sound or noise of the motion. And this sixth form is rightly called *Mercurius*; for it taketh its form, virtue, and beginning, in the aching or anxious harshness, by the raging of the bitterness; for in the rising it taketh the virtue of its mother, that is, the essence of the sweet harshness, along with it, and bringeth it into the fire-flash, from whence the light kindleth. And here the experience beginneth, one virtue beholding the other in the fire-flash, one virtue feeleth the other by the rising up, by the stirring they hear one another, in the essence they taste one another, and by the pleasant, lovely spring, or fountain, they smell one another, from whence the sweetness of the light springeth up out of the essence of the sweet and harsh spirit, which from henceforth is the water-spirit. And out of these six forms, now in the birth, or generating, cometh a sixfold self-subsisting essence, which is inseparable; where they continually generate one another, and the one is not without the other, nor can be, and without this birth or substance there could be nothing; for the six forms have each of them now the essences of all their sixfold virtue in it, and it is as it were only one thing, and no more; only each form hath its own condition.

For observe it, although now in the harshness there be bitterness, fire, sound, water, and that out of the springing vein of the water there floweth love, like oil, from whence the light ariseth and shineth; yet the harshness retaineth its fifth property, and the bitterness its property, the fire its property, the sound or the stirring its property, and the overcoming the first harsh or tart anguish or the water-spirit, its property, and the springing fountain, the pleasant love, which is kindled by the light in the tart or sour bitterness, (which now is the sweet source or springing vein of water) its property; and yet this is no separable essence parted asunder, but all one whole essence or substance in one another. And each form or birth taketh its own form, virtue, working and springing up from all the forms; and the whole birth now retaineth chiefly but these four forms in its generating or bringing forth; viz. the rising up, the falling down, and then through the turning of the wheel in the sour, harsh, tart essence, the putting forth on this side, and on that side, on both sides like a cross; or, as I may so say, the going forth from the centre towards the east, the west, the north, and the south: For from the stirring, moving, and ascending of the bitterness in the fire-flash, there existeth a cross birth. For the fire goeth forth upward, the water downward, and the essences of the harshness sideways.

Of the endless and numberless manifold engendering or birth of the eternal nature

THE GATES OF THE GREAT DEPTH

Reader, understand and consider my writings aright, we have no power or ability to speak of the birth of God, for it never had any beginning from all eternity; but we have power to speak of God our Father, what he is, and how he is, and how the eternal generation is.

And though it is not very good for us to know the austere, earnest and original birth, into the knowledge, feeling and comprehensibility of which our first parents have brought us, through the instigation and deceit of the devil, yet we have very great need of this knowledge, that thereby we may learn to know the devil, who dwelleth in the most strong birth of all, and that we may learn to know our own enemy *Self*, which our first parents awakened and purchased for us, which we carry within us, and which we ourselves now are.

And although I write now, as if there were a beginning in the eternal birth, yet it is not so; but the eternal nature thus begetteth itself without beginning. My writings must be understood in a creaturely manner, as the birth of man is, who is a similitude of God. Although it be just so in the eternal being, yet that is both without beginning and without end; and my writing is only to this end, that man might learn to know what he is, what he was in the beginning, how he was a very glorious eternal holy man, that should never have known the gate of the cruel birth in the eternity, if he had not suffered himself to lust after it through the infection of the devil, and had not eaten of that fruit which was forbidden him; whereby he became such a naked and vain man in a bestial form, and lost the heavenly garment of the divine power, and liveth now in the kingdom of the devil, and feedeth upon the infected food. Therefore it is necessary for us to learn to know ourselves, what we are, and how we might be redeemed from the anguishing austere birth, and be regenerated or born anew, and live in the new man which is like the first man before the fall in Christ our Regenerator.

For though I should speak or write never so much of the fall, and also of the regeneration in Christ, and did not come to the root and ground, what the fall was, and by what it was we came to perish, and what that property is which God abhorreth, and how that was effected, contrary to the command and will of God, what should I understand of the thing? Just nothing! And then how should I shun or avoid that which I have no knowledge of? Or how should I endeavour to come to the new birth, and give myself up into it, if I knew not how, wherein, nor wherewith to do it?

FURTHER OF THE BIRTH

The birth of the eternal nature is like the thoughts or senses in man, as when a thought is generated by somewhat, and afterwards propagateth itself into infinite many thoughts, or as a root of a tree generateth a stock and many buds and branches, as also many roots, buds, and branches from one root, and all of them from that one first root. Therefore observe what is mentioned before, whereas nature consisteth of six forms or properties, so every form generateth again a form out of itself of the same quality and condition of itself, and this form now hath the quality and condition of all the forms in itself.

But understand it well: the first of the six forms generateth but one source like itself, after the similitude of its own fountain-spirit, and not like the first mother the harshness, but as one twig or branch in a tree putteth forth another sprout out of itself. For in every fountain-spirit there is but one centre, wherein the fire-source or fountain ariseth, and the light ariseth out of the flash of the fire, and the first sixfold form is in the source or fountain.

But mark the depth, in a similitude which I set down thus:

The harsh spring in the original is the mother out of which the other five springs are generated, viz. Bitterness, Fire, Love, Sound, and Water. Now these are members of this birth [of their mother], and without them there would be nothing but an anguishing dark *vacuum*, where there could be no mobility, nor any light or life: But now the life is born in her by the kindling of the light, and then she rejoiceth in her own property, and laboureth in her own tart sour quality to generate again; and in her own quality there riseth a life again, and a centre openeth itself again, and the life cometh to be generated again out of her in a sixfold form, yet not in any such anguish as at the beginning, but in great joy.

For the spring of the great anguish, which was in the beginning before the light, in the harshness, from which the bitter sting or prickle is generated, that is now in the sweet fountain of the love in the light changed from the water-spirit, and from bitterness or prickliness is now become the fountain or spring of the joy in the light. Thus now henceforth the fire-flash is the father of the light, and the light shineth in him, and is now the only cause of the moving birth, and of the birth of the love. That which in the beginning was the aching source, is now SUL, or the oil of the lovely pleasant fountain, which presseth through all the fountains, so that from hence the light is kindled.

And the sound or noise, in the turning wheel, is now the declarer or pronouncer in all the fountains, that the beloved child is born; for it cometh with its sound before all doors, and in all essences; so that in its awakening, all the virtues or powers are stirring, and see, feel, have smell, and taste one another in the light, for the whole birth nourisheth itself in its first mother, viz. the harsh essence, being now become so pure, meek, sweet, and full of joy, and so the whole birth standeth in very great joy, love, meekness, and humility, and is nothing else than a mere pleasing taste, a delighting sight, a sweet smell, a ravishing sound to the hearing, a soft touch, beyond that which any tongue can utter or express. How should there not be joy and love, where, in the very midst of death, the eternal life is generated, and where there is no fear of any end, nor can be?

Thus in the harshness there is a new birth again; understand, where the tart sour astringency is predominant in the birth, and where the fire is not kindled according to the bitter sting or prickle, or from the beginning of the anguish: But the rising and exulting joy, is now the centre and kindling of the light, and the astringency hath now in its own quality the S U L, oil, and light of the father: Therefore now the birth out of the twig or branch of the first tree is modified altogether according to the harsh fountain; and the fire therein is a tart fire; and the bitterness a tart bitterness; and the sound a tart sound; and the love a tart love; but all in unalloyed perfection, and in a totally glorious love and joy.

And thus also the first bitter sting or prickle, or the first bitterness (after the light is kindled, and that the first birth standeth in perfection) generateth again out of its own quality a branch wherein there is a centre, where also a new fountain of source springeth up in a new fire or life, having the condition and property of all the qualities, and yet the bitterness in this new sprout is chiefest among all the qualities; so that there is a bitter bitterness, a bitter tartness, a bitter water-spirit, a bitter sound, a bitter fire, a bitter love, yet all perfectly in the rising up of great joy.

And the fire generateth now also a fire, according to the property of every quality; in the tart spirit it is tart; in the bitter, bitter; in the love, it is a very hearty yearning, kindling or the love, a total, fervent, or burning kindling, and causeth very vehement desires; in the sound it is a very sharp ringing fire, wherein all things are very clearly and properly distinguished, and where the sound in all qualities telleth or expresseth, as it were with the lips or tongue, whatsoever is in all the fountain-spirits, what joy, virtue, or power, essence, substance, or property [they have] and in the water it is a very drying fire.

The propagation of the love is most especially to be observed, for it is the loveliest, pleasantest, and sweetest fountain of all. When the love generateth again a whole birth, with all the fountains of the original essences out of itself, so that the love in all the springing veins in that new growth be predominant and chief, so that a centre ariseth therein, then the first essence, viz. the tartness, is wholly desirous or longing, wholly sweet, wholly light, and giveth itself forth to be food to all the qualities, with a hearty affection towards them all, as a loving mother hath towards her children, and there the bitterness may be rightly called joy, for it is the rising or moving thereof. What joy there is here, there is no other similitude of it, than when a man is suddenly and unexpectedly delivered out of the pain and torment of hell, and brought into the light of the divine joy.

So also the sound, where the love is predominant; it bringeth most joyful tidings or news into all the forms of the birth, as also the fire in the love, that kindleth the love rightly in all the fountain-spirits, as is mentioned above; and the love kindleth love in its essence. When the love is predominant in love, it is the sweetest, meekest, humblest, most loving fountain of all that springeth in all the fountains; and it confirmeth and fixeth the heavenly birth, so that it is a holy divine essence or substance.

You must also mark the form of the water-spirit; when that generateth its like, so that it is predominant in its regeneration or second birth, and that a centre is awakened in it, (which itself in its own essence doth not awaken, but the other fountain-spirits do it therein), the water-spirit is still and quiet as a meek mother, and suffereth the others to sow their seed into it, and to awaken the centre in it, so that the fire riseth up, from whence the life beginneth to stir. In this form the fire is not a hot burning fire, but cool, mild, soft, and sweet; and the bitterness is no bitterness, but cool, mild, budding, and flowing forth, from whence the form- ing or figuring and beauteous shape in the heavenly glory proceedeth, and is a most beautiful substance; for the sound also in this birth floweth forth most pleasantly and harmoniously, all as it were palpably or feelingly; or in a similitude, as a word that cometh to be an essence, or a comprehensible substance. For in this regeneration that is brought to pass in the water-spirit, that is, in the true mother of the regeneration of all the fountain-spirits, all is as it were comprehensible or substantial; although no comprehensibility must be understood here, but spirit.

Of the True Eternal Nature, that is, of the numberless and endless generating of the birth of the Eternal Essence, which is the Essence of all essences; out of which was generated, born, and at length created, this world, with the stars and elements, and all whatsoever moveth, stirreth, or liveth therein.

THE OPEN GATE OF THE GREAT DEPTH

Here I must encounter with the proud and seeming conceited wise, who doth but grope in the dark, and knoweth or understandeth nothing of the spirit of God, and must comfort both him and also the desirous longing Reader who loveth God, and must shew them a little door to the heavenly essence; and shew them in what manner they should understand these writings, before I come to the chapter itself.

I know very well, and my spirit and mind sheweth me as much, that many will be offended at the simplicity and meanness of the author, for offering to write of such high things; and many will say to themselves he hath no authority to do it, and that he doth very sinfully in it, and runneth clean contrary to God and his will, in presuming, being but a man, to go about to speak and say what God is.

For it is lamentable, that since the fall of *Adam*, we should be so continually cheated and befooled by the devil, to think that we are not the children of God, nor of his essence. He continually putteth the monstrous shape or form into our thoughts, as he did into our mother *Eve*, which she gazed too much upon, and by her representing it in her imagination, she became a child of this world, wholly naked and vain, and void of understanding: And so he doth to us also still continually; he would bring us to see ourselves in a different way, as he did *Eve*, that we might be ashamed to appear in the presence of the light and power of God, as *Adam* and *Eve* were, when they hid themselves behind the trees (that is, behind the monstrous shape or form), when the Lord appeared in the centre of the birth of their lives, and said, Where art thou, *Adam*? And he said, I am naked, and am afraid; which was nothing else, but that his belief [or faith] and knowledge of the holy God was extinguished; for he beheld the monstrous shape which he had to himself by his imagination and lust, by the devil's instigation, and false pretending, to eat of the third Principle wherein corruption was.

And now when he saw and knew by that which God had told him, that he should die and perish, if he did eat of the knowledge of good and evil, it made him continually imagine that he was now no more the child of God, and that he was not created out of God's own essence or substance, out of the first Principle. He conceived that he was now but a mere child of this world, when he beheld his corruptibility, and also the monstrous image which enveloped him; and that the paradisical understanding, delight, and joy were departed from him, so that his spirit and perfection were driven out of paradise (that is, out of the second Principle of God, where the light or the Heart of God is generated from eternity to eternity, and where the Holy Ghost proceedeth from the Father and the Son), and that he now lived no more merely by the Word of God, but did eat and drink, viz. the birth of his life henceforward consisted in the third Principle, that is, in the kingdom, or dominion of the stars and elements, and he must now eat of the virtue and fruit thereof, and live thereby: And thereupon he then supposed, that he was past recovery, and that the noble image of God was destroyed. And besides, the devil also continually represented his corruptibility and mortality to him, and himself could see nothing else, because he was gone out of paradise, that is, out of the incorruptible holy protection of God; wherein he was God's holy image and child, in which God created him to continue therein for ever. And if the merciful love of God had not appeared to him again in the centre of the birth of his life, and comforted him, he would have thought that he was wholly departed, or quite separated from the eternal divine birth, and that he was no more in God, nor God any more in him, and that he was no more of God's essence.

But the favourable love (that is, the only begotten Son of God, or that I may set it down so that it may be understood, the lovely fountain where the light of God is generated) sprang up, and grew again in *Adam* in the centre of the birth of his life, in the fifth form of his birth; whereby *Adam* perceived that he was not broken off from the divine root, but that he was still the child of God, and repented him of his first evil lust: And thereupon the Lord shewed him the Treader upon the Serpent, who should destroy his monstrous birth; and so he should from the monstrous birth be regenerated anew, in the shape, form, power and virtue of the Treader upon the Serpent, and be brought with power again into paradise, into the holy birth, and eat of the Word of the Lord again, and live eternally, in spite of all the gates of the wrathfulness, wherein the devil liveth; concerning which there shall be further mention made in its due place.

Your monstrous appearance indeed is not God, nor of his essence, or substance, but the hidden man, which is the soul, is the proper essence of God, forasmuch as the love in the light of God is sprung up in your own centre, out of which the Holy Ghost proceedeth, wherein the second Principle of God consisteth: How then should you not have power and authority to speak of God, who is your Father, of whose essence you are? Behold, is not the world God's? and the Light of God being in you, it must needs be also yours, as it is written, *The Father hath given all things to the Son, and the Son hath given all to you.*

Why will you be fooled by Antichrist, by his precepts and pratings? Where will you seek God? in the deep above the stars? You will not be able to find him there. Seek him in your heart, in the centre of the birth of your life, and there you shall find him, as our father *Adam* and mother *Eve* did.

For it is written, *You must be born anew through the water and the spirit, or else you shall not see the kingdom of God.* This birth must be done within you: The Heart, or the Son of God must arise in the birth of your life; and then the Saviour Christ is your faithful Shepherd, and you are in him, and he in you, and all that he and his Father have is yours, and none shall pluck you out of his hands; and as the Son (viz. the Heart of the Father) is one with the Father, so also the new man is one in the Father and the Son, one virtue or power, one light, one life, one eternal paradise, one eternal heavenly birth, one Father, Son, and Holy Ghost, and thou his child.

For if any would attain salvation, he must be born again, through the water in the centre of the birth of his life, which springeth up in the centre in the light of God; for which end God the Father hath by his Son commanded Baptism, that so we might have a law, and a remarkable sign of remembrance, signifying how a child void of understanding receiveth an outward sign, and the inward man the power and the new birth in the centre of the birth of life; and that there ariseth the confirmation, which the light of God brought into *Adam*, when the light of God the Father, in the centre of the fifth form of the birth of the life of *Adam*, brake forth or sprang up. Thus it is both in the baptism of an infant or child, and also in the repenting convert, that in Christ returneth again to the Father.

The Last Supper of Christ with his disciples is just such another covenant as the [Paedobaptism of] infants. That which is done to the infant in baptism, that is done also to the poor sinner which awaketh from the sleep of Antichrist, and cometh to the Father in and through Christ; as shall be handled in its place.

I have therefore been desirous to warn you, and tell you beforehand, that you must not look upon flesh and blood in these high things, nor upon the worldly wisdom of the universities, or other places of learning; but that you should consider, that this wisdom is planted and laid down by God himself in the first, and last, and in all men: And you need only to return with the prodigal lost son to the Father, and then he will clothe you with a new garment, and put a seal-ring upon the hand of your mind; and in this garment only you have power to speak of the birth of God.

But if you have not gotten this garment on, and will prattle and talk much of God, then you are a thief and a murderer, and you enter not into the sheepfold of Christ by the door, but you climb over into the sheepfold with Antichrist and the robbers, and you will do nothing but murder and steal, seek your own reputation, esteem, and pleasure, and are far from the kingdom of God. Your university learning and arts will avail you nothing: it is your poison, that you are promoted by the favour of man to sit in great authority and place, for you sit upon the stool of pestilence; you are but a mere servant or minister of the Antichrist. But if you be new born, and taught by the Holy Ghost, then your place or office is very pleasing and acceptable to God, and your sheep will hear your voice, and you shall feed them and bring them to the chief Shepherd; God will require this at your hands, therefore take heed what you teach and speak of God without the knowledge of his spirit, that you be not found to be a liar.

NOW HERE FOLLOWETH THE CHAPTER

The eternal generating is an unbegining birth, and it hath neither number nor end, and its depth is bottomless, and the band of life, incorruptible: The astral [psychic] spirit of man cannot discern it, much less comprehend it; it only feeleth it, and seeth a glimpse of it in the mind; which mind is the chariot of the soul, upon which it rideth in the first Principle in its own seat in the Father's eternal generating; for its own substance is altogether crude, without a body, and yet it hath the form of the body in its own spiritual form, understand according to the image; which soul, if it be regenerated in the light of God, it seeth in the light of the Father, in the eternal birth, wherein it liveth and remaineth eternally.

Understand and consider it aright, O man! God the Father made man; the beginning of whose body is out of the one element, or root of the four elements, from whence they proceed, which [one] element is the fifth essence [or quintessence] hid under the four elements, from whence the dark chaos had its being, before the times of the earth; whose original is the spring of water, and out of which this world with the stars and elements, as also the heaven of the third Principle, were created.

But the soul was breathed into man purely out of the original birth of the Father by the moving spirit (understand, the Holy Ghost which goeth forth from the Father out of the light of the Father). Which original birth is before the light of life, which is in the four aching properties, out of which the light of God is kindled, wherein is the original of the name of God; and therefore the soul is God's own essence or substance.

And if it elevate itself back into the anguish of the four forms of the original, and will horribly breathe forth out of pride in the original of the fire, knowing itself shall so become powerful; it so becometh a devil: For the devils also with their legions had this original, and they out of pride would live in the fierce wrath of the fire, and so they perished, and remained devils.

Yet if the soul elevate its imagination forward into the light in meekness and comeliness or humility, and doth not as Lucifer did use the strong power of its fire, in its qualification, then it will be fed by the Word of the Lord, and get virtue, power, life, and strength, in the Word of the Lord, which is the Heart of God; and its own original wrathful source of the birth of the eternal life becometh paradisical, exceeding pleasant, friendly, humble, and sweet, wherein the rejoicing and the fountain of the eternal songs of praise spring up: and in this imagination it is an angel and a child of God, and it beholdeth the eternal generating of the indissoluble union; and thereof it hath ability to speak (for it is its own essence or substance), but it is not able to speak of the infinite generating, for that hath neither beginning nor end.

THE VERY SUBLIME GATE OF THE HOLY TRINITY, FOR THE CHILDREN OF GOD

If you lift up your thoughts and minds, and ride upon the chariot of the soul, as is before mentioned, and look upon yourself, and all creatures, and consider how the birth of the life in you taketh its original, and the light of your life, whereby you can behold the shining of the sun; and also look with your imagination, without the light of the sun, into a huge vast space, to which the eyes of your body cannot reach, and then consider what the cause might be that you are more rational than the other creatures, seeing you can search what is in every thing; and consider farther, from whence the elements fire and air take their original, and how the fire cometh to be in the water, and generateth itself in the water; and how the light of your body generateth itself in the water; and then if you be born of God, you attain to what God and the eternal birth is.

For you see, feel, and find, that all these must yet have a higher root from whence they proceed, which is not visible, but hidden; especially if you look upon the starry heaven which endureth thus unchangeably; therefore you ought to consider from whence it is proceeded, and how it subsisteth thus, and is not corrupted, nor riseth up above, nor falleth down beneath, though indeed there is neither above nor beneath there. Now if you consider what preserveth all thus, and whence it is, then you find the eternal birth that hath no beginning, and you find the original of the eternal Principle, viz. the eternal indissoluble union: And then, secondly, you see the separation, in that the material world, with the stars and elements, are out of the first Principle, which containeth the outward and third Principle in it; for you find in the kingdom of the elements, a cause in every thing, wherefore it is, generates, and moves, as it doth: But you find not the first cause, from whence it is so: There are therefore two several Principles; for you find in the visible things a corruptibility, and perceive that they must have a beginning, because they have an end.

Where is it then that men may find God?

Here open your noble mind, see and search further. Seeing God is only good, from whence cometh the evil? And seeing also that he alone is the life, and the light, and the holy power, as it is undeniably true, from whence cometh the anger of God? From whence cometh the devil, and his evil will? Also hell-fire, from whence hath that its original? Seeing there was nothing before the time of this world, but only God, who was and is a spirit, and continueth so in eternity, from whence then is the first *materia*, or matter of evil? For reason giveth this judgment, that there must needs have been in the spirit of God a will to generate the source or fountain of anger.

But now the Scripture saith, *The devil was a holy angel.* And further, it saith, *Thou art not a God that willeth evil.* And in *Ezekiel, As sure as I live, I will not the death of a sinner.* This is testified by God's earnest severe punishing of the devils, and all sinners, that he is not pleased with death.

What then moved the devil to be angry and evil? What is the first matter of it in him, seeing he was created out of the original eternal spirit? Or from whence is the original of hell, wherein the devils shall remain for ever, when this world, with the stars, and elements, earth, and stones, shall perish in the end?

Beloved Reader, open the eyes of your mind here, and know, that no other [anguish] source will spring up in him [and torment him] than his own inherent nature; for that is his hell out of which he is created and made; and the light of God is his eternal shame, and therefore he is God's enemy, because he is no more in the light of God.

Now you can here produce nothing more, that God should

ever use any matter out of which to create the devil, for then the devil might justify himself, that he made him evil, or of evil matter. For God created him out of nothing, but merely out of his own essence or substance, as well as the other angels. As it is written, *Through him, and in him, are all things*: And his only is the *kingdom*, the *power*, and the *glory*; and all in him, as the holy Scripture witnesseth. And if it was not thus, no sin would be imputed to the devil, nor men, if they were not eternal, and both in God, and out of God himself.

Only (Reader) I advise you sincerely, if you be not in the way of the prodigal, or lost son, returning to his Father again, that you leave my book alone, and read it not, for it will do you harm. For the great prince will not forbear to deceive you; because he standeth naked in this book before the children of God, and is exceedingly ashamed, as a man that is put to open shame before all people for his misdeeds; therefore be warned. And if you love and favour the tender delicate flesh still, do not read my book; but if you will not take warning, and a mischief befall you, I will be guiltless, blame nobody but yourself; for I write down what I know at present, for a Memorial to myself; yet God knoweth well what he will do with it, which in some measure is hidden from me.

And now being to speak of the Holy Trinity, we must first say, that there is one God, for he is called the Father and Creator of all things, who is Almighty, and All in All, whose are all things, and in whom and from whom all things proceed, and in whom they remain eternally. And then we say, that he is three in Persons, and hath from eternity generated his Son out of himself, who is his Heart, light, and love; and yet they are not two, but one eternal essence. And further we say, as the holy Scripture telleth us, that there is a Holy Ghost, which proceedeth from the Father and the Son, and there is but one essence in the Father, Son, and Holy Ghost, which is rightly spoken.

For behold, the Father is the original essence of all essences. And if now the second Principle did not break forth and spring up in the birth of the Son, then the Father would be a dark vacuum. And thus you see, that the Son (who is the Heart, the love, the brightness, and the mild rejoicing of the Father) in whom he is well-pleased openeth another Principle in his birth, and maketh the angry and wrathful Father (as I may say, as to the originality of the first Principle) reconciled, pleased, loving, and as I may say, merciful; and he is another manner of Person than the Father; for in his centre there is nothing else but mere joy, love, and pleasure. And yet you may see that the Holy Ghost proceedeth from the Father and the Son, for when the Heart or light of God is generated in the Father, then there springeth up (in the kindling of the light in the fifth form) out of the water-source in the light, a very pleasant sweet smelling and sweet tasted spirit; and this is that spirit which in the original was the bitter sting or prickle in the harshness [or tartness], and that maketh now in this water-source many thousand centres, without number or end; and all this in the fountain of the water.

Now you may well perceive that the birth of the Son taketh its original in the fire, and attaineth his personality and name in the kindling of the soft, white, and clear light, which is himself; and himself maketh the pleasant smell, taste, and satisfaction in the Father, and is rightly the Father's Heart, and another Person; for the openeth and produceth the second Principle in the Father; and his own essence is the power or virtue and the light; and therefore his is rightly called the power or virtue of the Father.

But the Holy Ghost is not known in the original of the Father before the light breaketh forth; but when the soft fountain springeth up in the light, then he goeth forth as a strong almighty spirit in great joy, from the pleasant source of water, and from the light, and he is the power and virtue of the source of water, and of the light; and he bringeth about now the forming of images or species; and he is the centre in all essences; in which centre the light of life, in the light of the Son, or Heart of the Father, taketh its original. And the Holy Ghost is a distinct Person, because he proceedeth (as a living power and virtue) from the Father and the Son, and confirmeth the birth of the Trinity.

Thus God is one only undivided essence, and yet threefold in personal distinction, one God, one will, one Heart, one desire, one pleasure, one beauty, one almightiness, one fulness of all things, neither beginning nor ending; for if I should go about to seek for the beginning or ending of a small point or *punctum*, or of a perfect circle, I should miss and be confounded.

Therefore, O child of man, consider what thou art in this time; esteem not so slightly or poorly of thyself, but consider that you remain in paradise, and put not out the divine light in you; or else you must hereafter remain in the original source of anger or wrath in the valley of darkness; and your noble image, outside of God, will be turned into a serpent and dragon.

For you must know, that as soon as the divine light went out in the devils, they lost their beauteous form and image, and became like serpents, dragons, worms, and evil beasts; as may be seen by *Adam's* serpent; and thus it is also with the damned souls. For this we know in the original of the first Principle very well. If you ask, How so? Read this following:

A description of the Devil, how he is in his own proper form, and also how he was in the Angelical form.

Behold, O child of man! All the angels were created in the first Principle, and by the flowing spirit were formed and bodified in a true angelical and spiritual manner, and enlightened from the light of God, that they might increase the paradisical joy, and abide therein eternally. But seeing they were to abide eternally, they must be formed out of the indissoluble union, out of the first Principle, which is an indissoluble band; and they ought to look upon the Heart of God, and feed upon the Word of God, and this food would be their holy preservation, and would make their image clear and light; as the Heart of God, in the beginning of the second Principle enlighteneth the Father (that is, the first Principle); and there the divine power, paradise, and the kingdom of heaven spring up.

Thus it is with those angels that continued in the kingdom of heaven in the true paradise, they stand in the first Principle in the indissoluble band, and their food is the divine power, in their imagining. The will of the Holy Trinity in the Deity is the confirmation of their life, will, and doings, in the power of the Holy Ghost.

This sport of love was spoiled by Lucifer himself (who is so called, because of the extinguishment of his light, and of being cast out of his throne), who was a prince and king over many legions, but is become a devil, and hath lost his bright and glorious image. For he, as well as other angels, was created out of the eternal nature, out of the eternal indissoluble band, and hath also stood in paradise, also felt and seen the birth of the holy Deity, the birth of the second Principle, of the Heart of God, and the confirmation of the Holy Ghost; his food should have been of the Word of the Lord, and therein he should have continued an angel.

But he saw that he was a prince, standing in the first Principle, and so despised the birth of the Heart of God, and the soft and very lovely influence thereof, and meant to be a very potent and terrible lord in the first Principle, and would work in the strength of the fire; he despised the meekness of the Heart of God. He would not set his imagination therein or his thoughts upon it, and therefore he could not be fed from the Word of the Lord, and so his light went out; whereupon presently he became a loathsomeness in paradise, and was spewed out of his princely throne, with all his legions that depended on him.

And now when the Heart of God departed from him, the second Principle was shut up to him, and so he lost God, the kingdom of heaven and all paradisical knowledge, pleasure, and joy; he also presently lost the image of God, and the confirmation of the Holy Ghost, because he despised the second Principle, wherein he was an angel and image of God. Thus all things departed from him, and he remained in the valley of darkness, and could no more raise his imagination up into God; but he continued in the four anguishes of the originalness.

And when he raised up his imagination, then he kindled to himself the source or root of the fire, and then when the root of the fire sought for the water (viz. the true mother of the eternal nature), it found the astringent harshness, and the mother in the aching death; and the bitter sting formed the birth to be a fierce raging serpent, very terrible in itself, rising up in the indissoluble band, an eternal enmity, a will striving against itself, an eternal despair of all good; the bitter sting also formed the mind to be a breaking striking wheel, having its will continually aspiring to the strength of the fire, and to destroy the Heart of God, and yet could never at all be able to reach it.

For his is always shut up in the first Principle (as in the eternal death), and yet he raiseth himself up continually, thinking to reach the Heart of God, and to domineer over it; for his bitter sting in the birth climbed up thus eternally in the source of the fire, and affordeth him a proud will to have all at his pleasure, but he attaineth nothing; his food is the fountain of poison, viz. the brimstone-spirit, which is the most aching mother, from which the indissoluble band is fed and nourished; his refreshing is the eternal fire, and eternal freezing in the harsh mother, and eternal hunger in the bitterness, an eternal thirst in the source of the fire; his climbing up is his fall, the more he climbeth up in his will, the greater is his fall; like one that standing upon a high cliff, would cast himself down into a bottomless pit, he looketh still further, and he falleth in further and further, and yet can find no ground.

Thus he is an eternal enemy to the Heart of God, and all the holy angels; and he cannot frame any other will in himself. His angels and devils are of very many several sorts, all according to the eternal birth. For at the time of his creation he stood in the kingdom of heaven in the place (where the Holy Ghost in the birth of the Heart of God, in paradise, did open infinite and innumerable centres), in the eternal birth; in this seat or place, he was given shape and form, and hath his beginning in the opening of the centres in the eternal nature.

Therefore, when the birth of life sprang up, every essence had again a centre in itself, according to its own property or quality, and figureth a life according to its essences, viz. harshness, bitterness, fire, and sound; and all further according to the ability of the eternal birth, which is established in the kingdom of heaven.

Seeing then that they stood in heaven in the time of their creation, therefore their quality was also manifold; and all should have been and continued angels, if the great fountain Lucifer (from whence they proceeded) had not destroyed them. And so now also every one in his fall continueth in his own essences, only the second Principle is extinguished in them; and so it is also with the soul of man, when the light of God goeth out in it; but so long as that shineth therein, it is in paradise, and eateth of the Word of the Lord, of which shall be clearly spoken in its due place.

Of the Heaven and its Eternal Birth and Essence, and how the four Elements were generated; wherein the Eternal Band may be the more and the better understood, by meditating and considering the Material World.

THE GREAT DEPTH

Every spirit seeth no further than into its mother, out of which it hath its original, and wherein it standeth; for it is impossible for any spirit in its own natural power to look into another Principle, and behold it, except it be regenerated therein. But the natural man, who in his fall was captivated by the matrix of this world, whose natural spirit wavereth between two Principles, viz. between the divine and the hellish, and he standeth in both the gates, into which Principle he falleth, there he cometh to be regenerated, whether it be as to the kingdom of heaven, or the kingdom of hell; and yet he is not able in this life time to see either of them both.

He is in his own essence and substance a twofold man. For his soul (in its own substance) is out of the first Principle, which from eternity hath no ground nor beginning; and in the time of the creation of man in paradise, or the kingdom of heaven, the soul was truly bodified by the fiat in a spiritual manner; but with the first virtue or power which is from eternity, in its own first virtue or power it hath remained inseparably in its first root, and was made shining bright by the second Principle, viz. by the *Heart of God*; and therewith standing in paradise, was there, by the moving spirit of God, breathed into the matrix of the third Principle, into the starry and elementary man. And now therefore he may understand the ground of heaven, as also of the elements and of hell, as far as the light of God shineth in him; for if that light be in him, he is born in all the three Principles; but yet he is only a spark risen from thence, and not the great source, or fountain, which is God himself. And therefore it is that Christ saith: *If you had faith as a grain of mustard-seed, you might say to the mountain, Cast thyself into the sea, and it shall be done.* And in this power men have raised the dead, and healed the sick, by the word, and the virtue and power of the spirit, or else they could not have been able to have done such things, if they had not stood in the power of all the three Principles.

For the created spirit of man, which is out of the matrix of this world, that ruleth (by the virtue of the second Principle in the virtue of the light) over and in the virtue of the spirit of the stars and elements very mightily, as in that which is its proper own. But in the fall of *Adam* we lost this great power, when we left paradise, and went into the third Principle, into the matrix of this world, which presently held us captive in restraint. But yet we have the knowledge of that power by a glance or glimmering, and we see as through a dim or dark glass the eternal birth.

And although we move thus weakly or impotently in all the three births, and that the gate of paradise is so often darkened to us, and that the devil doth so often draw us into the hellish gate, and that also the elements cover the sidereal gate, and wholly cloud them, so that we oftentimes move in the whole matrix, as if we were deaf, dumb, or half dead, yet if the paradisical light shineth to us, we may very well see into the mother of all the three Principles; for nothing can hinder us, the threefold spirit of man seeth every form and quality in its mother.

Therefore though we speak of the creation of the world, as if we had been present, and had seen it, none ought to marvel at it, nor hold it for impossible. For the spirit that is in us, which one man inherits from another, that we breathed out of the eternity into *Adam*, that same spirit hath seen it all, and in the light of God it seeth it still; and there is nothing that is far off, or unsearchable: For the eternal birth, which standeth hidden in the centre of man, that doth nothing that is new, it knoweth, worketh and doth even the same that ever it did from all eternity; it laboureth for the light and for the darkness, and worketh and doth even the same that ever it did from all eternity; it laboureth for the light and for the darkness, and worketh in great anguish; but when the light shineth therein, then there is mere joy and knowledge in its working.

For as the soul of man moveth and swimmeth between the

virtue of the stars and elements, so the created heaven also moveth between paradise and the kingdom of hell, and it swimmeth in the eternal matrix; its limit reacheth as far as the *ethera* or skies and hath yielded itself up to the creation, so far as the kingdom of Lucifer did reach, where yet no end is to be found. For the virtue or power of God is without end, but our sense reacheth only to the fiery heaven of the stars, which are a propagation in the fifth form of the eternal mother (or *quinta essentia*), wherein the separation in the time of the third Principle (or in the beginning of this world), the virtue or power of the matrix was separated, where now the separation is thus moved: And then every essence in the propagation, in the manifold centres of the stars, hath a longing desire, one after another, and a continual will to impregnate; and the one essence, or virtue, is the meat and drink, as also the receptable of the other.

For as in the paradisical Principle the Holy Ghost in the Trinity of the Deity continually goeth forth, and floweth very softly, immovably and imperceptibly as to the creature, and yet formeth and fashioneth all in the paradisical matrix, so also doth the third Principle. After that the matrix hath had a great attractive longing towards another, a continual springing, blossoming, and fading again like a bud, or some boiling seething matter, wherein the sourness, coldness, and fierce strongness, attract without ceasing; and this attracting, prickle [or sting], stirreth always without ceasing, and striveth, so that the sour matrix (because of the inward, hellish, or most original matrix) standeth continually in anguish, with a great desire of the light, which it espieth in the root of the fire, and is continually affrighted at it, and becometh mild, soft, and material; whereby the elementary water is continually generated.

In this manner you must understand the four elements, which yet are not four divided things, but one only essence: And yet there are four differences, or distinctions in this birth; and each element lieth in the other, as in a chest, and as it is its own receptacle, so also it is a member therein. Understand and consider the ground aright, which followeth: The astringency is the root of the mother, and a cause of all things, which in its own substance is very dark, cold, and as nothing; but the eternal Deity being there, and speculating or beholding itself in the sourness, therefore the dark sourness is desirous after the divine virtue, and attracteth; although there is no life or understanding in the sourness, yet it is the ground of the first essence, and the original whence something cometh to be: Here we can search no further into the ground of the Deity, for it confoundeth us.

Now the sourness (in its lust or great longing after the light) attracteth continually, and in its own substance it is nothing else but a vehement hunger, very dry, and as a *vacuum* or nothing at all, a desiring will, as the darkness after the light; and its hunger, or attracting, maketh the bitterness, the woe that it cannot be satiated, or mollified, from whence the anguish ariseth, so that the will, or prickle is rubbed, [or struck] in itself, as steel and a flint strike fire, from the lust of the desiring, and it will not yield itself to the dark nothing, or dead will, but setteth its desire and anguish, and also its eager will so very hard towards the hidden light of God, that thereby the will becometh a twinkling flash, like a sparkling or crackling fire, as when you throw water into the fire, whereby the sourness, that is so very aching, is continually filled, and as it were deadened, whereby the sour spirit cometh to be soft, sweet, and material, even water.

But the bitterness being so very much affrighted at the flash of fire in the sourness, it catcheth its mother (the sourness) which is become material from the crack, and flieth out, and is overshadowed or impregnated from the material sourness, as if it also were material, and moveth, and strengtheneth itself continually in the mother; and that is the element called air in this world, which hath its original in the water mother, and the water hath its original from the air, and the fire hath its original from the longing anguish; and the earth and stones took their beginning in the strong attraction at the fall of Lucifer, when the sourness was so fierce, strong, rising, and attractive, which attraction is stopped again by the light in the third Principle.

Thus it may very plainly be understood, that the light of God is a cause of all things, and you may hereby understand all the three Principles: For if the power, virtue, and light of God were not, then there would be also no attractive longing in the dark eternity, and also the sour desire (which is the mother of the eternity) would be nothing at all; and it may be understood, that the divine virtue shineth in everything, and yet it is not the thing itself, but the spirit of God in the second Principle; and yet the thing is his ray which thus proceedeth from the longing, or attracting will. But now the Heart of God is in the Father, [in] the first will, and the Father is the first desiring or longing after the Son, and the Son is the virtue and brightness of the Father, from whence the eternal nature becometh always longing; and so from the Heart of God, in the eternal dark matrix, it generateth the third Principle. For so God is manifest, but otherwise the Deity would remain hidden eternally.

O that I had but the pen of man, and were able therewith to write down the spirit of knowledge. I can but stammer of the great mysteries like a child that is beginning to speak; so very little can the earthly tongue express what the spirit comprehendeth and understandeth; yet I will venture to try whether I may procure some to go about to seek the Pearl, whereby also I might labour in the works of God, in my paradisical garden of roses; for the longing of the eternal matrix driveth me on to write and exercise myself in this my knowledge.

If you will meditate on God, take before you the eternal darkness, which is without God; for God dwelleth in himself, and the darkness cannot in its own power comprehend him; which darkness hath a great [desire of] longing after the light, caused by the light's beholding itself in the darkness, and shining in it. And in this longing or desiring, you find the source, and the source taketh hold of the power or virtue of the light, and the longing maketh the virtue material, and the material virtue is the inclosure of God, or the heaven; for in the virtue standeth the paradise, wherein the spirit which proceedeth from the Father and the Son worketh. All this is incomprehensible to the natural man, but not impossible to be found in the mind; for paradise standeth open in the mind of a holy soul.

Thus you may see how God created all things out of nothing, but only out of himself; and yet the out-birth is not from his essence, but it hath its original from the darkness. The source of the darkness is the first Principle, and the out-birth, generated out of the darkness by the virtue of the light, is the third Principle;

and that is not called God: God is only the light, and the virtue of the light, and that which goeth forth out of the light is the Holy Ghost.

Now mark, when God would manifest himself by the material world, and the matrix stood in the anguishing birth, wherein the Creator moved the first Principle to the creating of angels, then the matrix stood undivided in the inward essence; for there was then no comprehensibility, but spirit only and the virtue of the spirit. The spirit was God, and the virtue was heaven, and the spirit wrought in the virtue, so that thereby the virtue became attracting and longing, for the spirit beheld itself in the virtue; and therein the spirit created the virtue from whence the angels came to be. And thus the virtue became the dwelling of the angels, and the paradise wherein the spirit wrought; and the spirit longed after the light, and the light shone in the virtue; so there is a paradisical joy, and pleasant sport therein; and thus God is manifested.

Now thus the eternal light, and the virtue of the light, or the heavenly paradise, moveth in the eternal darkness; and the darkness cannot comprehend the light; for they are two several Principles; and the darkness longeth after the light, because that spirit beholdeth itself therein, and because the divine virtue is manifested in it. But though it hath not comprehended the divine virtue and light, yet it hath continually with great longing lifted up itself towards it, till it hath kindled the root of the fire in itself, from the beams of the light of God; and there arose the third Principle: And it hath its original out of the first Principle, out of the dark matrix, by the beholding of the virtue [or power] of God. But when the kindled virtue in this springing up of the third Principle in the darkness became fiery, then God put the fiat therein, and by the moving spirit, which goeth forth in the virtue of the light, created the fiery source in a bodily manner, and severed it from the matrix, and the spirit called the fiery created properties stars, for their quality.

Thus it is plain to our sight how the starry heaven (or as I may better render it to the enlightened Reader), the quintessence (or the fifth form in the birth), is separated from the watery matrix; or else there would have been no ceasing from the generating of stones and earth, if the fiery nature had not been separated: But because the eternal essence (viz. God) would manifest himself in the dark matrix, and hath desired to make the nothing something, therefore he hath severed the kindled virtue, and made the matrix clear or pure.

And thus now the matrix standeth incomprehensibly, and longeth after the fiery nature [or condition], and the fiery nature longeth after the matrix. For the spirit of God (which is a spirit of meekness) beholdeth itself in the watery matrix; and the matrix receiveth virtue from thence. Thus there is a constant will to generate and work, and the whole nature standeth in a great longing and anguish, willing continually to generate the divine virtue, God and paradise being hidden therein, but it generateth after its kind, according to its ability. *The Genesis story of creation is continued in like manner.*

For all things are come to be something out of nothing: And every creature hath the centre, or the circle of the birth of life in itself; and as the elements lie hidden in one another in one only mother, and none of them comprehendeth the other, though they are members one of another, so the created creatures are hidden and invisible to one another. For every creature looketh but into its mother that is fixed [or predominant] in it. The material creature seeth a material substance, but an immaterial substance (as the spirits in the fire and in the air) it seeth not; as the body seeth not the soul, which yet dwelleth in it; or as the third Principle doth not comprehend, nor apprehend the second Principle wherein God is; though indeed itself is in God, yet there is a birth between: As it is with the spirit of the soul of man, and the elementary spirit in man, the one being the case or receptacle of the other; as you shall find about the creation of man.

3

MAN AND NATURE

Of the creation of man, and of his soul, also of God's breathing in.

THE PLEASANT GATE

I have perused many masterpieces of writing, hoping to find the Pearl of the Ground of Man; but I could find nothing of that which my soul longed for. I have also found very many contrary opinions. And partly I have found some who forbid me to seek, but I cannot know with what ground or understanding, except it be that the blind grudge at the eyes of them that see. With all this my soul is become very disquiet within, and hath been as full of pain and anguish as a woman at her travail, and yet nothing was found in it, till I followed the words of Christ, when he said, *You must be born anew, if you will see the kingdom of God:* which at first stopped up my heart, and I supposed that such a thing could not be done in this world, but that it should first be done at my departure out of this world. And then my soul first was in anguish to the birth, and would very willingly have tasted the Pearl; and give itself up in this way more vehemently to the birth, till at last it obtained a jewel. According to which I will write, for a Memorial to myself, and for a light to them that seek. For Christ said, *None lighteth a candle and putteth it under a bushel, but setteth it upon a table, that all that are in the house may see by the light of it.* And to this end he giveth the Pearl to them that seek, that they should impart it to the poor for their health, as he hath very earnestly commanded.

Indeed Moses writeth, *That God made man of the dust of the earth*. And that is the opinion of very many: And I should also not have known how that was to be understood, and I should not have learned it out of *Moses*, nor out of the glosses which are made upon it; and the veil would have continued still before my eyes, yet in great trouble. But when I found the Pearl, then I looked *Moses* in the face, and found that *Moses* had written very rightly, and that I had not rightly understood it.

For after the fall God said also to *Adam* and *Eve*, *Earth thou art, and to earth thou shalt return again*: And if I had not considered the *limbus* (out of which the earth was), I should have been so blind still: That *limbus* shewed me the ground of what *Adam* was before and after the fall.

For no such earth or flesh as we carry about us can subsist in the light of God: Therefore also Christ said, *None goeth to heaven, but the Son of Man who is come from heaven, and who is in heaven*. Thus our flesh before the fall was heavenly, out of the heavenly *limbus*. But when disobedience came, in the lust of this world, to generate itself in another centre, then the flesh became earthly; for by the biting of the earthly apple in the Garden of *Eden*, the earthly kingdom took its beginning: And the mother of the great world instantly took the man, or microcosm or little world into its power, and made it to be of a bestial kind, both in form and in substance.

And if the soul had not been within it, then *Adam* would have continued to be an unreasonable beast; but because the soul out of the *limbus* had been breathed into *Adam* by the Holy Ghost, therefore now the mercifulness (viz. the Heart of God) must do its best again, and bring again the centre out of the heavenly *limbus*, and himself become flesh, and by the fiat generate the new man in the soul, which is hidden in the old. For the old belongeth only to the corruptibility, and goeth into its ether, and the new remaineth for ever. But how this came to pass, you have the following fundamental information of it, wherein, if you be regenerated from God, you may see the old and new man into the very heart, because you have the Pearl; but if not, then you shall scarce see here the old *Adam*, and you shall not so much as look upon the new.

Men must not think, that man before his fall had bestial members to propagate with, but heavenly members, nor any entrails; for such a stink, and filthy source or property, as man hath in his body, doth not belong to the Holy Trinity in paradise, but to the death; it must go again into its ether. But man was created immortal, and also holy, like the angels; and being he was created out of the *limbus*, therefore he was pure. Now in what manner he is, and out of what he was made, it followeth further:

Behold, when God had created the third Principle, after the fall of the devils, when they fell from their glory (for they had been angels, standing in the place of this world) yet nevertheless he would that his will and purpose should stand; and therefore he would give to the place of this world and angelical host again, which should continue to stand for ever. And now he having created the creatures, whose shadows after the changing of the world should continue for ever, yet there was no creature found that could have any joy therein, neither was there any creature found that might manage the beasts in this world; therefore God said, *Let us make man an image like unto us, which may rule over all the beasts, and creatures upon the earth; and God created man to be in his image, after the image of God created he him.*

Now the question is: What is God's image? Behold, and consider the Deity, and then you will light upon it. For God is not a bestial man; but man should be the image and similitude of God, wherein God should dwell. Now God is a spirit, and all the three Principles are in him: And he would make such an image, as should have all the three Principles in him, and that is rightly a similitude of God.

But the *limbus* out of which he created him is the matrix of the earth; and the earth was generated out of it; yet the *materia* [or matter] out of which he created him was a *massa*, a *quinta essentia*, out of the stars and elements; which instantly became earthly, when man awakened the earthly centre, and did instantly belong to the earth and corruptibility.

But yet this *massa* was out of the heavenly matrix, which is the root of the out-birth, or the root of the earth. The heavenly centre ought to remain fixed; and the earthly ought not to be awakened. And in this virtue [and power] he was lord and ruler over the stars and elements; and all creatures should have stood in awe of him, and he should have been incorruptible; he had the virtue and properties of all manner of creatures in him, for his virtue was out of the virtue [or power] of the understanding. Now then he ought to have all the three Principles, if he were to be the similitude of God [viz.] the source of the darkness, and also of the light, and also the source of this world: And yet he should not live and act in all three, but in one of them only, and that in the paradisical property, in which his life [quickened] arose, [or did exist].

Now that this is demonstratively and certainly thus, [appeareth] in that it is written, *And God breathed into him the living breath, whereby man became a living soul.* All other creatures which were produced out of the corruptible *limbus* by the fiat, in all those the will in the fiat had awakened the spirit in their centre, and every creature's spirit went forth out of the essence and property of its own self, and mixed afterwards with the spirit of the great world of the stars and elements, and that ought not to have been in man; his spirit ought not to have mixed itself [or been united] with the spirit of the stars and elements. The two Principles (viz. the darkness and the spirit of the air) ought to have stood still in such a substance as should be the image of God; and therefore he breathed into him the living breath; understand God's breath, that is, the paradisical breath or spirit, viz. the Holy Ghost; that should be the breath of the soul, in the centre of the soul. And the spirit which went forth out of the *limbus*, or out of the *quinta essentia* (which is of the same nature as the stars) that was to have power over the fifth essence of this world. For man was in one only essence, and there was also but one only man that God thus created, and he could have lived for ever. And although God had brought the stars again into their ether, and also had withdrawn the matrix of the elements, and the elements also, back into nothing, yet man would have continued still. Besides, he had the paradisical centre in him, and he could have generated again out of himself, out of his will, and have awakened the centre; and so should have been able, in paradise, to generate an angelical host, without misery or anguish, also without dividing of himself; and such a man he ought to have been, if he must continue in paradise, and be eternal without decay; for paradise is holy, and in that respect man also ought to have been holy, for the virtue and power of God and paradise consisteth in holiness.

THE DEEP GATE OF THE SOUL

The soul of man, which God hath breathed into him, is out of the Eternal Father; yet understand it aright; there is a difference [to be observed, you must] understand, [that it is] out of his unchangeable will, out of which he generateth his Son and Heart from eternity, out of the divine centre, from whence the fiat goeth forth, which maketh separation, and hath in it all the essences of the eternal birth [or all manner of things which are in the eternal birth]. Only the birth of the Son of God, that very centre which the Son of God himself is, he hath not; for that centre is the end of nature, and not creaturely. This is the highest centre of the fire-burning love and mercy of God, the perfection [or fulness]. Out of the centre no creature cometh, but it appeareth [or shineth] in the creature, viz. in angels, and in the souls of holy men; for the Holy Ghost, and the omnipotence [or almightiness] which frameth the eternal will in the eternal Father, goeth forth out of this centre.

Now therefore the soul standeth in two gates, and toucheth two Principles, viz. the eternal darkness, and the eternal light of the Son of God, as God the Father himself doth. Now as God the Father holdeth his unchangeable eternal will to generate his Heart and Son, so the angels and souls kept their unchangeable will in the Heart of God. Thus the soul is in heaven and in paradise, and enjoyeth the unutterable joy of God the Father which he hath in the Son, and it heareth the inexpressible words of the Heart of God, and rejoiceth at the eternal, and also at the created images, which are not in essence [or substance], but in figure.

When God had created *Adam* thus, he was then in paradise in the joyfulness; and this clarified [or brightened] man was wholly beautiful, and full of all manner of knowledge; and there God brought all the beasts to him (as to the great lord in this world), that he should look upon them, and give to every one its name, according to its essence and virtue, as the spirit of every one was figured in it. And *Adam* knew all of what every creature was, and he gave every one its name, according to the quality [or working property] of its spirit. As God can see into the heart of all things, so could *Adam* also do, in which his perfection may very well be observed.

And *Adam* and all men should have gone wholly naked, as he then went; his clothing was the clarity in the virtue; no heat nor cold touched him; he saw day and night clearly with open eyes; in him there was no sleep, and in his mind there was no night, for the divine virtue and power was in his eyes; and he was altogether perfect. He had the *limbus*, and also the matrix in himself; he was no male or man, nor female or woman; as we in the resurrection shall be neither. Though indeed the knowledge of the marks of distinction will remain in the figure, but the *limbus* and the matrix not separated, as now they are.

Now man was to dwell upon the earth as long as it was to stand, and manage rule and order the beasts, and have his delight and recreation therein: But he ought not to have eaten any earthly fruit, wherein the corruptibility did stick.

If *Adam* had continued in innocency, then he should in all fruits have eaten paradisical fruit, and his food should have been heavenly, and his drink should have been out of the mother of the heavenly water of the source [or fountain] of the eternal life. The out-birth touched him not, the element of air he had no need of in this manner as now; it is true, he drew breath from the air, but he took his breath from the incorruptibility, for he did not mingle with the spirit of this world, over the stars, and over the sun and moon, and over the elements.

This must be *Adam's* condition; and thus he was a true and right image and similitude of God. He had no such hard bones in his flesh [as we now have], but they were strength, and such [a kind of] virtue; also his blood was not out of the tincture of the watery mother, but it was out of the heavenly matrix. In brief, it was altogether heavenly, as we shall appear and be at the Day of the Resurrection. For the purpose of God standeth, the first image must return and come again and continue in paradise; and seeing it could be done in no other form, nor that which was lost be restored again, therefore God would rather spend his own Heart; his eternal will is unchangeable, that must stand.

THE SECRET GATE OF THE TEMPTATION OF MAN

Since many questions fall to be in this place (for the mind of man seeketh after its native country again, out of which it is wandered, and would return again home to the eternal rest) and since it is permitted to me in my knowledge, I will therefore set down the deep ground of the fall, wherein men may look upon the eyes of *Moses*: If you be born of God, then it may well be apprehended in you, but the unenlightened mind cannot hit the mark; for if the mind desireth to see what is in the house, it must then be within that house; for from hearsay, without seeing it oneself, there is always doubting whether a thing be as is related. But what the eye seeth, and the mind knoweth, that is believed perfectly, for the eye and the mind apprehendeth it.

The mind searcheth wherefore man must be tempted, whereas God had created him perfect; and seeing God is omniscient, the mind therefore always layeth the blame upon God; and so do the devils also; for the mind saith, If the Tree of Knowledge of Good and Evil had not sprung up, then *Adam* had not fallen.

O beloved reason! if you understand no more than so, then shut up the eyes of your mind quite, and search not; continue under patience in hope, and let God alone, or else you will fall into the greatest unquietness, and the devil will drive you into despair, who continually pretendeth or giveth it forth, that God did will evil, and that he willeth not that all men should be saved, and therefore he created the tree of anger.

Beloved mind, put such thoughts away from thee, or else thou wilt make of the kind and loving God, an unmerciful and hostile will, but leave off such thoughts of God, and consider thyself what thou art; in thyself thou shalt find the Tree of the Temptation, and also the will to have it, which made it spring up; yea the source whence it sprang up standeth in thee, and not in God; this must be understood that when we will speak of the pure Deity (which manifesteth itself in the second Principle through the Heart of God) it is thus, and not otherwise.

But when we consider the original of the first Principle, then we find the nature of the tree, and also the will of the tree. We find there the abyss of hell and of anger and wrath; and moreover we find the will of all the devils, we find the envious will of all the creatures of the world, wherefore they all are the enemies of one another, and do hate, bite, worry, kill, and devour one another. My beloved reason, here I will shew you the Tree of the Temptation, and you shall look *Moses* in the face: Keep your mind steadfast, that you may apprehend it.

I have often given you to understand in this book already, what the essence of all essences is; but because it is most of all highly necessary in this place to know the ground thereof, therefore I will set it you down all at large, and very fundamentally, so that you shall know it in yourself; yea you shall understand it in all creatures, and in all things that are, or that you look upon, or at any time may possibly think on; all these shall be witnesses. I can bring heaven and earth, also the sun, stars, and elements for a witness, and that not in bare words and promises only, but it shall be set before you very convincingly and very powerfully in their virtue and essence; and you have no power in your body; that shall not convince you and witness against you; but do not suffer the lying spirit, the old serpent, to darken your mind, who is the inventor of a thousand tricks.

When he seeth that he cannot catch man, by making him doubtful of the mercy of God, then he maketh him careless, so that he accounteth all as nothing. He maketh his mind very drowsy, so that he esteemeth very lightly of himself, as if all were not worth the looking after: Let things be as they will, he will not break his heart or trouble his head with it. Let the Pope look after it, they must answer for it. Thus the mind carelessly passes it over, like a whirlwind or stream of water; concerning which Christ said, The devil stealeth the word out of their hearts, that they do not apprehend it, nor believe it, that they might be saved; so that it taketh no root.

Or else if the Pearl should grow, and the lily bud forth, he should be revealed, and then every one would fly from him, and he should stand in great shame. This trade he hath driven ever since the beginning of the world: And though he resisteth never so vehemently, yet a lily shall grow in his supposed kingdom, whose smell reacheth into the paradise of God, in spite of all his raging and tyranny; this the spirit of God doth witness.

Behold, thou child of man, if thou wilt easily draw near to this knowledge, take but thy mind before thee, and consider it, and therein thou wilt find all. You know, that out of it proceedeth joy and sorrow, laughter and weeping, hope and doubting, wrath and love, lust to a thing and hate of the thing; you find therein wrath and malice, also love, meekness, and well-doing.

Now the question is, May not the mind stand in one only will (viz. in mere love) like God himself? Here sticketh the mark, the ground, and the knowledge: Behold, if the will were in one only essence, then the mind would also have but one only quality that could give the will to be so, and it should be an immovable thing, which should always lie still, and should do no more but that one thing always: in it there would be no joy, no knowledge, also no art or skill of anything at all, and there would be no wisdom in it: also if the quality were not *in infinitum*, it would be altogether a nothing, and there would be no mind nor will to anything at all.

Therefore it cannot be said, that the total God in all the three Principles is in only will and essence; there is a distinction to be observed: Though indeed the first and the third Principles be not called God, neither are they God, and yet are his substance, out of which from eternity the light and Heart of God is always generated, and it is one essence, as body and soul in man are.

Therefore now if the eternal mind were not, out of which the eternal will goeth forth, then there would be no God. But now therefore there is an eternal mind, which generateth the eternal will, and the eternal will generateth the eternal Heart of God, and the Heart generateth the light, and the light the virtue, and the virtue the spirit, and this is the Almighty God, which is one unchangeable will. For if the mind did no more generate the will, then the will would also not generate the Heart, and all would be a nothing. But seeing now that the mind thus generateth the will, and the will the Heart, and the Heart the light, and the light the virtue, and the virtue the spirit, therefore now the spirit again generateth the mind; for it hath the virtue, and the virtue is the Heart; and it is an indissoluble band.

THE DEPTH

Behold now, the mind is in the darkness, and it conceiveth its will to the light, to generate it; or else there would be no will, nor yet any birth: This mind standeth in anguish, and in a longing or is in labour; and this longing is the will, and the will conceiveth the virtue; and the virtue fulfilleth the mind. Thus the kingdom of God consisteth in the virtue, which is God the Father, and the light maketh the virtue longing to be the will, that is God the Son, for in the virtue the light is continually generated from eternity, and in the light out of the virtue goeth the Holy Ghost forth, which generateth again in the dark mind the will of the eternal essence.

Now behold, dear soul, that is the Deity, and that comprehendeth in it the second or the middlemost Principle. Therefore God is only good, the love, the light, the virtue. Now consider, if the mind did not stand in the darkness, there would be no such eternal wisdom and skill; for the anguish in the will to generate, standeth therein; and the anguish is the quality, and the quality is the variety, and maketh the mind, and the mind again maketh the multiplicity.

Now, dear soul, see all over round about you, in yourself, and in all things: What find you therein? You find nothing else but the anguish, and in the anguish the quality, and in the quality the mind, and in the mind the will to grow and generate, and in the will the power, and in the power the light, and in the light its forth-driving spirit; which maketh again a will to generate a twig, bud, or branch, out of the tree like itself; and this I call in my book the *centrum*, where the generated will becometh an essence, and generateth now again another such essence; for thus is the mother of the genetrix.

Now therefore in the anguishing mind of the darkness, is the inexpressible source from whence the name quality existeth, as from many sources into one source, and out of these many sources running into one source springeth forth the plurality of skill, so that there is a multiplicity. And the spirit of God out of the light cometh to help every skill or science, or knowledge, and in every skill of the sources in the quality (by its kind infusion of the love) it maketh again a centre, and in the centre a source is generated again, as a twig out of a tree, where again there springeth forth a mind in the anguish. And the spirit of love, with its infusing of kindness, maketh all, every thought in the will, and that essentially.

For the will in the centre climbeth aloft till it generateth the fire, and in the fire is the substance and essentiality generated. For it is the spirit thereof, and the end of the will in the dark mind, and there can be nothing higher generated in the anguish than the fire, for it is the end of nature, and it generateth again the anguish and the source, as may be perceived. Now therefore the dark anguishing mind hath not only one substance, viz. one being in itself, but many, or else no quality could be generated; and yet it is truly but one substance, and not many.

Thou dear soul, thus saith the high spirit to thee; yield up thy mind here, and I will shew it thee. Behold, what doth comprehend thy will, or wherein consisteth thy life? If thou sayest, In water and flesh: No, it consisteth in the fire, in the warmth. If the warmth were not, then thy body would be stiff with cold, and the water would dry away; therefore the mind and the life consisteth in the fire.

But what is the fire? First, there is the darkness, the hardness, the eternal cold, and the dryness, where there is nothing else but an eternal hunger. Then how cometh the fire to be? Dear soul, here in the fire's coming to be, the spirit of God (viz. the eternal light) cometh to help the hunger; for the hunger existeth also from the light: Because the divine virtue beholdeth itself in the darkness, therefore the darkness is desirous and longing after the light; and the desirousness is the will.

Now the will or the desirousness in the dryness cannot reach the light; and therein consisteth the anguish in the longing after the light; and the anguish is attractive, and in the attracting is the woe, and the woe maketh the anguish greater, so that the anguish in the harshness attracteth much more, and this attracting in the woe is the bitter sting, or the bitterness of the woe; and the anguish reacheth after the sting with attracting, and yet cannot grasp it, because it resisteth, and the more the anguish attracteth, the more the sting raveth and rageth.

Now therefore the anguish, bitterness, and woe in the [sting or] prickle, are like a brimstone-spirit, and all spirits in nature are brimstone: They cause the anguish in one another, till that the light of God cometh to help them; and then there cometh to be a flash, and there is its end, for it can climb no higher in nature; and this is the fire, which becometh shining in the flash, in the soul, and also in the mind. For the soul reacheth the virtue of the light, which doth put it into meekness; and in this world it is the burning fire: In hell it is immaterial, and there it is the eternal fire, which burneth in the quality.

Now, thou dear soul, here you see in a glass how very near God is to us, and that he himself is the heart of all things, and giveth to all virtue, power and life. Here Lucifer was very heedless, and became so very proud, that when this brimstone-spirit in the will of the mind of God was created, then he would fain have flown out above the end of nature, and would drive the fire out above the meekness; he would fain have had all burn in the fire; he would have ruled. The sparks of fire in the brimstone-spirit did elevate themselves too high; and these spirits pleased not the Creator, or the spirit in the fiat, and therefore were not established angels, although in the first mind (when the centre was opened to the creation of the spirits) he came to help them, and beheld them as well as the other angels. But they indeed generated a fiery will, when they should have opened their centre to the regeneration of their minds, and so should have generated an angelical will.

The first will, out of which they were created, that was God's, and that made them good; and the second will, which they as obedient children should have generated out of their centre in meekness, that was evil: And therefore the generator, for the will which he generated, was thrust out from the virtue of God, and so he spoiled the angelical kingdom, and remained in the source of the fire: And because the evil child of their mind did turn away from the meekness, therefore they attained what they desired. For the mind is the god and the creator of the will; that is free from the eternal nature, and therefore what it generateth to itself, that it hath.

Now if you ask, Wherefore came not the love of God to help

them again? No, friend, their mind had elevated itself, even to the end of nature, and it would fain have gone out above the light of God; their mind was become a kindled source of fire in the fierce wrath, the meekness of God cannot enter into it, the brimstone spirit burneth eternally: In this manner he is an enemy of God, he cannot be helped; for the centre is burning in the flash: his will is still, that he would fain go out above the meekness of God; neither can he create any other will, for his source hath revealed the end of nature in the fire, and he remaineth an unquenchable source of fire; the heart of God in the meekness, and the Principle of God, is close shut up from him, and that even to eternity.

To conclude, God will have no fiery spirit in paradise, they must remain in the first Principle, in the eternal darkness; if they had continued as God had created them (when the meekness appeared to them), and had put the centre of their minds into the meekness, then the light of God should for ever have shone through them, and they should have eaten of the *Verbum Domini*; and they should, with the root of their original, have stood in the first Principle, like God the Father himself; and with the will in the mind they should have stood in the second Principle: Thus they should have had a paradisical source, and an angelical will; and they should have been friendly in the *limbus* of Heaven, and in the love of God.

What the body of Man is; and why the Soul is capable of receiving Good and Evil.

Scholar: What then is the body of man?
Master: It is the visible world; and image and quintessence, or compound of all that the world is; and the visible world is a manifestation of the inward spiritual world, come out of the eternal light, and out of the eternal darkness, out of the spiritual compaction or connection; and it is also an image or figure of eternity, whereby eternity hath made itself visible; where self-will and resigned will, viz. evil and good, work one with the other.

Such a substance is the outward man. For God created man of

the outward world, and breathed into him the inward spiritual world for a soul and an intelligent life; and therefore in the things of the outward world man can receive and work evil and good.

Of the destruction of the World; of Man's body, in and after the Resurrection; whereby Heaven and Hell shall be; of the Last Judgement; and wherefore the strife in the creature must be.

Scholar: What shall be after this world, when all things perish and come to an end?

Master: The material substance only ceaseth; viz. the four elements, the sun, moon, and stars. And then the inward world will be wholly visible and manifest. But whatsoever hath been wrought by the will or spirit of man in this world's time, whether evil or good. I say, every such work shall there separate itself in a spiritual manner, either into the eternal light, or into the eternal darkness. For that which is born from each will penetrateth and passeth again into that which is like itself. And there the darkness is called hell, and is an eternal forgetting of all good; and the light is called the kingdom of God, and is an eternal joy in and to the saints, who continually glorify and praise God, for having delivered them from the torment of evil.

The last judgment is a kindling of the fire both of God's love and anger, in which the matter of every substance perisheth, and each fire shall attract into itself its own, that is, the substance that is like itself: Thus God's fire of love will draw into it whatsoever is born in the love of God, or love-principle, in which also it shall burn after the manner of love, and yield itself into that substance. But the torment will draw into itself what is wrought in the anger of God in darkness, and consume the false substance; and then there will remain only the painful aching will in its own proper nature, image, and figure.

Scholar: With what matter and form shall the human body rise?

Master: It is sown a natural gross and elementary body, which in this lifetime is like the outward elements; yet in this gross body there is a subtle power and virtue. As in the earth also there is a subtle good virtue, which is like the sun, and is one and the same with the sun; which also in the beginning of time did spring and proceed out of the divine power and virtue, from whence all the good virtue of the body is likewise derived. This good virtue of the mortal body shall come again and live for ever in a kind of transparent chrystalline material property, in spiritual flesh and blood; as shall return also the good virtue of the earth, for the earth likewise shall become chrystalline, and the divine light shine in everything that hath a being, essence, or substance. And as the gross earth shall perish and never return, so also the gross flesh of man shall perish and not live for ever. But all things must appear before the judgement, and in the judgement be separated by the fire; yea, both the earth, and also the ashes of the human body. For when God shall once move the spiritual world, every spirit shall attract its spiritual substance to itself. A good spirit and soul shall draw to itself its good substance, and an evil one its evil substance. But we must here understand by substance, such a material power and virtue, the essence of which is mere virtue, like a material tincture (such a thing as hath all figures, colours, and virtues in it, and is at the same time transparent), the grossness whereof is perished in all things.

Scholar: Shall we not rise again with our visible bodies and live in them for ever?

Master: When the visible world perisheth, then all that hath come out of it, and hath been eternal, shall perish with it. There shall remain of the world only the heavenly chrystalline nature and form, and of man also only the spiritual earth; for man shall be then wholly like the spiritual world, which as yet is hidden.

Scholar: Shall there be husband and wife, or children or kindred, in the heavenly life, or shall one associate with another, as they do in this life?

Master: Why art thou so fleshly-minded? There will be neither husband nor wife, but all will, like the angels of God, viz. masculine virgins. There will be neither son nor daughter, brother nor sister, but all of one stock and kindred. For all are but one in Christ, as a tree and its branches are one, though distinct as creatures; but God is all in all. Indeed, there will be spiritual knowledge of what every one hath been, and done, but no possessing or enjoying, or desire of possessing earthly things, or enjoying fleshly relations any more.

Scholar: Shall they all have that eternal joy and glorification alike?

Master: The Scripture saith, 'Such as the people is, such is their God'. And in another place, 'With the holy thou art holy, and with the perverse thou art perverse'. And St Paul saith, 'In the resurrection one shall differ from another in glory, as do the sun, moon, and stars'. Therefore know, that the blessed shall indeed all enjoy the divine working in and upon them; but their virtue, and illumination or glory, shall be very different, according as they have been endued in this life with different measures and degrees of power and virtue in their painful working. For the painful working of the creature in this lifetime is the opening and begetting of divine power, by which that power is made moveable and operative. Now those who have wrought with Christ in this lifetime, and not in the lust of the flesh, shall have great power and transcendent glorification in and upon them. But others, who have only expected, and relied upon, an imputed satisfaction, and in the meanwhile have served their belly-god, and yet at last have turned, and obtained grace; those, I say, shall not attain to so high a degree of power and illumination. So that there will be as great a difference of degrees between them, as is between the sun, moon, and stars; or between the flowers of the field in their varieties of beauty, power, and virtue.

Scholar: How shall the world be judged, and by whom?

Master: Jesus Christ, that 'word of God which became man', shall by the power of his divine stirring or motion separate from himself all that belongeth not to him, and shall wholly manifest his kingdom in the place or space where this world now is; for the separating motion worketh all over the universe, through all at once.

Scholar: Whither shall the devils and all the damned be thrown, when the place of this world is become the kingdom of Christ,

and such as shall be glorified? Shall they be cast out of the place of
this world? Or shall Christ have, and manifest his dominion, out
of the sphere or place of this world?

Master: Hell shall remain in the place or sphere of this world
everywhere, but hidden to the kingdom of heaven, as the night is
hidden in and to the day. 'The light shall shine for ever in the
darkness, but the darkness can never comprehend, or reach it.'
And the light is the kingdom of Christ; but the darkness is hell,
wherein the devils and the wicked dwell; and thus they shall be
suppressed by the kingdom of Christ, and made his footstool,
viz. a reproach.

Scholar: How shall all people and nations be brought to judgement?

Master: The eternal word of God, out of which every spiritual
creaturely life hath proceeded, will move itself at that hour,
according to love and anger, in every life which is come out of the
eternity, and will draw every creature before the judgement of
Christ, to be sentenced by this motion of the world. The life will
then be manifested in all its works, and every soul shall see and
feel its judgement and sentence in itself. For the judgment is,
indeed, immediately at the departure of the body, manifested in
and to every soul: And the last judgement is but a return of the
spiritual body, and a separation of the world, when the evil shall
be separated from the good, in the substance of the world, and of
the human body, and everything enter into its eternal receptacle.
And thus is it a manifestation of the mystery of God in every
substance and life.

Scholar: How will the sentence be pronounced?
Master: Here consider the words of Christ.

He will say to those on his right hand, Come, ye blessed of my Father,
inherit the kingdom prepared for you from the foundation of the
world. For I was hungry, and ye gave me meat; I was thirsty, and yet
gave me drink; I was a stranger, and ye took me in; naked, and ye
clothed me. I was sick, and ye visited me, in prison, and ye came unto
me.

Then shall they answer him, saying, Lord, when saw we thee

hungry, thirsty, a stranger, naked, sick, or in prison, and ministered thus unto thee?

Then shall the King answer and say unto them; Inasmuch as ye have done it to one of the least of these my brethren, ye have done it unto me.

And unto the wicked on his left hand he will say, Depart from me, ye cursed, into everlasting fire, prepared for the devil and his angels. For I was hungry, thirsty, a stranger, naked, sick, and in prison, and ye ministered not unto me.

And they shall also answer him, and say, When did we see thee thus, and ministered not unto thee?

And he will answer them, Verily I say unto you, inasmuch as ye have not done it unto one of the least of of these, ye did it not to me.

And these shall depart into everlasting punishment, but the righteous into life eternal.

Scholar: Loving master, pray tell me why Christ saith, 'What you have done to the least of these, you have done to me; and what you have not done to them, neither have you done it to me'. And how doth a man this so, as that he doth it to Christ himself?

Master: Christ dwelleth really and essentially in the faith of those that wholly yield up themselves to him, and giveth them his flesh for food, and his blood for drink; and thus possesseth the ground of their faith, according to the interior or inward man. And a Christian is called a branch of the vine Christ, and a Christian, because Christ dwelleth spiritually in him; therefore whatsoever good any shall do to such a Christian in his bodily necessities, it is done to Christ himself, who dwelleth in him. For such a Christian is not his own, but is wholly resigned to Christ, and become his peculiar possession, and consequently the good deed is done to Christ himself. Therefore also, whosoever shall withhold their help from such a needy Christian, and forbear to serve him in his necessity, they thrust Christ away from themselves, and despise him in his members. When a poor person that belongeth thus to Christ, asketh anything of thee, and thou deniest it him in his necessity, thou deniest it to Christ himself. And whatsoever hurt any shall do to such a Christian, they do it to Christ himself. When any mock, scorn, revile, reject, or thrust away such a one, they do all that to Christ; but he that receiveth him, giveth him meat and drink, or apparel, and assisteth him in his necessities, doth it likewise to Christ, and to a fellow-member of his own body. Nay, he doth it to himself if he be a Christian; for we are all one in Christ, as a tree and its branches are.

Scholar: How then will those subsist in the day of that fierce judgement, who afflict and vex the poor and distressed, and deprive them of their very sweat; necessitating and constraining them by force to submit to their wills, and trampling upon them as their footstools, only that they themselves may live in pomp and power, and spend the fruits of this poor people's sweat and labour in voluptuousness, pride, and vanity?

Master: Christ suffereth in the persecution of his members. Therefore all the wrong that such hard exactors do to the poor wretches under their control, is done to Christ himself; and falleth under his severe sentence and judgement: And besides that, they help the devil to augment his kingdom; for by such oppression of the poor they draw them off from Christ, and make them seek unlawful ways to fill their bellies. Nay, they work for, and with the devil himself, doing the very same thing which he doth; who, without intermission, opposeth the king-dom of Christ, which consisteth only in love. All these oppress-ors, if they do not turn with their whole hearts to Christ, and minister to, or serve him, must go into hell-fire, which is fed and kept alive by nothing else but such mere self, as that which they have exercised over the poor here.

Scholar: But how will it fare with those, and how will they be able to stand that severe trial, who in this time do so fiercely contend about the kingdom of Christ, and slander, revile, and persecute one another for their religion, as they do?

Master: All such have not yet known Christ; and they are but as a type or figure of heaven and hell, striving with each other for the victory.

All rising, swelling pride, which contendeth about opinions, is an image of self. And whosoever hath not faith and humility, nor liveth in the spirit of Christ, which is love, is only armed with the anger of God, and helpeth forward the victory of the imagin-ary self, that is, the kingdom of darkness, and the anger of God.

For at the day of judgement all self shall be given to the darkness, as shall also all the unprofitable contentions of men; in which they seek not after love, but merely after their imaginary self, that they may exalt themselves by exalting and establishing their opinions; stirring up princes to wars for the sake of the same, and by that means occasioning the desolation of whole countries of people. All such things belong to the judgement, which will separate the false from the true; and then all images or opinions shall cease, and all the children of God shall dwell for ever in the love of Christ, and that in them.

All whosoever in this time of strife, namely, from the Fall to the Resurrection, are not zealous in the spirit of Christ, and desirous to promote peace and love, but seek and strive for themselves only, are of the devil, and belong to the pit of darkness, and must consequently be separated from Christ. For in heaven all serve God their Creator in humble love.

Scholar: Wherefore then doth God suffer such strife and contention to be in this time?
Master: The life itself standeth in strife, that it may be made manifest, sensible, and palpable, and that the wisdom may be made separable and known.

The strife also constituteth the eternal joy of the victory. For there will arise great praise and thanksgiving in the saints from the experimental sense and knowledge that Christ in them hath overcome darkness, and all the self of nature, and that they are at length totally delivered from the strife; at which they shall rejoice eternally, when they shall know how the wicked are recompensed. And therefore God suffereth all souls to stand in a free will, that the eternal dominion both of love and anger, of light and of darkness, may be made manifest and known; and that every life might cause and find its own sentence in itself. For that which is now a strife and pain to the saints in their wretched warfare here, shall in the end be turned into great joy to them; and that which hath been a joy and pleasure to ungodly persons in this world, shall afterwards be turned into eternal torment and shame to them. Therefore the joy of the saints must arise to them out of death, as the light ariseth out of a candle by the destruction and consumption of it in its fire; that so the life may be freed from the painfulness of nature, and possess another world.

And as the light hath quite another property than the fire hath, for it giveth and yieldeth itself forth; whereas the fire draweth in and consumeth itself; so the holy life of meekness springeth forth through the death of self-will, and then God's will of love only ruleth, and doth all in all. For thus the Eternal One hath attained feeling and separability, and brought itself forth again with the feeling, through death in great joyfulness; that there might be an eternal delight in the infinite unity, and an eternal cause of joy; and therefore that which was before painfulness, must now be the ground and cause of this motion or stirring to the manifestation of all things. And herein lieth the mystery of the hidden wisdom of God.

'Every one that asketh receiveth, every one that seeketh findeth; and to every one that knocketh it shall be opened. The grace of our Lord Jesus Christ, and the love of God, and the communion of the Holy Ghost, be with us all. Amen.'

Hebrews 12:22–4:

Thank ye the Lord, for ye are now come to Mount Zion, to the city of the living God, to the heavenly Jerusalem, to the innumerable company of angels, and to the general assembly and church of the first born, who are written in heaven.

And to God the Judge of all; and to the spirits of just men made perfect; and to Jesus the mediator of the new covenant.

And to the blood of sprinkling, that speaketh better things than that of Abel. Amen.

Praise, glory, and thanksgiving; honour, wisdom and power, be unto him that sitteth on the throne, to our God, and the Lamb for ever and ever. Amen.

Of the enmity of the Spirit and of the Body, and of their cure and remedy.

Everything is in itself senseless, and as a dead thing or being; it is only a manifestation of the spirit, which is in the body: The spirit is signed with the body; whatever the spirit is in itself in an incomprehensible [imperceptible] operation, the same is the body in the comprehensible and visible working. There is one form of the seven forms of nature superior and chief; the other hand to it, and give their signs also, according as each of them is strong in the essence; and as the forms stand in their order in each thing, so they sign the body of every thing and creature in its generation [or kind]: This is the manifestation of the divine wisdom in the expressed word of love and anger.

There is not anything but it has its soul in it according to its property, and the soul is a kernel to another body: Whatever lives and grows has its seed in it; God has comprehended all things in his word, and spoken them forth into a form, as the will has formed itself in the desire, the expressed word is a platform of the speaking, and has again the speaking in it; this same speaking is a seed to another image according to the first, for both work, viz. the speaking, and the spoken [word].

The speaking works in itself, viz. in the eternity, and the spoken also in itself, viz. in the time; the speaking is the master, and the spoken is the instrument; the speaking makes the nature of eternity, and the spoken makes the nature of time; each makes in its comprehension two properties, viz. light and darkness, wherein the element of all beings consists, which in the expressed word operates itself into four elements, but in the speaking word there is but one: The element in itself is neither hot nor cold, also neither dry nor moist; but it is a *lubet*, viz. a desiring will, wherein the divine wisdom makes the different and various colours; all according to the desire's property, in which there is neither number nor end: But in the four elements there is number and end; for with the expressing (in that they become self-full) they have taken a beginning, and have formed themselves into a model or platform of a time, which runneth as a watch-work; it forms, frames, and destroys.

This watch-work consists of seven forms, or properties (as is before mentioned), which make in themselves a threefold spirit, viz. a vegetative, sensitive, and rational: The vegetative consists in the four elements; the sensitive in the seven forms of nature, and the reasoning power in the constellation; but the understanding proceeds only from God, for it rises out of the eternal nature;

all life whatever, which has its limit in the expressed word, consists in Sal, Sulphur, and Mercury; for therein consist the seven properties of every life of this world; and also the spirit of vegetation, sensation, and reason.

Sulphur is the mother of all spirituality and corporality; Mercury manages the dominion therein; and Sal is the house of its habitation, which Mercury itself makes in Sulphur: Reason arises in the oil of the Sulphur, whereinto the constellation gives its desire, viz. the essence of its property, from whence immediately the senses and thoughts arise; but the understanding proceeds from the oil of the element, viz. in the free *lubet* in the speaking Mercury.

Now then, seeing it is very necessary for us poor children of Eve to know from whence the disease and enmity of our life arise, and what that is in us which makes us our own enemies, and vex, perplex, and plague us in ourselves; much more necessary it is to know the cure, whereby we may cure ourselves in our selfhood, and bring ourselves into the limit of rest.

This we will delineate and declare, if there be any one that has a mind to enter upon it, and truly prove and try it; and we will set forth from whence evil and good arise originally, and how they arise, and give occasion to the understanding searcher to seek: And we will shew how the will to evil and good arises, and how the evil is the death of the good, and on the contrary the good the death of the evil.

When we consider what the mercurial life is, then we find that it consists in Sulphur; for Sulphur is a dry hunger after matter, which makes an austere impression, and in its austere impression it has the fire, and also in its impression the oil, from whence the life burns. Now the impression makes coldness, and its compunction or attraction makes heat, so that now there is a cold fire and a hot fire in one thing; the cold makes in itself hardness and darkness, and the heat makes in itself the light, and yet there could be no light, if the oil in the Sulphur did not die in hot anguish, as the candle in the fire.

Now there is a twofold dying in the Sulphur, from whence also a twofold life is generated; First, the impression or desire does draw in, contract, enclose, make hard, cold, thick; and the hardness, viz. the enclosed, causes a death in the enclosed being, and yet in that spirit there is no death, but pricking, raging, and anxious cold fire-life, which is generated with the impression, and is the life of the darkness.

Secondly, in the same anguish, in the austere desire, the hot fire is generated, which consumes the substance, which the coldness, viz. the impression of the desire to nature makes: Thus there remains in the fire the contention betwixt the cold and the heat; the cold will have its life according to its property, and in that it strives for life, it enkindles the heat in its impression, and immediately the heat deprives the cold of its might, and consumes the cold substance, and then also the fire-spirit cannot subsist; for unless it has substance it goes out, therefore it must continually, and without intermission, die in itself in the fiery anxious desire: So long as it has the cold's substance to live upon, its life arises, and yet it is nothing but a constant dying and consuming, and in its devouring is the greatest hunger after substance; the same [hunger] passes forth through and with the devouring out of the drying of the fire, and dwells in the nothing, yet it may not be a nothing, and also it cannot be a nothing, therefore it draws the fire again into itself; for its own desire is bent towards its mother: But seeing it is once dead to the fire-source, it cannot die any more in the fire of the heat or cold, but it continually proceeds forth from the fire, and the fire draws it again continually into itself, and so it is the life of the fire; and this is the air, which in the fire is rightly called wind, by reason of the strength and force; and in that which is proceeded forth it is properly called air, by reason of its life of meekness.

And in the dying of the fire we are to understand the oil, whence the fire receives its shining light, in which the true life is understood; for that which proceeds forth in the fire-death with the desire to be delivered and freed from the fire-source, that is a desire of meekness, and takes its original in the first will to nature, in which the eternal nothing brings itself with its *lubet* into a desire.

This *lubet* brings forth itself through the cold and hot death (through both the dyings) again into the liberty, viz. into the NOTHING; and so it is manifested in the austere impression through the fire, and brought into a principle, and yet it is not either of the fire or of the cold, but so is its manifestation.

But seeing the eternal *lubet* to nature introduce itself with nature into a desire; thereupon this desire cannot die either in the cold or heat, for it takes its origin neither in the heat or cold, but in the nothing; and so it is, after it proceeds from the dying in the fire, again desiring, namely of its own property, and impresses itself, for in the fire it has taken the impression.

Now it cannot conceive anything in its impression but an essence according to its desire, which is now water; understand according to the dark impression's property it is water, and according to the fire [light] it is oil; and that which in the cold impression is wholly enclosed in the hardness, as a conception according to the wrath's property, is earth.

Thus the wrathful fiery desire draws continually the same air, water, and oil into itself, and devours it, and so the fire-wrath is changed in the air, and oil, and water, into a shining light; for the nothing desires nothing else but power and lustre, and so makes itself manifest, and brings itself into essence: And the spirit which proceeds forth out of the fire burning in the oil, viz. in the light from the fire and light, gives reason and understanding; for it has originally taken its rise in the nothing, and was the desire to nature; and has brought itself through all the properties of nature, through heat and cold, through the dying in the fire through the light, and dwells again in the nothing.

It is a prover and knower of all the properties, for it is generated through all, and proceeded forth from all; it is as a NOTHING, and yet has all things, and passes through heat and cold, and yet none of them apprehend it; as we see that the life of the creature dwells in heat and cold, and yet the right life is neither hot nor cold.

Now therefore understand us right: This birth in the eternity is spiritual, but in the time it is material; for I cannot say of God that he is darkness and fire, much less air, water, or earth; but in his eternal desire he has so formed himself with the time in the place of this world into such an essence, which he formed in the speaking MERCURY according to the properties of the will, and brought with the expressed word into such a formation according to the properties of the desire in the eternal nature, viz. in the *verbum fiat*.

Now the expressed word, viz. the eternal nature's property is understood in Sulphur, for therein is the sevenfold wheel of the birth, which in the spirit, viz. in the first conception to nature, is a constellation, and divides itself out of the constellation in its own peculiar birth into seven properties, and out of the seven properties into four elements.

This constellation is a chaos, wherein all things lie, but hidden; and it is the first body, but spiritual; and the sevenfold wheel is the first explication [or working forth] of the chaos, and makes the second body, viz. the reason; the second manifests the first, and it is also a spiritual body, the third body is elementary, a cabinet of both the first, and is a visible tangible body.

The first body, viz. the chaos, or the first constellation, seeing it is spiritual, is the word expressed out of the eternal conception; the same has again its speaking in itself, which is the mercurial wheel in the Sulphur with the seven forms, which speaks forth again from itself the four elements.

Thus the one proceeds forth from the other; the first before the chaos is the *lubet* of eternity in the abyss, which takes in itself a will to its own manifestation; this is all God; and the will conceives in itself a desire in the *lubet*; this is the chaos, or first *astrum*, wherein consists the eternal nature, which with the desire to nature introduces itself into seven forms, as is before mentioned, and so manifests the chaos, viz. the eternal hidden wisdom of God; and with the desire in the mercurial wheel the element is formed, being a spiritual body of the mercurial life.

Now all this is twofold, viz. the desire makes in itself in its impression the darkness, wherein is the strong might of the enkindling of nature, and it is painful; and the free *lubet* to the desire makes in itself through the enkindling of the desire, light and pleasing motion; the light is the power and lustre, and the element is its body, or essence; whereas yet it is only spiritual: Thus the fire-desire is a joyfulness in the free *lubet*, and in the darkness it is an aching painful source.

Out of this whole essence man was created to the image of God, and understand us right, he stood after and in the creation in the dominion of the element; the mercurial wheel in Sulphur stood in the light, and in the free *lubet* of eternity; but he departed further with his desire into the four elements, viz. into the centre of darkness, from whence heat and cold arise.

His desire in the beginning was bent [inclined] into the liberty of God, viz. into the element, where he was resigned in God; and then God's love-will ruled him with the free *lubet*'s property, but he departed out of the free *lubet* of God, out of the resignation into a self-will, which he forged in the centre to nature, from whence the pain and torture arise, viz. heat and cold, so also astringency, sour, bitterness, and all the properties of the dark impression.

Even there he fell into the eternal death, viz. into the dying source, in which the mercurial life in the Sulphur rules in the poison, where one form in the mercurial sphere does envy, hate, annoy, and destroy the other, where there is mere anguish, aching, tormenting, and enmity; for the free *lubet* was quenched in him, wherein the holy element, viz. the divine body consists, and there arose in the same pure element the four elements of the outward source; there the image of God was cursed, which is nothing else but that God's love-will, which ruled in the image of his likeness, withdrew from man, and so man fell into the dominion of nature: And seeing the four elements have a temporal beginning and end, and must again enter into the end, therefore also the human body, which is now become wholly earthly in the four elements, must fall again into the four elements, and be destroyed therein: And therefore now we are to consider of his cure and restoration, how he may again be delivered from death, and be again introduced with the body into the pure element, and with the spirit into the dominion of God's will.

Now there is no other remedy but that he with the spirit which arises in the chaos, and was inspired by God's will-spirit into the created image, does again depart out of his self-hood, viz. out of his natural will, and resign himself up fully and freely into the first will, which in the beginning formed him into an image: He must wholly die to his self-hood in himself in the death of the dark impression (as far as he lives therein to his own will in the self-desire of the outward life of the four elements) and cast himself with total resignation into God's will, viz. into God's mercy, that he may no longer live and will to himself, but to God, viz. to the first will of God, which created him in its image, whereby God manifested himself in an image; and so he is with the first astrum, viz. with the chaos of the soul, again in the same comprehension wherein God created him to his image.

But seeing the self-hood, viz. the self-will, strives against this, and will in no wise die to its selfhood (understand the will of the outward world, which is from the outward stars and four elements), therefore God's food must be given to the inward will of the spirit to eat of, that it may live without need and hunger as to the outward being, that it may continually mortify and break the will of the earthly selfhood, till the earthiness, viz. the earthly body, does freely unloose or dissolve itself in death, and also enter again into the mother, from whence it was created, and forsake its selfhood, that the pure body of the element (in which the true life in God's will-spirit does again enkindle the soul in the resigned will) and the disappeared body from the pure element may become a mansion of the soul, viz. a paradisical budding [or bloomy renovation in the eternal springtime of paradise].

And that the own will of the soul might be able to do this, viz. that it might break itself off from its selfhood, and willingly enter into the death of its selfhood, and become a nothing in its selfhood, the free will of God, viz. the eternal *lubet* to the chaos of the soul, which is the eternal Mercury in the power of the majesty, is again entered into the disappeared image of God proceeded from the pure element, viz. into the virgin-like life, and draws the will of the soul to itself, and gives it again out of love and grace the heavenly corporality of the pure element of food, and the water in that element in the tincture of the fire and light, viz. of the eternal life, for drink: and it has incorporated itself in the humanity, and freely tenders itself to all souls with full desire: That soul which dies to its selfhood, and brings its hunger again into God's mercy may enjoy this food, whereby it again becomes the first creature in God's love.

Now we are to consider how the poor soul captivated in God's anger, being void of the heavenly food, lives in mere anguish, and distress, and restless pain; as the outward earthly body in its properties lives in its hunger in mere anguish, distress, and oppressing pain, unless the soul with the pure element does so overpower and keep it under, that it does not fully domineer in its own dominion of the outward astrum and four elements in the poisonful mercurial wheel, according to the dark impression, by reason of the influence of the element: If the universal does withstand it, then it may stand in quiet rest, but yet no longer than the inward penetrates the outward [body], and tinctures it: There is in the four elements no perfection, till the body is changed again into the pure element; therefore it must enter again into that from whence the four elements arise.

Now in this time of the four elements there is mere pain and vexation; the soul amuses itself on the outward astrum, which forces into it, from whence its false imagination arises, and the body stirs up the poisonful mercurial wheel, from whence sickness and pain befall it; therefore the soul must be cured with the inward perfection, viz. by the speaking word, wherein it stands in God's hand, which alone is able to tincture the soul, and bring it to rest: The outward body must be tinctured and healed with the expressed Mercury; and if the outward Mercury does also stand in the curse as a poison-wheel, then he must be tinctured with his own light in his mother in the body [or womb] of Sulphur: Mercury's own will and hunger must be broken that the envious odious hunger may become a love desire.

And now to know how this may be brought to pass, we must consider the generation in Sulphur, from whence joy and sorrow do arise; for the poisonful Mercury may not otherwise be resisted, and also nothing can resist it, but its own mother which brings it forth, in whose womb it is couched: As nothing can resist the cold but the heat only, and yet the heat is the cold's son; so also the poisonful Mercury must be resisted with its own child, which he himself generates in his mother's womb out of heat and cold out of himself.

As the love proceeding from the heart of the Father, which is his Son, withstands the anger of the Father, whereby the Father is merciful; so likewise it is in the expressed word of Mercury.

Now understand it thus: I do not mean that the cold poison of Mercury should be, or could be resisted with the enkindled heart; no, but if the cold poison be enkindled, then the remedy must be from the same likeness; but it must be first freed from the coldness, viz. from the enflamed cold wrath, and brought into meekness, and then it does also still and appease the hunger of the cold's desire in the disease of the body: For if enkindled heat be administered to the enkindled cold, then the cold is dismayed at the heat, and falls into a swound, viz. into death's property; and so the heat becomes in this death's property a poison-life, viz. an anxious sting; and the mercurial wheel runs into sadness, viz. into sickness, or a crazy dotage, wherein all joy is forgotten.

For if the life shall subsist in its own right, then the heat and cold must stand in equality, that so they may accord one with another, and no enmity or disaffection be at all in any of them; the one must not exceed or over-top the other, but they must stand in one will; for the enkindled cold desires no heat but only likeness: Every hunger desires only likeness for its food, but if the hunger be too strongly enkindled in the cold, such a cure is not to be given it which is so enkindled; indeed it must be in as high a degree in the cold; but the violent force must be first taken away from it; so that it may be only as the mother which generates it, not according to the enkindled poison-source, but according to the mother's joy; and so the sickness, viz. the poison in the anguish, will be likewise changed into such a joy, and so the life receives again its first property.

The raw opposite body does not belong to the cure, but its oil, which must be mollified with its own love, understand with a meek essence, which also belongs to the same property; for the seven forms of nature are only one in the centre: Therefore that oil must be brought so far in the wheel, till it enters into its highest love-desire, and then it is rightly fit for cure; for there is nothing so evil but it has a good in it, and that very good resists its evil [or poisonful malignity].

Thus also in the same sickness it may withstand the enkindled wrath in the body; for if the cold poison be enkindled in the body, then its good falls into faintness; and if it cannot obtain the likeness of its essence for its help, it remains in faintness; and then the enkindled wrath also does immediately consume itself, and falls also into faintness; and so the natural death is in both, and the moving life in the body ceases; but if it attains the likeness, then it gathers strength again, and the enkindled hunger of the disease must cease.

In like manner also we are to consider of the heat, which needs no cold property, but the likeness; yet it must be first freed from the wrath of the same likeness, and brought into its own highest joy and good, so that this likeness does not effectually operate either in heat or cold, but in its own love-desire, viz. in its best relish, and so it will bring the heat in the body into such a desire: All corruptions in the body proceed from the cold; if the brimstone be too vehemently enkindled by the heat, then the right and property of the cold dies, and enters into sorrow.

Mercury is the moving life in all, and his mother is Sulphur; now the life and death lie in Sulphur, viz. in the wrestling mercurial wheel. In the Sulphur there is fire, light, and darkness; the impression causes darkness, coldness, and hardness, and also great anguish: and from the impression of the attraction Mercury takes his rise, and he is the sting of the attraction, viz. the motion or disquietude, and arises in the great anguish of the impression, where coldness, viz. a dark cold fire, by reason of its hardness, arises in the impression; and in the sting of anguish, viz. in the disquietude, a hot fire arises.

Now Mercury is the wheel of motion, and a stirring up of the cold and heat; and in this place it is only a painful aching source in heat and cold, viz. a cold and hot fiery poison-anguish, and forces forward as a wheel, and yet it is a cause of joy, and all life and motion; but if it shall be freed from the anguish, and introduced into joy, then it must be brought forth through death.

Now every sickness and malady is a death's property; for Mercury has too much enkindled and enflamed himself either in heat or cold, whereby the essence or flesh, which he has attracted to himself in his desire, viz. in his mother in the Sulphur, is burnt, whereby the earthliness arises both in the water and flesh: Even as the matter of the earth and stones, viz. the grossness of the same, is nothing else but a burnt Sulphur, and water in Mercury is his property, where the *salniter* in the *flagrat* of the mercurial wheel, from whence the manifold salts arise, is burnt [or too vehemently enflamed], from whence come the stink and evil taste.

Otherwise if the Mercury did so effectually operate therein in the oil of Sulphur, that he might be brought through the death of the impression from the heat and cold, then the earth would be again in paradise, and the joy-desire would again spring [or bloom afresh] through the anguish of the cold's impression: And this is the cause that God laid a curse upon the earth; for the mercurial wheel was deprived of its good (viz. the love-desire, which arises in the eternal liberty, and manifests itself with this mercurial wheel through cold and heat, and proceeds forth through the fire, and makes a shining of the light) and the curse was brought thereinto, which is a withdrawing of the love-desire.

Now this Mercury, being a life in the Sulphur of its mother, stands in the curse, viz. in the anguish of heat and cold, and makes in his *flagrat*, or salnitral walm, continually salts, according to such property as he is in each place, and as he is enkindled in each body; these salts are only the taste in the seven properties.

Now if the Mercury be too vehemently enkindled in the cold, then he makes in the salnitral *flagrat* in his mother in the Sulphur a cold hard impressive salt, from whence melancholy, darkness, and sadness arise in the life of the Sulphur; for observe what salt is in each thing, such a lustre of the fire, and such a vital shining from the fire is also therein; but if Mercury be enkindled in immoderate heat, he then burns up the cold essence, and makes raging pains and achings according to the impression, and according to the sting's property, from whence arises in the Sulphur great heat and inflammation; he dries up and consumes the water, so that the desire's hunger or sting has then no food to satisfy its wrathful hunger, upon which he rages and tears in the salt, as it is the poison's property [so to do], from whence the painful distemper in the flesh arises.

But if he obtains the likeness again in the property as he stands in the centre of his mother, viz. in the Sulphur, understand as she has generated him in the beginning, viz. as he at first came forth to the natural life in both tinctures of man and woman, understand in the child where his life did enkindle, then he is freed from all anguish, and enters again into the likeness from the very womb, yet the combat is first raised up after the beginning of the life: In the life's beginning the life enters into its highest joy; for the gates of the three principles are opened in equal accord; but the strife soon begins about the conquest between the darkness and the light.

But now we are to consider what is to be done to Mercury, if he be enkindled either in heat or cold, whereby he raises up sickness and pains: Now it were very good that men had the right cure; but alas! it will remain hidden and covered by reason of the curse of the earth, and the abominations and sins of men, because they awaken this poison in Mercury with their immoderate bestiality.

Yet the poor captive has need of deliverance; and though men have not the high universal, which reaches the centre, and brings the wheel of life into its first property, yet men must take from the mercurial walm of the earth its fruits thereunto, seeing the body is also become earthly: A man must accord (or assimilate) one likeness with another, one salt with another, according as the inflammation is in the salt of the body: For observe, in what property the brimstone is enkindled, either in heat or cold, in melancholy or falling sickness (whether it be yet fresh and burning), even such a herb, such a brimstone belongs to the cure, lest the heat or cold be terrified in the salniter, where the salt arises, by a strange might which comes into it, and generates a mort salt, and sets upon more and more the house of sadness: But it is not sufficient and powerful enough in its wild nature and property as it grows out of the walm of the earth; it is not able to master the root of the enkindled Mercury in the brimstone, but it does more vehemently enkindle it in such a source and property.

That which thou desirest should happen to the body, the same must first happen to that which shall cure the body: To the cure of a foul sickness there belongs a foul brimstone, and so to a cold or hot sickness the like is to be understood; for look in what degree of the fire or cold Mercury is enkindled, and in what form among the seven properties of nature; that is, what salt soever among the seven salts is enkindled, such a salt belongs to the cure: For sickness is nothing else but a hunger; now the hunger desires nothing else but its likeness; but now the property of that life, which in its beginning of its rise stood in joy, is the root; and the sickness is its immoderate enkindling, whereby the order [or temperature] is broken and divided: Thus the root desires in its hunger the likeness, but the inflammation has taken it away; now the inflammation is stronger than the root, therefore the hunger of the inflammation must be appeased, and that which itself is must be administered to it.

But as God cured us with his love, and restored to us the salvation of the soul, when we had enkindled the same in the poisonful Mercury of his anger; in like manner also this likeness must be first cured and circulated in the mercurial wheel, and freed from the heat and cold; indeed not taken away from them (this cannot be, and it were also unprofitable), but it must be brought into his highest joy, and then it will make such a property in the body in the Mercury of the brimstone and salt; for the root of life does again quicken itself therein, and lifts up the first desire, so that now the hunger vanishes in the fall of the inflammation.

Now it behoves the physician to know how he may deal with the medicaments in the likeness, so that he does not enrage them, and bring them into another property; for in their property they are even as a man's life is: He must take care that they remain in their degree, as they are originally brought forth in their mother; for nothing can come higher than it is in the centre of its original according to the hiddenness; but if it shall come higher, then it must assume another property to itself; and so it is not in its own degree, and has not its proper virtue, but an improper one; which indeed may very well be, but it has lost its nature-right, wherein it stands in joy, and is not able to effect any proper operation in the assimulate of its own nature.

Therefore there is nothing better than to let everything remain in its innate genuine virtue; only its wrath must be changed into its own joy, that so its own virtue according to the good part may be advanced into its dominion, and then in the likeness it is powerful enough in all sicknesses without any other mixture: For the original in the life desires no other multiplicity, but only its likeness, that it may stand, live, and burn in its own power and property.

The power of the Most High has given to all things (to every one according to its property) a fixed perfection; for 'all was very good', as Moses says, but with the curse the *turba* is introduced, so that the properties stand in the strife of Mercury; yet in each property, in every herb, or whatever is, in whatever grows or arises out of the walm of the four elements, there is a fixity hidden; for all things which are in the four elements are originally sprung forth out of the eternal element, in which there is no strife, neither heat nor cold, but all things were in equal weight of all the properties in a love-play, as it is so now in paradise; and the same [paradise] sprung forth in the beginning of this world before the curse through the earth: Thus it is also yet hidden in all things, and may be opened by understanding and art, so that the first virtue may overcome the enflamed malignity.

Though we men have not full power to do it in self-might, yet it may be done in God's permission, who has again turned his mercy towards us, and again opened paradise and its comprehension in man: Hath God given us power to become his children, and to rule over the world? Why then not over the curse of the earth? Let none hold it for impossible; there is required only a divine understanding and knowledge thereunto, which shall blossom in the time of the lily, and not in Babel, for whom we also have not written.

Christianity and other religions

For God hath not sent his Son to condemn the world (John 3:17), viz. the poor corrupt man, but he hath therefore sent him into the world among the Godless crew of evil men, to reach and call them; and those who have a willing desire to hear he will save. Even those that have but a sparkle of the divine being in them, which is capable of hearing, the quickening and renewing voice of Christ doth cry and call in that little spark which is in all these; that is, it bloweth up that little spark, that it may become a divine fire.

And that we may open wide the eyes of the blind, self-named Christendom, and also of the Jews in their boasting, that they may not so brag, and stand upon their knowledge, as if they alone were the children of God, because they know the name of God, and flatter themselves with the knowing it, and condemn other people, who are deprived of knowing as they know, and have introduced another knowledge, as they, alas! do most blindly; in so much, that one nation and people doth evilly entreat another: Know, that Cain, Ham, Ishmael, and Esau, are the types of the Turks and heathen, whom God blessed in Ishmael; and gave them to possess the princely dominions in his kingdom of this world, and cast them out in their own contrived knowledge from the knowledge of the sonship of Christ; as he cast out Ishmael; but recalls them in the womb, by the angel of the great counsel, unto the fire, viz. to God's goods, that they should return to him.

For they lie shut up under the veil of Christ, as Christ did under the Levitical priesthood under Moses; Children of Israel under the Law were not justified through the Law, but through him who was hidden under the Law, and thus they are now hidden under the true knowledge, and lie as it were shut up in the mother's womb.

But the angel of the great counsel calls them by their mother, Hagar, viz. by the kingdom of nature; that she (the mother and her child) should return home to Sarah, viz. to the free, that is, to the one only God, who hath born his Son of the free. Thus they come as it were under the veil in the mother's womb to the free, viz. to the one only God; who hath born unto them, of the free woman, the true Lord, (unto whose goods they, being strangers, are received in grace), as sojourners.

For as Ishmael did not go to Isaac for the inheritance, which did of right belong to Isaac (because the Lord was in him, who freely bestowed it upon him, and set him as a steward), but would have it of the Father; even so the Turks have turned themselves from Isaac, viz. from the Son, to the Father, and will have the inheritance of God from the Father.

Now the Father is manifested to us in the Son; and when they now do call upon the Father, he heareth them only in his Son, viz. in his voice manifest in the human property, and they yet serve the Son in the Father.

For we men have no other God at all without Christ the Son; for the Father hath manifested himself towards us with his voice in the Son, and heareth us only through his voice manifested in the Son.

Now when the Turks worship the Father, he heareth them in the Son, and receiveth them to adoption only in the Son, in whom God hath only alone once more manifested himself in the human property, and in no other property besides.

Now saith reason, how can they attain to the adoption of Christ, when as they will not have the Son to be the Son of God, and say, that God hath no Son. Hear, O man, Christ said, *Whosoever speaketh a word against the Son of Man, to him it shall be forgiven; but he that blasphemeth the Holy Ghost, to him it shall never be forgiven* (Matthew 12:32): that is, as much as if he should say:

Whosoever reproacheth the humanity of Christ in ignorance, considering of it as his own flesh, to him it may be forgiven; for he knoweth not what the humanity of Christ is. But he that blasphemeth the Holy Ghost, viz. the only God, who hath manifested himself in the humanity, wherein Father, Son, and Holy Ghost, are one only God, he hath no forgiveness for evermore. That is, he that rejecteth the only God, he hath quite broken himself off from him, into an ownhood of self.

Now the Turks do not blaspheme the Holy Spirit, who manifested himself in the humanity, but they reproach the humanity, and say a creature cannot be God.

But that God hath wrought, and done wonders in Christ, that they confess, and blaspheme not the Spirit which hath wrought in Christ, viz. in the humanity. Blindness is happened unto them, so that they walk under a veil.

Now saith reason, God hath taken away the candlestick from them, and rejected them. Hear, O man, what was the cause that God (as he threatened by St John) did take away the candlestick from them, and shut them up under the veil. Thinkest thou that it was done without his foreknowledge, without his will? No, it was done with his will.

He permitted the kingdom of nature to give them a doctrine of reason; seeing Christendom became blind in their reason, in respect of Christ's person, and did wrangle and jangle about Christ's humanity, and put all manner of scorn, reproach, and disgrace upon his person; as it fell out among the Arians, when they denied his deity, and the bishops in their covetousness did apply his merits in his humanity for the belly's sake to their belly orders, and did practice all manner of lewdness and profaneness, even with swearing, cursing, and juggling and sorcery by his suffering and holy wounds; so that there the holy name of God, which had manifested itself in the humanity, was abused; thereupon God did hide himself from them in their understanding, so that first they became blind with the Arians in respect of the deity of Christ.

But afterwards, when as they would be only blind beasts, he hid himself also from them in respect of the humanity by the Turkish religion, the doctrine of Mahomet, or the Koran, so that they were wholly deprived of the candlestick of the world, and it went with them, as the prophet said to Israel under their king: *Ah! I must give theee judges, as in former times* (Isaiah 1:26).

Thus the king of light in the humanity was withdrawn from them, and the judicature of nature was given them again for a guide and governor; so that they returned again into the mother's womb, viz. into the root, out of which man was created, that is, to the only God; so that the name and knowledge of the holy humanity of Christ is yet put out with them.

And that they might not use the same so vainly, and uneffectually for swearing, and false defence, they must again enter into Hagar, as into the mother's womb; and have now verily been a long time a people run away in their mother Hagar from Abraham's house, viz. from the humanity of Christ.

But know and declare this as a word of the Most High, known in the sound of his trumpet, which he hath prepared to awaken all nations, and to visit the face of the whole earth: That the angel of the great counsel, viz. the holy voice of Christ, is not departed from them, eternally to forget them, so little as a mother can forget her child, that she should not have pity upon the son of her womb, albeit he were disobedient to her.

For as the angel came to Ishmael, being yet in the womb, when his mother fled from Sarah, and did enrich him with a blessing and wordly dominions, and bade the mother with the child return to Sarah; thus likewise when the Eastern Countries entered again into the mother's womb, with their knowledge of religion, God gave unto them, in the kingdom of nature, power and authority over the princely dominions of the world, for to possess and rule them under the light of nature, till its time; and then they shall come in again with great joy, and with great humility, to Abraham, viz. to Christ.

And not in the form of the Babylonical, formal, literal Christendom, in their invented and contrived orders, which are only Christians (so that a testimony of Christ and his kingdom have still continued upon the earth), but they shall be born in spirit, and in power; for they are the lost son, which is wandered away from the Father, and is become the swineherd.

But when the angel shall bid them return, they come in the humility of the lost son returning to the Father. And then there will be great joy celebrated by Christ and his angels, that the dead is made alive, and the lost is again found, and the true golden jubilee-year of the marriage of the Lamb ariseth up among them.

And albeit the elder brother (who hath continued in the letter) doth grumble at it, in respect of the different form which he hath made to himself (for the most part for his belly and honour), yet they are not moved at it; they are merry with the Father.

Now then, if we truly compare counterfeit Christendom and the Turks together, and look upon them aright, then we see that they (since the Turks departed from them) have been but one people, before God in righteousness and holiness, with different names.

And they are the two sons, to one whereof the Father said, *Go and do this; and he said, Yea, but did it not; and to the other also, Do this, and he said, No, but did it* (Matthew 21:28–31). Which doth so highly advance or set forth the Turks in the kingdom of nature, which the blind Christian world doth not understand.

Not that we justify the Turks, and say that they should remain in their blindness. No, but to the counterfeit nominal Christians we declare, that they are alike with the Turks before God, in that they are as blind as to Christ's kingdom as the Turks. As it plainly shews itself, in that Christendom is full of strife and contention about Christ's deity, and humanity; and abominably profaneth the holy name in his humanity; and uses it only for a form and custom to swear also to idolatry and hypocrisy, and is gone from the sword of the Holy Spirit, unto a bloodthirsty confounding sword, wherein is nothing but contending, and condemning one another; and the whole titular Christendom is turned into mere sects and orders, where one sect doth despise and brand another for unrighteousness. And thus they have made of Christendom a mere murdering den, full of blasphemies about Christ's person; and have bound the spirit of Christ, (in which a Christian should live in deepest humility), to the forms and orders of disputation; and have set foolish reason to judge what the meaning of the Holy Spirit is in the Scripture above Christ's kingdom.

But ought we to speak so of Christendom and the Turks as if they were alike? Thus we say, the Turk is openly an Ishmaelite, and a mocker of Christ's humanity, and holdeth him not for the Son of God and for the son of man, jointly; for he understands not the heavenly ens in the person.

But the sects of Christendom do indeed cover themselves with Christ's mantle, but do attack him in his humanity and deity, and revile him in his whole person; tear and rend one another with words, and swords, about his person; the one will have it this way, another that way, every one will be master over his words and spirit; and deride Christ in his members, and are as revolting rebellious and fugitive Ishmaelites as the Turks, and live in their selfish will; and serve the kingdom of nature in their selfhood, and worldly interests and pleasure.

A Christian should be dead with Christ to self; and be risen again in Christ; and be born anew of Christ, and put on Christ; that so he might be a Christian in Christ, in the spirit and heavenly flesh of Christ, according to the internal spiritual man.

But instead hereof men have put on Babel and the Antichrist; and do boast themselves of their ordinances and of the divine orders in the performance of devout duties in lip-labour and much prating, and in the stone houses of the churches, cathedrals, and cloisters of Christendom; where indeed they do counterfeit somewhat of Christ, seeing that they there read the writings which the Apostles left behind them; but afterwards in their preaching, for the most part they foist in the kingdom and government of nature, with brawling, and disputing; and spend the time with disputing, confuting, and contending about sects and their different mental idols and opinions, in so much that one party is brought wholly to condemn another, and the ears and hearts of the hearers are so infected with gall and bitterness that one sect wilfully opposeth another, and cries it down for devilish; whence nothing but wars, and disdainful provocations do arise, to the desolating of countries and cities.

Thus they are alike before God, and lie as it were shut up in Hagar, in the dead reason; except the true children of God, which verily are here and there to be found among all nations and sects, but wholly simple, and despised; also covered under Christ's cross, to the reasonwise world.

For as the four elements receive the powerful influence of the sun, and we see in the substance the body, but not the sun, although it worketh therein; so likewise the spirit of God is hid in the children of God. But as a herb springing from the earth doth by the virtue of the sun put forth a fair blossom and fruit, so also God's children out of their disregarded form or homeliness, to the lewd world's prating hypocrite's eye, do bring forth the fair fruits of humility and piety.

LETTERS TO FRIENDS

**A letter to Paul Kaym, being an answer to him concerning
our last times.
Wherein he treateth of the first resurrection of the dead,
and of the thousand years Sabbath. Also, of the fall of
Babel, and of the new building in Zion.**

Light, Salvation, and Eternal Power flowing from the fountain
of the heart of Jesus Christ be our quickening consolation.

Worthy and much esteemed sir, and good friend in the
illumination of the Holy Spirit, and in the love of our Lord Jesus
Christ: Beloved brother, I received of Mr Carl von Ender the
letter you sent me, dated about the 20th of July, together with
two small treatises annexed; and therein I understand that you
have received and read some of my small manuscripts concerning the wisdom of God, and as you affirm, the same do rejoice
you; and withal you bear a great desire and longing to them,
being in the like exercise in the wisdom of God.

Which on my part doth likewise rejoice me to see that even
now the time is at hand that the right divine understanding and
true knowledge of God doth again spring forth in *Zion*; and that
the ruinate *Jerusalem shall again be built up*, and that man's true
image which disappeared and went out in *Adam*, doth again put
forth itself in *Zion* with a right human voice, and that God doth
pour forth His Spirit into us, that the precious pearl in the power
and light of the Holy Ghost is again known, sought, and found.

Whereby, then, we do clearly see and understand in what

blindness we for a long time have been in *Babel*, going astray in carnal, evil ways; whereby we have forsaken the true *Jerusalem* and shamefully misspent our patrimony, and lightly esteemed our angelical trophy or diadem (viz. the fair image), and wallowed in the filth of the devil; and under a show of divine obedience have played with the serpent and walked on in mere erroneous ways. Thus the divine light doth at present set before our eyes, and exhorts us to return with the lost son and enter into the true Zion.

Not with historical supposals, opinions, or blind persuasions, as if we had apprehended and understood the same very well; this is not *Zion*, but *Babel*, which confesseth God with the mouth and maketh devout speeches to Him from the lips, but in the heart hangeth unto the *great Babylonical whore*, unto the *dragon* of self-love, pride, covetousness, and pleasure, and yet will set forth herself as if she were a virgin. No, this is not the virgin in *Zion*, it must be seriousness.

We must be born of God in *Zion*, and know and also do His will, God's Spirit must bear witness to our spirit that we are God's children; not only in the mouth with knowledge and conjectures, but in the heart in very deed; not in an holy seeming way without power [in formal ways of word-worship and rounds of lip-labour, wherein the captivated conscience placeth the power of godliness]; this the devil mocks at and cares not for; but we must put on the helmet of righteousness and of love, also of charity and purity, if we intend to wage battle against the Prince of this world; he careth not a whit for any outward show, it must be power that shall overcome him, and that power must shine forth in *goodness, and holy fruits of Christianity*; and so we may fight for the noble prize or crown of life.

For we have a powerful warrior against us; he sets upon us in body and soul, and soon casts us down, and there is no other way to overcome him but with power in humility, which alone is able to quench his poisonful fire, wherewith he fighteth us without and within against our noble image.

Therefore, beloved sir and brother in Christ, seeing you do apply yourself to the divine wisdom and labour in the same, it is right and requisite that we exhort one another to be vigilant to withstand the devil, and continually set before our eyes the way which we ought to walk, and also go on in the same, else we effect nothing. If we know that the world is blind in *Babel* and goeth astray, then we must be the first that effectually *go out* of Babel, that the world may see that we are in earnest.

It is not enough that we lay open and manifest Babel, and yet be found doing as Babel doth; for if we do so, we thereby testify that God discovereth His light unto us, so that we see, but we will do nothing but the works of darkness. And that very light which enlighteneth our understanding shall witness against us, that the Lord hath called us and shown us the way, but we would not walk in the same.

It is *well* that we lay open Babel, but we must *take heed* in what spirit and mind, and in what kind of knowledge, the same is done. It is *good* that we be zealous, but the heart must be *upright* towards God, else we run without being sent. And in our course we are not known or acknowledged of God; but so acting, the devil mocks us, and leads us into by-paths of error.

Besides, the Holy Scripture doth declare that our works and words shall follow us (Revelation 14:13). Therefore we are seriously to consider in what spirit and knowledge we set upon the high mysteries; for he that will pull down a thing that is evil must set up a better in the room, otherwise he is none of God's builders, also he laboureth not in Christ's vineyard; for it is not good to pull down, unless a man knows how to make up the building again in a better frame and form.

For God only is the Master Builder of the world. We are but servants. We must take great heed how we labour if we will receive reward; and also that we have learnt His work in His school, and not run without being sent, when as we are not yet capable of His service, else we shall be found to be unprofitable servants. This I speak in good affection, and in all faithfulness, to instruct and direct one another what we ought to do, that so our labour may be accepted of God.

For the dark mysteries are no other way at all to be known, save only in the Holy Ghost. We cannot make conclusions upon hidden things, unless we have the same in real knowledge, and *experimentally find in the illumination of God*, that what we aver is the truth and will of God; and that *it is also agreeable to His Word and grounded in the light of Nature, for without the light of Nature there is no understanding of the divine mysteries.*

The great building of God is manifest in the light of Nature; and therefrom he whom God's light doth illuminate may search out and know all things. Albeit, knowledge is not in one and the same say and measure; for God's wonders and works are boundless, infinite, and immense, and they are revealed to every one according to his gifts, and he to whom the light shineth hath mere joy in God's works.

And also that which is old and past above a thousand years ago is as nigh and as easily to be known in the light as that which is done today; for a thousand years before God are scarce so much as a minute or the twinkling of an eye is before us. Therefore, all things are nigh and manifest to His spirit, both that which is past and that which is to come.

And if we see in His light, then we must declare His wonders and manifest and praise His glorious name, and *not bury* our talent in the earth; for we must deliver it unto our Master with *increase.* He will require an account of us—how we have traded with it. And without knowledge or certain illumination from God no man must presume to judge, or be a doctor or master, in the great mystery; for it is not committed to, or commanded him, but he must labour to attain the true light, and then he goeth rightly to work in the school of God.

For there be many masters to be found who presume to judge in the mystery, and yet they are not known or sent by God; and therefore their *school* is called *Babel*, the mother of whoredom upon earth. They flatter on both sides, they play the hypocrites with God, and also serve the devil; *they call themselves* the shepherds and pastors of Jesus Christ; they run and yet are not sent, much less doth God own them; and what they do they do for their honour and belly's sake, and they would not run either, if they did not obtain it in their *course* of spiritual whoredom and hypocrisy.

They have turned the right and exceeding precious mystery of God to a mystery of their whoredom and pleasure. And, therefore, the spirit calleth it *Babel*—a confusion—where men do practice an hypocritical service and worship of God, acknowledging Him with the tongue but denying Him in the power; where men do dissemble and flatter God with the lips, but in the heart they embrace and love the dragon (in the *Revelation*).

Such as these we must not be, if we would obtain the divine mystery, and be capable of the light. But wholly approve our way to God, and resign ourselves up to Him, that God's light may shine in us; that He may be our intelligence, knowing, willing, and also doing; we must become His children if we will speak of His being, and walk or labour in the same, for He commits not His work unto a stranger, who hath not learnt His work, or the mystery of His *wonders in nature and grace.*

I have read over your books, and therein have found your great diligence with very much labour, in that you have gathered together the texts of the Holy Scripture in great abundance; I understand likewise that you are in good earnest about it, and that you would fain clearly prove and set forth thereby the dark terms and places of the Scripture concerning the last times, also concerning the first resurrection of the dead, and also concerning the thousand years Sabbath; likewise you would manifest and set forth the ruin of *Babel*, and the new building of *Zion* of which the Scripture speaketh in many places.

First, what concerneth *Babel*; how it hath grown up, and how it shall again be destroyed, is sufficiently manifest; the *destroyer is already on foot*, and is now about the work; he hath long since made a beginning; however, the world will not see or take any notice of it.

Men cry murder, confusion, and destruction, to their adversaries, and yet there is no strange enemy, but it is the *Turba* only which hath grown up in the midst of Babel in her wickedness and unrighteousness; that hath found the limit, and destroyeth only that which for a long time hath been naught, useless, and selfish, the which should at all times have been rejected, for where God should have been honoured, and loved, and our neighbour also as a man loveth himself, there men have set up in God's stead the abominable and bestial covetousness, deceit, falsehood, and wicked craft under an hypocritical show and pretence of holiness, and have minded and loved falsehood in the place of God, and so have made of the mystery an abominable vicious Babel full of reproachings, revilings, and contentions, where they have with sweet speeches and enticing words of man's wisdom, blindfolding our eyes, and binding our consciences, have led up captive in a very deceitful way to the glory and magnificence of the great whore, so that she hath fatted her adulterous brat, and domineered over our body and soul, goods and estate.

This bastard is now at odds with himself about the great prey and spoil, and doth itself discover its own wickedness and great shame, so that we may see what good ever was in her, for the great wickedness which she hath committed doth plague her; and no strange thing, whereby it may be seen that her whoredom hath been manifold, and that the devil had beset and caught us in manifold nets, and that one whoredom runs in opposition to another, and are malicious, biting, devouring, destroying, and slaying each other in a hostile manner.

For the great pain is come upon her, and she shall now bring forth the great iniquity, wherewith she is become fully pregnant, and therefore she crieth out, because of her travail and woe, which is fallen upon her; and she speaketh of the child which she shall bring forth, viz. of murder, covetousness, and tyranny; she uncovereth her fair feature, and showeth what she is in the heart; now he that will not know her, there is no remedy for him.

The *Revelation* saith, *Go out from her, My people, that you may not be partakers of her plagues*, for she hath filled her cup full with the abominations of her whoredom in the anger of God, the same she shall drink of, and be forced to burst herself thereby.

And this is that which I say of *Babel*, that she is a whore, and shall suddenly break in pieces and be destroyed, and no stranger shall do it; the spirit of her own mouth doth strangle her; her own *Turba* destroyeth her; she crieth for vengeance and murder upon heresy, and yet she doth it not for God's sake, but for her *adulterous brat and belly-god*: for otherwise if it were for God, she would enter into His command and will of *love*, where Christ saith, *Love one another, for thereby men shall know that you are My disciples*.

The kingdom of God doth not consist in war and revilings, or in an eternal show in delicious days; herein the children of God are not to be found, but in love, in patience, in hope, in faith, under the cross of Jesus Christ; thereby groweth the Church of God unto the sacred Ternary, and the new angelical man, hidden in the old, springeth forth in God; and this is my certain knowledge briefly comprised concerning this article; in my writings you may see further of it.

Secondly, concerning *Zion*, I speak and declare according to my knowledge, even as the Spirit showeth it to me; that there shall *surely come an ending and removal of the deceit, and Zion shall be found only of the children of faith*; not in general, as if there should be no wicked man.

For the oppressor shall be a cause that *Zion* is born: when men shall see how *Babel* is a whore; then many children shall be found in *Zion* and seek the Lord, but the oppressor shall dog them and cry them down for heretics; also, persecute and put to death, and where one is killed there shall be ten, yea a hundred, rise up in his room.

But in general *Zion* appeareth first in greatest misery; when *Babel* cometh to ruin, then it shall stand desolate and miserable, and the children of *Zion* shall then say: How hath the Lord forsaken us? Come, we beseech you, let us seek His face; let us cease from strife and war. Have we not, alas! Made our country desolate? Is not all store and *provision wasted and spent?* Are we not brethren? *Wherefore do we fight?* We will now enter into love and unity and seek the Lord, and no more fight and destroy ourselves; we will be content; are we not here altogether pilgrims and strangers, and seek our native country?

In this time a *Zion* verily shall be found, and the heaven shall drop down its dew, and the earth yield her fatness; yet, not so as if wickedness should be wholly done away, for it shall continue unto the end, of which Christ saith: *Thinkest thou that when the Son of Man shall come that there will be faith upon the earth?* And though the children of *Zion* shall have a fiery deliverance, that they shall remain, despite the will of the devil; insomuch that God will work great things, *as at the time of the Apostles*, yet it endureth not unto the end; for as it was in the days of *Noah* when he entered into the Ark, so shall the coming of the Son of Man be, as it is written.

But that the Holy Ghost shall be in the hearts of the faithful in *Zion*, I acknowledge and I know it, for *Zion* shall not be from without, but in the new man; it is already born; he that would seek it, let him but seek himself, and depart from the old *Adam* into a new life, and he shall find where Jesus be born in him.

If he finds it not, let him enter into himself, and seriously consider himself; and so he shall find Babel, and her workings in him; these he must destroy and enter into God's covenant; and then *Zion* will be revealed in him, and he shall be born with Christ in Bethlehem of Judaea in the dark stable, *not in Jerusalem*, as reason fain would have it, that Christ should be born in the old ass; the old ass must become servant, and serve the new man in *Zion*.

But that in *four hundred years* there shall be a mere golden age, I know nothing of it, it is not revealed to me; also, the *limit* of the world's end is *not revealed to me*. I cannot speak of any *four hundred years*, for the Lord hath not commanded me to teach it. I commend it to God's might, and leave it for those to whom God would vouchsafe the knowledge of it; seeing, therefore, I have not as yet apprehended it, I rest satisfied in His gifts; yet I despise no man, if he had a knowledge and command so to teach.

For the fourth book of Esdras is not sufficient, as I understand, to give a positive assurance to it; yet, I wait for my Saviour, Jesus Christ, and rejoice that I may find my Lord; when I have Him, then I hope after the death of my old Adam fully to recreate myself in the still rest of Zion, and to wait in my God, expecting what He will do with me in His and my Zion; for if I have but Him, then I am in and with Him in the eternal Sabbath, where no strife or contention of the ungodly can any more reach me, me in my *new man*, at this I do, in the meantime, rejoice in this miserable *Vale of Tabernacles*.

The first resurrection of the dead to the thousand years Sabbath (of which there is mention in the *Revelation*) is not *sufficiently* made known to me, how the same may be meant, seeing the Scripture doth not mention it elsewhere, and Christ also and his Apostles give not a hint of it in other places, save only *John* in his Revelation; but whether they shall be in a thousand *solar* years, or how it may be referred, seeing I have not full assurance, I leave it to my God, and to those to whom God shall vouchsafe the right understanding of it, till God is pleased to open my eyes concerning these mysteries.

For they be secrets, and it belongeth not to man to make conclusions about them without the command and light of God; but if any had knowledge and illumination of the same from God, I should be ready and willing to learn, if I could see the ground thereof in the light of nature.

But seeing it behoveth me not to hide my knowledge of it, so far as I apprehend it in the light of nature, I will therefore set down some suppositions, or considerable opinions, which are in my mind, not positively to affirm, but give it to consideration, for good and wholesome instructions may be drawn forth thereby, and 'tis also profitable for man *so to search.* I will do it in all sincere uprightness, to see if we might attain somewhat nearer the matter, and perhaps there may be some to whom God shall bestow such a gift, stirred up thereby to write more clearly.

As first, whether or no it be certain that the world must continue *seven thousand years*, and one thousand of them should be a mere Sabbath. Seeing that God created all in six days, and began the rest on the sixth day towards evening, whence the Jews begin their Sabbath on Friday evening; and *Elias* also saith that the world should stand but *six thousand years*, and Christ likewise declareth that the days of tribulation shall be shortened for the elect's sake, else no man should be saved, which you apply to the fall of *Babel*, and to the time of *Zion*; but it seems as if Christ spake of the fall of the *Jews* and the end of the world, and foreshoweth an evil end.

Also Christ saith, that it shall be at the time of His coming to judgement as it was in the days of *Noah*, where men did marry, and were given in marriage; now we know very well (as the Scripture testifieth) what manner of wicked world was in the days *Noah*, that the deluge must come and destroy them. (This would intimate and denote a very *mean Sabbath.*)

And though a man should otherwise expound the words of Christ concerning His coming, yet that would not be sufficient to prove it; being also that the disciples of Christ do always represent the end to be nigh, and *Paul* saith, that the end should come after the *Antichrist is revealed*.

But that the resurrection of the dead, and the last judgement, should be understood of both (namely, that the righteous shall arise to the thousand years Sabbath, and among them some ungodly; and that *Gog* and *Magog* at the end of the thousand years should fight against the saints), it seems to run quite contrary to the light of nature.

For first, I cannot apprehend how the first resurrection must come to pass, seeing the saints shall have their works follow them according to the words of the Spirit; besides, we know very well that all our works are sown into the great mystery; that they are first brought forth into the four elements, and so pass into the mystery, and are reserved to the judgement of God, where all things shall be tried by fire, and that which is false shall consume in the fire; and the figures shall fall into the centre of Nature, viz. the dark eternity.

But if men's work shall follow them in the first resurrection, as you affirm, then God must verily move the mystery (that is, Himself), which denotes *the last judgement*.

For God hath moved Himself but twice only from eternity; once in the creation of the world; and secondly, in the Incarnation of Christ according to His heart: the first motion belongeth to the Father of all beings, and the second to the Son, according to God's heart; now the third motion, of the Holy Ghost, is yet to be accomplished both in love and anger, according to the *Three Principles*; where all what ever hath been corrupted shall again be restored in the motion in the Holy Ghost, and each given unto its owner.

How can, then, the dead arise in their works without the motion of the Holy Spirit, both in love and anger? When as the restoration of life doth only consist in Him; moreover, I do not know how the first resurrection should come to pass, whether it should come to pass in the twofold man (which cannot otherwise be understood), that is, in good and evil; but what perfect Sabbath can we hold therein; was not *Adam* unable so to stand?

Now, if the new man only should arise, then he would not be

in the four elements of this world; moreover, the new body in Christ needs no resurrection; it liveth eternally without any want, necessity, or death, in Christ, and doth only wait when God shall move the mystery, where He shall *then* put on *the crown* of His wonders and works.

The manner of the resurrection is thus, the mystery shall restore whatever it hath swallowed up; man's works shall be put upon him, and therewith he shall pass through the fire, and it shall be tried what will endure the fire or not.

Now I *cannot* apprehend how this should agree with the *dwelling upon the earth*, for if it should be after a Paradisical manner that man should arise with the wonders, then it could not be done without the motion of the great mystery; for your writings say, that also some wicked men shall arise; this showeth that the mystery must be moved, and at the motion, the last judgement of fire must needs be; if now the mystery should be moved it would not only awaken and raise up some, and that in one source only, seeing that likewise some ungodly shall arise.

Besides, you say that they shall all die at the end of the *six thousand years*, then there must be a dwelling upon, or an inhabiting the earth, where the ungodly that arise should again marry, and build; of whom there should not be only some as according to your opinion, but according to the Scripture *they shall be as the sand upon the seashore*; whence else should Gog and Magog come, or how should they fight against the children of Paradise, for in the Paradisical children there is *no* strife.

Also, it were not necessary that they should die at the *end* of the six thousand years if they should arise in the twofold body, as we are now, but if they should arise in the new body, then no ungodly man can either see or touch them, like as we *now* do *not* see Paradise; even such is the new body, no ungodly man can fight against it.

What should they fight for? Are the saints in Paradise? Then they make no use of the external elements, but only of the internal element, wherein all the four are couched in unity, so that they have nothing to strive for, but they are separate in the source.

But should the ungodly die, and also arise again in the four elements; this seemeth much more strange, but if they should arise in the spiritual body, then the four elements could not contain it, but the *abyss*, and still they would be separate as light and darkness. What pleasure or liking should God have to bring the saints again into the combat and source of the four elements, unto which they have been so long dead? And yet should they then begin to fight with the wicked? Much more fit and agreeable were it for those who here have suffered nothing for Christ's sake; that is, for those who here upon the earth have not lost their lives for Christ's sake.

And though you would say that they should not fight, but the Lord for them, what liking could God take to raise up the saints and to set them again in the presence of the ungodly; or should not the joy in *Abraham's* bosom be much greater than this in the four elements, whence natural strife and contention do arise; but if they should dwell in Paradise without the four elements, then no strife or ungodly man can reach them.

Besides, to what end should the ungodly be upon the earth if there shall be such a *Sabbath*? Their source is not in the four elements but in the abyss, whether their soul goeth when the body dieth.

Besides, should none but those dwell in the Sabbath who have died for Christ's sake (of which verily there cannot be such a number as is set down in the *Revelation*), that they should be sufficient to possess the earth? and should the ungodly also dwell upon the earth and hold their *hellish Sabbath*? This runs directly against the light of Nature.

Moreover Christ saith, *that they shall marry, and be given in marriage*, as in the days of Noah. Also, two shall be grinding in one mill, and two sleeping in one bed, and the one shall be taken and the other let, *when the last day shall come*.

Besides, Christ saith also, That when He shall come to judge the world, *all generations and kindreds shall see Him*, and tremble before Him; and the wicked shall wait, and lament, and say to the wise virgins, give us of your oil; all this denotes a *general expectation* of the last judgement.

For if at the last trumpet two shall be lying in one bed (namely, one holy, the other ungodly), this shows no difference, and if the saints be mixed with the ungodly, then verily there must needs be a poor Sabbath.

When we look upon the words of Christ and His apostles, they will not in the least manner agree thereto, and though there is mention made of a thousand years in the *Revelation*, yet the same is hidden from us, and we know not *when they may begin* or *whether they are begun*; if the first resurrection be Pardisical, then it may be done without our knowledge.

They shall not dwell among us, also they shall not marry; for we die once from male and female, and we shall not arise male and female, but we shall live in Paradise in the form of angels (Matthew 22:30).

Besides, the wicked shall, in the appearance of Christ's coming, entreat the wise for oil of faith; and you write that the fire of God, being the anger and hellish source, shall be in them, and that they shall be tormented (here upon the earth in the four elements) in the anger of God, whereas the anger of God is *not manifest* in the four elements; for therein good and evil are mixed together.

But how shall he that is once dead to good, and cannot so much as have one good thought, entreat the saints for faith and comfort? It much rather declareth, that when Christ shall come to judge the world, that they shall all yet dwell together in the flesh in the four elements, where the one shall be received and the other rejected; and the sins of the wicked shall then come in his sight at the appearance of the severe countenance of God in the fiery zeal of the first principle, so that he shall be affrighted, and then would fain begin to be honest.

And though you mention that they shall only awake, and not arise, yet the uncorrupted are to be understood; now you say that they shall dwell upon the earth in the four elements and the saints in Paradise; when this cometh to be, then there will be no more any strife or controversy; but they are eternally separate.

But shall the saints dwell upon the earth in Paradise, as *Adam* before the fall, and the ungodly be opposed to them, then they are in danger as *Adam* was, that they should again eat of the forbidden fruit, whereof they should yet once die.

But shall they be hidden from the ungodly a thousand years

and also from the four elements, why should they then first at the end be manifest in the four elements, that *Gog* and *Magog* should then enter battle with the children of Paradise? It doth *neither agree with Scripture or reason.*

The first epistle of Saint *Paul* to the *Corinthians*, chapter 15 doth indeed teach of Christ's and also our resurrection, yet not of a third. But first of Christ's and then of ours; for he saith there, *That Christ is the first fruits*; and then we who belong unto Christ; this is the general resurrection; and though he saith, *that then cometh the end*, yet by the end he signifieth no resurrection, but the end is our resurrection; this is much rather to be understood, than that he should mean by the end another resurrection, or time; for just after our resurrection cometh the end of the world.

The dead shall first appear before the judgement ere that the end of this world and the four elements cometh, for the end is the *enkindling of the fire, and the last.*

Also, the apostles of Christ, and all teachers from God, have always represented the end as nigh at hand, for *John* himself saith in his Epistle, *that we are in the end*; he speaketh indeed of the last hour; but if the wicked were assured that he had yet four hundred years unto the end, how would he seek after riches for his children?

Besides, we are to look unto the end, for this world is confined and determined in the beginning of the creation; and then into the end where the creation ceased; all which was finished in *six days*; and in such a time the mystery of God's kingdom shall be *finished*, and a thousand years are before Him as one day.

Concerning the seventh day of rest, whether or no the world shall yet be in *rest a thousand years*; the same is hidden to mankind; we cannot certainly determine, we must leave it unto His might; I have no knowledge of it, seeing the Scripture doth not give clear evidence when the thousand years *begin*, or what *years* they be, or to what they have relation; therefore, I let it alone in its own worth, and will hinder none that hath a certain knowledge or command so to teach; this I give you to consider of, meaning it well unto you.

What I might further answer concerning this matter, you find sufficiently in my writings, although I could set down a large answer about it, yet I thought it not expedient, seeing *this* knowledge is *not* given to me; thereupon I let it alone, for I know that I must give an account of my works, and I send you by the bearer hereof your two books again, and give you thanks for them.

Concerning the end, of limit of *Babel's downfall* (viz. that *Babel* should be wholly destroyed about the year 1630, according to your computation, and albeit many more of the same mind), the same likewise is *not sufficiently* manifest to me.

To me indeed is given to know that the time is *nigh* and even now at hand, but the year and day I know not; thereupon I leave it to God's counsel, and to those to whom God shall reveal it; I cannot *conclude* anything *without certain knowledge*, otherwise I should be found a *liar* before God.

But I wait for my Saviour Jesus Christ, and will see what He will do; will He that I shall know it, then I will know it; if not, then I will not know it; I have committed my will, knowledge, understanding, and desire unto Him; He shall be my knowing, willing, and also doing; for without Him there is mere danger and uncertainty.

Man doth hardly reach that which is before his eyes, much less that which is hidden and mystical, except God be his light; this answer I give you out of good affection to consider of; albeit I am a simple mean man, and born of no art in this world [or not bred up in any *scholastic* learning].

But what I have, that is the gift of God, I have it not from any art or studying, but from the light of grace which I only sought for; and though my beginning was simple by reason of my childish understanding, yet God hath since that time, in His light, wrought somewhat in me and opened my childish eyes.

As for the book *Aurora* (which is the first), it were needful to be *better explained* in many places, for at that time the full apprehension was not born in me, for like as a sudden shower, whatsoever it lights upon it hits, even so it went with the fiery instigation.

Although I had no purpose at all that any should read it, I wrote only the wonders of God which were shown unto me for a memorial to myself, and it went abroad without my consent, and it was taken from me perforce and published without my knowledge; for I thought to keep it by me as long as I lived, and had no intent to be known with all, among such high persons, as now is come to pass.

But the Most High (in whose hands and power all things are) had another purpose therewith, as is now manifest, and as I am informed it is known in many cities and countries at which I do wonder, and also not wonder, for the Lord doth effect His work marvellously beyond and above all reason; although he should employ a shepherd in the work: and albeit the art and outward reason will give Him no room and place, yet however His purpose must stand against all the ragings of the devil.

And though I have not obtained many days of pleasure thereby, yet I must not therefore resist His will; I have written only according to the form as it was given to me, not according to other masters or writings.

And besides, my intent was only for myself, albeit the spirit showed me how it should fall out, yet my heart willed nothing, but committed the same to Him to do therewith what He pleased.

I have not run with it (*not being called*) and made myself known to any; for I can say also with truth that my acquaintance knew least of it, but what I have shown unto any, the same was done upon his entreaty and importunate desire.

And then, further, I give you to understand, seeing that you have my writings in hand to read, that you would not look upon them as coming from a great *master*, for art is not to be seen or found therein; but great earnestness of a zealous mind which thirsteth after God; in which thirst it hath received great things, as the illuminate mind shall well see, and without light no man shall rightly know and apprehend them, as the *reader* shall surely find.

And yet it could not be written more clearly and ready for the understanding, although I conceive that the same is clear and plain enough in such a depth; but yet, if there were anything that should seem too obscure and difficult, I might represent it in a more simple and plain manner if *it were mentioned to me*.

There are yet other books besides this, written concerning the wisdom of God, of a very deep sense and understanding, treating of the great depths of the wonders of God, which at present I have not at hand.

But that I give you not a large answer of my judgement upon your book concerning the thousand years Sabbath and the four hundred years in *Zion* (which you suppose to prove with many places of Holy Scripture) is, because I do not fundamentally and certainly know whether those *texts* may be applied to such a meaning.

For there be many sayings of Scripture which seem to intimate only *one general resurrection* of the dead; and they are clear, especially in the words of Christ in the four evangelists, which I hold for the most certain.

In like manner the cause stands with *Zion*, that wickedness shall continue to the end, and though a *Zion* shall be, yet it will not be *wholly* universal; *Babel* shall go to ruin, and get another form, yet they shall not all be children of God that are called children in *Zion*.

Also, I have no knowledge of the thousand years Sabbath; I know not sufficiently to ground it with Scripture, for we find one place seeming to cross another; men may interpret the Scripture as they are disposed, but, seeing I have *no command* from God of it, I let it alone, and leave every one to answer for his own opinion. This I tell you sincerely out of good affection, and am, however, your faithful friend in the love of Christ.

In your forty-second and forty-third pages, where you write of the mystery of the *departed souls*, you bring the opinion of *Theophrastus and others into question* and suspicion, as if they had not written aright of the mystery; it were better that had been left out, seeing you have not understood *their* opinion, as you say, and just so it seems. You shall find in my book of the *Forty Questions* concerning the last judgement, and also in other questions, sufficient and large information, if the same be read and rightly understood.

There is no need of *any* further searching; it is *there clear enough* what the mystery is that compriseth body and soul, and also what condition the separated souls are in, both with their expectation of the last judgement and also, in the meantime, in respect of their habitation, source, life, and difference: I had thought that it was so deeply and high grounded that the mind of man should be satisfied enough therewith; and if you neither have, nor cannot set forth anything more fundamental, then it remains of right in its own place, the thousand years Sabbath and the four hundred years in *Zion* will but find fault with all, and bring it into suspicion; and though many objections might be made, yet they would be of no service or esteem.

Moreover, the manifestation of the thousand years Sabbath is not of much importance or concernment to the world, seeing we have *not sufficient* ground of the same, it should of right rest in the Divine Omnipotence, for we have enough in the Sabbath of the new birth; for that soul that obtains this Sabbath will, after the death of the earthly body, have Sabbath enough in Paradise. We may very well leave and commend the other unto the Divine Omnipotence, and wait on God what He will do with us when we shall be in Him and He in us.

For I suppose there should be a better Sabbath in God than in this world, and if man should dwell upon the earth in Paradise, then must God restore that which in his curse entered into the mystery, as is to be seen in the forty questions.

But that you suppose that the righteous shall *not* be brought with their works before the judgement, is *contrary* to the words of Christ, who saith, *that all things shall be proved through the fire.*

I say *not* (that they shall come) *into* the judgement, for the judgement is in the wicked, understand the judgement of anger, of which the Scripture saith, the righteous, or as Christ saith, *He that believeth in Me cometh not unto judgement*; He understands hereby the source of pain of the judgement His words do hold forth, that they shall all come together before the judgement, and every one hear his sentence: The ungodly depart hence, and the righteous come hither, etc.

Also, every one shall stand forth with his own works in the mystery, and themselves be judged according to their works; now you know very well that our works in this world have been wrought in good and evil, and shall be proved and separated in the fire of God. How shall they then, being unseparated, follow the saints in the resurrection to the Sabbath, and *they* hold Sabbath therein? But if they shall follow them, then they must be tried and separated in the fire, and then they shall have no more any need to come before the judgement; but if they should keep a Sabbath without their works, then they are not perfect.

If we would speak of *Paradise* and apprehend the same, then we must have clear eyes to see into it, for the internal Paradisical world and the external world do hang one within another, we have only turned ourselves out of the internal into the external, and so we work in two worlds.

Death cannot separate our works, the fire of God must do it, for they remain in one mystery till the judgement of God; every one at the hour of the resurrection shall come forth in his own mystery, and he shall see his works before him and feel them in him.

It is not understood that they shall answer for their selves with words, for the kingdom of God consists and proceeds in power, and albeit the ungodly shall cry out, woe upon his abominations and seducers; yet every man's work shall be *summoned in power*, which shall either rejoice or torment him.

Now, the old body of his world is the mystery of this world, and the new body is the mystery of the Divine light world, and the soul is the mystery of God the Father, and the earth with the elements hath also both mysteries, which shall be moved through the principle of the Father.

And then the doors of the mysteries shall be set open, and each shall give and set forth its *figures* which it hath swallowed up, for the principle of the soul must stand before the judgement with both the mysteries.

Happy are they which shall have the body of Christ in the mystery of the wrath of God's anger, they shall have the soul's fire, or the principle of the Father surrounded with the light world, and illustrate with the majesty, they shall feel no pain or hurt, and shall pass insensibly through the fire, and there the outward or third principle shall be proved, and all earthliness or falsehood shall remain in the fire; but the works shall be renovated in the fire, and freed from their earthly source and soul; and then the *earthly mystery* remaineth in the fire, and is a *food* of the fire, whence the light ariseth and the *righteous loseth nothing*.

For the works of love which were brought forth in the new body do pass with the spirit of the soul through the fire, and remain in the Divine image in the source of the light; and they of the third principle, that is, of this world, do remain in the fire source of the soul.

But that which hath been wrought and acted in a wholly evil and malicious manner in the third principle, and yet in this world hath not been renewed by earnest repentance and reconcilement toward his brother, and falleth unto the *centre of nature*, that is, the root of the dark world.

But the works of the ungodly shall not be able to remain in the fire, for the fire swalloweth them down in itself to the dark centre; viz. the original of nature wherein the *devils dwell*, and thither also goeth their souls' fire, being the Father's principle, for this fire of the soul shall have no matter to make it burn aright; but it shall be as a quenched, dark, painful source-fire, only as an anguish that would fain produce fire; this is called *God's wrath* (and not a principle), a death, or a dying source.

For the principle of the Father, wherein the right and true soul consists, is a flaming fire which giveth light, and in the light is the precious image of God, for that light doth qualify and sweeten the burning light with the essentiality of *love*, so that it is a pleasing delight, and a cause of *nature* and of life.

Therefore I tell you that you should not think it strange or misunderstand it when I or any other (let it be *Theophrastus* or who it will) write, that man shall stand before the judgement *with his body which he had here*. I perceive very well that you have not as yet understood my writings in the book of *The Threefold Life*, and also in the book of *The Incarnation of Jesus Christ* (which treateth of Christ's suffering, dying, and rising again, and how we must enter into His death and arise out of His death), you shall find it clear enough explained and enlarged; but seeing you have them not yet at hand, be pleased to have patience, you may very likely get them to read, and then you will be *freed* from your perplexity and deep searching in this manner.

For they lay their ground much deeper than your apprehension is in this; do but read them right, you shall verily find that the mystery is, what the magical *byss* and *abyss* is; also, what the Being of all beings is; there needs no consulting with one or another. He that understands the great mystery whence all beings have proceeded and do still proceed, he doth not encumber himself with such large circumstances.

You have undertaken a very hard labour which doth nothing but perplex, eat up, and consume your life; it is wholly needless; he that findeth and knoweth the great mystery, he findeth all things therein; there need no literal demonstration; God, Christ, and the eternity with all wonders do lie therein; the *Holy Ghost is the key to it*; are you in the new birth as you say, then there is no need of such hard seeking, with such hard labour; seek only Christ in the manger, in the dark stable; when you find Him, then you shall indeed find where He sitteth at the right hand of God.

Searching only doth nothing; the *philosophers' stone* is a very dark, disesteemed stone, of a grey colour, but therein lieth the highest tincture; would you search out the *mysterium magnum*, then take before you only the earth with its metals, and so you may well find what the magical or cabalistical ground is.

The deep and mystical numbers, which otherwise no man is able to fathom or find out, lie all in the mystery, but he that finds it, searcheth not after the numbers, he taketh gold for earth, and doth as one that hath a costly treasure lying in an obscure place; the manger and swaddling clothes of Christ are more acceptable to him than the whole world with its external pomp and glory; he hides the *numbers themselves*, for the outward kingdom must accomplish its wonders.

Wherefore should the earthly mystery be unveiled *before the time*, inquire of the *Magi*, who have understood the heavenly and earthly *magia*; wherefore they have kept the *tincture* secret, and not revealed it; there is no other cause at all, but that the world *is not* worthy of it, so likewise it *is not* worthy of the *numbers* of the mystery.

Therefore God hath hidden them from us, that the earthly mystery might accomplish and fulfil all its wonders on us, and that all the vials of God's anger be poured forth on us. How can a man undertake to reveal such secret things *without the consent* of the mystery; indeed he tampereth about the outside of the mystery, but if he comes in he must have the will of the mystery.

The outward instigation to manifest and reveal the mystery proceedeth from the *stars*, for they would fain be freed from vanity, and they drive mightily in the *magical children* to manifestation, therefore we must prove and examine the instigation, whether it proceed from God's light, from God's spirit, or from the dominion or government of the stars.

For God's spirit speaketh plainly of His mystery; He only declareth the *Turba*, and letteth the *numbers* alone; He hath once signed and sealed the mystery with the might of the first principle in the *seven forms of nature* to the wonders of God; and again He hath signed it in the love in the humanity of Christ, with the *seven golden candlesticks* and lights, and therewith He continues until the judgement; each number manifests itself *in its own age*; no creature hath power to manifest the same, for he that hath it *dares not*, else he transgresseth the magical order, and becomes a loathing to the mystery.

And therefore the prophets, and also Christ Himself, have spoken all in parables, after a magical manner, and even to this day *none* who is capable of the mystery *dare* speak otherwise unless there be a *peculiar purpose* of God, that the *number* shall be plainly revealed; as *Daniel* who did clearly denote the *time* of Christ with its *own number*; he had *command* so to do; this I tell you sincerely and in all faithfulness, also in right Christian love towards you, not out of contempt, but from my knowledge and gifts, seeing you desired it of me; I have given you a short hint, what you are to do herein, and entreat you to look upon it in a brotherly way.

But yet what I am able to serve you in, with my few gifts, if you shall further desire, it shall be done with a good will, provided I shall perceive you are in good earnest, and that it shall serve to the honour of God and the welfare of mankind, and so I commend you into the love of *Jesus Christ*.

Dated, Gorlitz, 14th of *August*, Anno Dom, 1620.

Another letter to Paul Kaym concerning the Way to True Knowledge and the Regeneration in Christ: Likewise concerning the thousand years Sabbath, and how the mysteries in the Revelation are to be understood.

Worthy and much respected sir, and in Christ beloved brother, I have received your last letter, and therein I have once more understood, and well observed your zealous inflamed mind in your intended labour and hard study, and then your anxious earnest desire after the light of the true knowledge thereof; and thirdly, the great thirst after the fountain and well-spring of Christ, wherein the mind is refreshed, quickened, comforted, satisfied, and appeased; and considering that I am a servant to my brethren, and no less than a debtor in the love of Christ to them; therefore, I shall in the same love show and impart to you what I know, and what is given to me, seeing your desire also requireth it.

Christ said, 'I am the vine, ye are the branches; he that abideth in Me, and I in him, shall bring forth much fruit; for without Me you can do nothing; also, he that abideth in Me and hath My words abiding in him, he bringeth forth much fruit'. Herein lieth the whole ground, and it is the only root or spring to the fountain whence the *Divine understanding* floweth; there is *no other* seeking, studying, or searching doth avail anything.

For every spirit searcheth only its own depth and apprehendeth that wherein it doth enkindle itself, and though it doth search in its own enkindling, yet it findeth no more but a type or representation of things like a shadow or dream; it is not able to behold the Being itself, for if it would see the Being, then it must be in the Being, and the Being in it, that so it may be capable of the Being, and see really in the Being itself.

Now then, seeing that we are dead in *Adam* to the divine essence, and are become blind and estranged, we have no power in us *as from ourselves*, we know nothing of God in our *reason*, but only the history that there is a God; we do neither feel His power nor see His light unless we return and become like unto children, which know nothing, but are guided and ruled; and as a child looks upon its mother and longeth after her, and she also cherisheth and bringeth it up, so must the external reason be blinded, beaten down, and quite quashed.

And the desire must resign and cast itself into the grace and love of God, and not regard the opposition and contradiction of the outward reason which saith, it is nothing so. God is afar off. You must search, meditate, and represent Him only to yourself by your apprehension; you must seek after His will, how He hath *revealed Himself*; so He will be known, and not otherwise; thus the external, historical, astral reason doth judge, and it ruleth also the whole world except a very small number of God's children.

Christ said, *You must abide in Me; for without Me you can do nothing*; you can neither know nor search out anything really and fundamentally of God? *for he that cometh to Me, him I will in no wise cast out; in Me you shall bring forth much fruit; now every branch groweth* on its own tree, and hath the sap, power, influence, virtue, and property of the tree, and beareth fruit according to the quality, kind, and property of the tree.

Thus, likewise, he who desireth to be taught of God, and to have Divine knowledge, must stand in the tree whereinto God hath engrafted us through the *Regeneration*; he must have the sap and virtue of the tree, else he bringeth forth strange, unsavoury, wild fruit, which hath not the taste and relish of the good tree; we must become like unto a child which understands nothing, but only knoweth its mother and longeth after her.

We must drink of the new milk of Christ's incarnation, that so we may be made partakers of His flesh and spirit; His virtue and sap must be our virtue and sap, we must become God's children in *divine eating and drinking*.

Nicodemus said: *How can it be that a man should be born again in his old age?* Yes, good *Nicodemus*, and good external earthly reason; how could it be that *Adam*, who was a perfect image of God, did perish in his perfection, and became earthly; did it not come to pass by *imagination*, because he induced his desire, longing, and lust into the outward, astral, elemental, and earthly kingdom, whereupon he in his desire, lust, and imagination was forthwith impregnated, and became earthly, and thereby he fell into the sleep of the external *Magic*, and thus it is also with the *new birth*.

Through *imagination, and an earnest serious desire*, we become again impregnated of the Deity, and receive the new body, in the old; the new doth not mix itself with the old, like as gold in the gross and rough stone is quite another thing, and hath *another tincture and spirit*, than the rough matter in the stone; thus also is the new man in the old. The rough stone knoweth nothing of the gold, and so likewise the earthly *Adam* knoweth nothing of the Divine heavenly *Adam*, and therefore there is strife in man, and man is contrary to himself.

The earthly *Adam* will see, feel, and taste, but he receiveth only a ray, type, and twinkling reflex from the internal man, where he indeed at sometimes tasteth somewhat of the divine Man, but not essentially, but as the light of the sun doth disperse, or swallow up the sad darkness, so that it appeareth as if there were no darkness more at all, and yet the darkness is really hidden in the light, which again is manifest when the light of the sun withdraweth.

Thus oftentimes the new man doth in the divine power swallow up the old, that the old man supposeth that he hath apprehended the Deity, whereas he is not capable of that essence, but the spirit of God from the new man doth pass through the old; but when the same entereth again into its mystery, then the old man knoweth not what happened unto it, but it seeketh ways to come to God, and searcheth after the purpose and will of God, and yet findeth nothing but invention, fiction, and opinion, and it is very zealous in its opinions, and knoweth not what it doth; it findeth not the root for it is not capable or worthy of it, and this showeth that it must die and perish.

But the new man, which in an earnest, serious will and purpose, ariseth through imagination, abideth steadfast in the rest of Christ, even in the tree (which God the Father by His motion, when He moved Himself the second time, according to His heart, did ingraft into the human soul), and it springeth forth in the life of God, and doth grow and flourish in the power, virtue, and sap of the divine essentiality in God's love; this receiveth divine knowledge and skill, not according to the measure of the external will, what the external man will know and search out, but according to the measure of the internal heaven; the internal Heaven doth enkindle and enlighten the external, so that the understanding or intellectual faculty of the soul doth comprehend and understand the external.

For God, who is a spirit, and also a being, hath manifested Himself by the external world in a similitude, that the spirit might see itself in the being essentially, and not so only, but that the creature likewise might contemplate and behold the being of God in the figure, and know it.

For no creature is able to see the being of God without itself; the spirit seeth God in the essence and lustre of the majesty, and the same likewise in itself, and its own fellow-creatures like itself; for God is Himself the spirit of all beings (I mean heavenly beings), so that when we see the divine creature, then we see an image or likeness proceeded from God's being; and when we see the will and working of that Creature, then we see the will and working of God.

Thus also is the new man born of God; what it willeth and doth, that is God's will and work; its knowing is God's knowing, for we know nothing of God without God's spirit.

The external cannot see the internal, but if the internal draweth the external by a glimpse into itself, then the external apprehendeth the mirror or resemblance of the internal for an instruction and direction, to show that the external world taketh its rise and original from the internal, and that *our works shall follow us in the mystery*; and that by the separation of God's judgement, by the fire of the Principle, they shall be set into the eternal world.

To which end God hath created angels and men, namely, for His deeds of wonders, that the wisdom of the *divine power* might appear, and that God might behold Himself in the resemblances and ideas of the creatures, and have joy in Himself with the beings created out of His own wisdom.

Loving brother, take it not ill that I speak roundly to you; you complain that you are not always able to reach, comprehend, and keep the divine mysteries, and moreover you say that many times you get a glimpse of them, and that my writings are *hard* and difficult to be understood of you; I will therefore show unto you, according to the power and ability that I have received from God, how the being of your hidden mystery standeth, which at present you are not able to understand.

Your meaning and will is to keep in a continued steadfast comprehension; this is the will of the *external world* in you; it would fain be capable of the Deity, and be freed from vanity, but the spirit of the external world must stand in continual travail and earnest seeking, for by its seeking it findeth the wonders of its own *Magic*, namely, the type and resemblance of the internal world.

For God doth not always move Himself, but the *longing* and earnest travailing of the creature *moveth the mystery*, that the image, or idea of the divine wisdom, may be sought and found; therefore Christ commandeth us to *seek and knock*, and withal promiseth to give us the pearl or jewel *in the seeking*.

The external world likewise is of God, and from God, and man is to that end created into the external world, that he might bring the external figures into the internal, that he might bring the end into the beginning.

The more man longeth after God, and the more he panteth and runneth after Him, the more he cometh out of the end into the beginning, not only to God's wonder, but to his own edification, for the twig of the tree continually thirsteth after the sap and virtue of the tree, it travaileth in desire after the tree, and draweth its sap and influence into it, and so thereby it groweth up to be a great branch; thus the anxious hunger and earnest longing in the *human mystery* draweth the kingdom of God into itself; of which Christ said, *The kingdom of heaven suffereth violence, and the violent take it by force to themselves.*

A being or essence that is not attractive cannot grow up or get a body to itself, but it starveth and pineth away, as we see the fire of the candle draweth or attracteth the fat into itself, and devoureth it, and yet it affordeth from its devouring a shining light; thus it is with man, he is shut up and enclosed (with his first divine essence) in the darkness of death, but God hath again opened the same to the soul in Christ.

Now the poor captivated soul is this very hungry *magical* fire, which doth again attract to itself out of the *Incarnation* of Christ the divine disclosed essence; and so it feedeth on God's being, and taketh it into itself, and from this spiritual and essential eating, consuming, or digesting, it giveth forth a body of light, which is both like unto, and capable of the Deity; thus the poor soul becomes clothed with the body of light, as the fire in the candle, and in this body of light it findeth rest, but in the darkness of this world in its earthly carcase and clothing of clay, wherein the curse of God, and all evil inclinations and false desires do stick it hath anguish and trouble.

But now, seeing it is so, that it hath with *Adam* put upon itself the earthly image, it must therefore bear the same, as the fire of the candle must take its burning light from the dark lump of fat; if it had with *Adam* abode in God's being, and had not put on the earthly image, it needed not to have borne the same, but now it is bound to bear it.

For Saint *Paul* saith, *To whom you give yourselves as servants in obedience, his servants you are, be it to sin, unto death, or to the obedience of God, unto righteousness.* Now seeing the soul hath put on the earthly image, which worketh nothing but fruit to death, and hath yielded and devoted itself a servant to sin, it is therefore now become the *sinful servant* of death.

Wherefore is it fallen in love with a strange master that domineereth over it? Had it but remained a child, and had not lusted after the tree of knowledge of good and evil, it needed not then to have been in subjection to both governments, but being it would be as God in love and anger, according to both the principles of eternity, thereupon it must now bear the image, and undergo the force and sway of both, and so endure the fire burning till the day of separation.

Therefore it is called a bearing of the cross, for when the magical fire ariseth, it maketh a cross-like birth, and the one form of nature doth press and quite pierce through the other, that is, the one is contrary to the other, as sweet against sour, sharp against bitter, and the fire against them all.

And if the soul had let the body of light be only Lord and Master, and had not imagined on the external kingdom of this world (that is, on the spirit of the great world in the stars and elements), nor lusted after the earthly fruit, then the wrath had been as it were swallowed up in it; there would not have been any sense, perceivance, or feeling of the same; but seeing it is departed from the meekness of the light and gone out of the love of God, *therefore* it feeleth now the wrath or burning anger of the eternal nature.

And therefore it must work, labour, and endeavour to obtain the light again; whence it is that the life of man standeth in such anguish, in painful seeking, in continual abstinence and repentance; it earnestly desireth the divine rest, and yet is held back by the wrath of nature.

The more the life desireth to fly from the wrath, the *more strong* and vehement the strife groweth in the life, besides that which the devil by his poisonful incantations, magical imaginations, representations, and insinuations, doth stir up and bring into his *nest*, being the centre of the soul, he continually representeth before the soul the magical image of the poisonful serpent, that the soul might still imagine upon it, and kindle or inflame itself in the poison of the same, which daily cometh to pass, and thus the fire of the soul becometh an evil, poisonful, burning, brimstony fire.

Yet, if the soul departeth from the serpent-like image of the devil, and rejecteth the evil earthly tree, which *tree* is pride, covetousness, envy, anger, and falsehood, and longeth not after it, but maketh itself as it were dead in this figure, as if it knew nothing of it, and casteth away the very concupiscence and imagination itself, and desireth only the love of God, submitting itself wholly to God's will and working, that he may be only its willing, working, and doing, then the divine light beginneth to shine in it, and it obtaineth an eye of the right seeing, so that it is able to behold its own natural form and feature, whereby it steppeth into plain, downright, and meek humility.

It willeth nothing, it also desireth nothing, but resigneth and casteth itself into the bosom of its mother, like a child that desireth nothing but its mother, inclining itself to her, and longing only after her; it doth not much esteem any art, subtle reason, or much knowledge; and though it knoweth much, yet it is not puffed up or elevated in its own conceit by its knowledge, but leaveth and resigneth the knowing, willing, and working wholly to its mother's spirit, that it might be both the will and work in it.

I speak according to my knowledge, that the devil in the power of God's anger doth continually shoot against and oppose this precious sprout of the soul after the root of nature, that is, after the forms of the fire-life in the first principle, and would continually by all means quite destroy the noble twig of grace. He continually shooteth his evil, poisonful rays into the soul's magical fire with evil lusts, concupiscence, and thoughts; and ministereth strange matter or fuel to the soul's fire to burn or feed upon, so that it might by no means attain to a shining light; he quencheth, suppresseth, and hindereth it, that his kingdom might not be known.

But, on the other side, the *noble twig* defendeth itself, and will *none* of the fierce, dark, and wrathful source; it ariseth and springeth forth like a plant out of the wild earth, yet the devil striveth continually against it.

Therefore, my dearly-beloved friend, there is such strife and contention in man; and hence he seeth the divine light as in a mirror, and sometimes he getteth a perfect glimpse thereof; for as long as the twig of the soul can defend itself against the poison of the devil, so long it hath the shining light.

For when the magical fire of the soul receiveth the divine essence (that is, the divine body, Christ's flesh), then the holy spirit doth *apparently* arise, and glance forth in the soul as a triumph, as he goeth forth from God the Father through the word or mouth of the Son (that is, from the heart of the sacred Ternary), out of the divine essentiality, and thus he goeth or proceedeth forth out of the being or essence of the noble lily-twig, which springeth forth and groweth out of the fire of the soul, which (lily-twig) is the *true Image* of God, for it is the new-born or regenerated spirit of the soul, the spirit of God's will, the triumphing chariot of the Holy Spirit, in which he rideth into the sacred Ternary, into the angelical world.

And with this twig or image of God renewed in us, as is before mentioned, we are in Christ out of this world, in the angelical world, of which the old Adam hath no understanding or perceivance; also, it knoweth it not, as the rough stone knoweth not the gold which yet groweth in it.

THE GATES OF THE TRUE KNOWLEDGE OF THE THREEFOLD LIFE

Man is the true similitude or image of God, as the precious man *Moses* testifieth, not only an earthly image (for the sake whereof God would not have become man, and put forth, unite, and espouse his heart and spirit after the fall unto it), but he is originally out of the Being of all beings, out of all the three worlds, viz. out of the innermost nature world, which is also the most outward, and is called the dark world, whence the principle of the fiery nature taketh its rise, as is declared *at large* in my book *of the Threefold Life*.

And secondly he is out of the light, or angelical world, out of the true Being of God, and then thirdly, he is out of this external world of the sun, stars, and elements, an entire image of God, out of the Being of all beings.

His first image stood in paradise, in the angelical world, but he lusted after the external world (that is, after the astral and elemental world), which hath swallowed up and covered the previous image of the internal heaven, and ruleth now in the similitude as in its own propriety.

Therefore 'tis said: *You must be born again, or else you cannot see the kingdom of God.* And therefore it is that the word or heart of God entered into the human essence, that we with our soul might be able in the power of the word, or heart of God, to beget, and bring forth again out of our soul, a new twig or image, like unto the first. Therefore the old carcase must rot, putrify, and perish, for it is unfit for the kingdom of God, it carrieth nothing but its own mystery into its first beginning, that is, its wonders and works, understand, in the essence of the first principle which is immortal and incorruptible, being the magical fire of the soul.

And not this alone, but he must bring and unite the end with the beginning, for the external world is generated out of the internal, and created into a comprehensible being, the wonders whereof belong unto the beginning, and they were known from eternity in the wisdom of God, that is, in the divine *Magic*, not in the being or essentiality, but in the mirror of the virgin-like wisdom of God, whence the *eternal nature* doth always arise from eternity.

And to this end the poor soul standeth in the prison of the astral and elemental kingdom, that it might be a *labourer*, and reunite the wonders of the external nature with the light world, and bring them into the beginning, and though it must now be bruised and pressed, and endure much, yet it is the *servant* in God's vineyard which prepareth the previous wine that is drunk in the kingdom of God, it is the *only* cause of the *understanding*, that the desire worketh in the mystery, and manifesteth and bringeth forth to light the hidden wonders of God, as we see plainly how man doth search out and reveal the wonders of nature.

Therefore we must not be amazed, and strangely perplexed, when as many times the noble image is hid, that we cannot receive any refreshment or comfort, but we must know that then the poor soul is put into the vineyard, that it should work and bring the fruit to be set upon God's table.

It hath then a twig or branch of the wild vine given unto it; it must trim and dress that, and plant it into the divine and heavenly mystery; it must unite it with the kingdom of God; this is to be understood thus:

As a plant or graft that is set doth work so long till it putteth forth its branches, and then its fruit, so much the graft of the soul, which standeth overshadowed in a dark valley, continually labour, that it might come to bring forth fruit, which is the noble and previous knowledge of God when the same is grown in it, that the soul *knoweth God*, then it yieldeth its fair fruits, which are *good doctrines, works, and virtues*; it leadeth to the kingdom of God, it helpeth to plant and build the kingdom of God, and then it is a right labourer in the vineyard of Christ.

And thus that of which I teach, write, and speak is nothing else but the same which hath been wrought in me, otherwise I could know nothing of it; I have not scraped it together out of histories, and so made opinions, as the Babylonical school doth, where men eagerly contend about words and opinions. I have by God's grace obtained eyes of my own, and am able in myself to work in Christ's vineyard.

I speak plainly and freely, that, whatsoever is patched together from conjecture and opinion (wherein man himself hath no divine knowledge whereupon he makes conclusions), that, I say, is Babel, a whoredom; for conceit or thinking must not do it; yea, not any opinion or conjectural apprehension, but the knowledge of God in the Holy Ghost.

The children of God *hath spoken as they were driven by the Holy Spirit*; they have planted many and divers trees, but they all stand upon one root, which is the internal heaven; none can find the same unless he likewise stand upon the same root, and therefore the external heaven cannot find them out or explain them by art.

The *words* of the holy children of God remain as a hidden mystery unto the earthly man, and though he thinks that he understands them, yet he hath no more than a darksome glimpse of them. As we see now-a-days how men do wrangle and contend about Christ's doctrine and worship, and fight about God's will, how He must be served whereas He is not served or worshipped with any opinion, but *in the spirit* of Christ, *and in truth*, men serve God.

It depends not on what ceremonies and manners we do use; every one laboureth in his work and gifts from his own *constellation and property*, but all are driven, and lead from one and the *same spirit*, otherwise God should be *finite* and measurable, if the gifts were only one. But He is a pure *wonder*; whosoever apprehends Him, he walketh in His wonders.

This I do impart unto you in all sincerity, out of a true Christian zeal, from my fountain, gifts, and knowledge; and I do exhort you to understand it in a right sense as it is meant. I do not extol or set up myself, but I speak brotherly to your mind, to stir you up and to comfort you; that you should not think the yoke of Christ to be heavy, when oftentimes the external man doth cloud the internal, that the poor soul mourneth for its image, which yet is purified, and truly begotten, and brought forth under *tribulation*. It is even so with me and other Christians besides; think not *strange* at it.

It is very good when the poor soul is in combat, much better than when it is imprisoned, and yet playeth the hypocrite, and maketh devout shows. It is written, *That all things shall serve for the best to them that love God.*

Now when the combat of the soul doth arise and proceed, that it would fain see God, and yet cannot at all times attain the same; then know that it frighteth for the *noble trophy*, of which the external man knoweth nothing; yea, the Spirit of God fighteth in the natural soul for that which is supernatural, that so He may lead the creature into God. He would always fain crown the soul with the previous image, if the blind reason soul but give Him room, and suffer the understanding to co-operate.

We must labour and strive against the external reason, and also against the flesh and blood, and wholly oppose the assaults and objections of the devil, always breaking them and casting them away, and resist the *evil thoughts, motions, and influences*, and effectually with prayer, supplication, or internal resignation, press into God's mercy.

Thus the precious grain of mustard seed is sown, which, if it be well preserved, becometh great like a tree, upon which tree the fruits of Paradise do afterwards grow, on which the soul feedeth, when it will *prophesy and speak of the kingdom of God*; when as it beholdeth the *divine Magic*, even then it *speaketh of the wonders of God*.

For the Being of God is undivided; it needeth not any room or place, but it ariseth in the *spirit of understanding* as the splendour of the sun in the air; it shooteth, or glanceth into the image, like lightning, whereby the *whole body is oftentimes enkindled and enlightened*.

Moreover, know that we in this life are labourers and not idle persons, for the birth of life is a continual strife and labour. The more we labour in God's vineyard, the more fruit we shall obtain and eternally enjoy; and it maketh for our own edification, for our labour remaineth in our own mystery to God's deeds of wonder, and to our own eternal *crown and glory* before God; as in my other writings is set forth at large.

For we are with Christ in God, we are together with Him planted into His death; we are buried in Him, and arise with the new man out of the grave with Him, and live eternally in our own being or essence, understand, in his corporiety. We are with and in Christ in God, and God in us.

Moreover, God is not a God of evil, that desireth revenge or torment, that He should out of His vengeance torment and plague the wicked a thousand years before the judgement. The wicked tormenteth himself in his own life's birth; the one form of life is enemy to the other. And that shall be indeed his hellish torment; and God hath no blame in it.

He hath never desired the fall of man, but the wrathful nature got the upper hand, and the spirit of man's will (which is free, as God Himself) did freely and willingly yield itself up into the combat, supposing to domineer and rule.

It was out of pride that the devil fell, and man also. If they had stayed in humility, God would have continued in them; but they themselves departed both away from God. But God did so exceedingly love man's image, that He Himself, out of love, did *re-enter* into the image of man. Why should He then desire his torment?

In God there is no evil desire, but *His wrath*, which is the dark world, is a desire of evil and destruction, which hath brought the devil and also man to fall. The *dark world* caused the devil to fall, and the *external wrathful nature* caused man to fall, and yet both these are tied and bound one to another, which we should well see and feel, if the sun were taken out of this world.

Therefore I yet say; that the righteous keepeth Sabbath in Abraham's bosom, in Christ's rest; for Christ hath destroyed the wrathful death for us that held us captive. He hath opened life, that we in a new man are able to spring forth, blossom, and rest in Him.

But the old man of the stars and elements must abide in his own region, in his house of torment and misery, *till* he be committed to the earth, and then all passeth into its own mystery again, and the soul abideth in its principle *till the judgement* of God, where God shall again move and enkindle the mystery, and then everything severeth itself into its own property. Each world shall take in its own harvest, be it good or bad; it shall part itself as light and darkness.

And therefore I do entreat you wholly as a brother and a

Christian, that you would be pleased to have a care that you *apprehend the Sabbath in the rest of Christ*; and be not so moved by the enkindling of the spirit, but search whether you be able to ground the same in the light of nature; if you be able to ground, and reach it in the light of the eternal nature, then indeed you may go on; but show it us plainly that we may see it, else our mind will be *unsatisfied*, unless it finds the ground.

It is not to be proved with Scriptures, which might be seemingly alleged for it; they give as well the contrary, and may well be otherwise applied; if my mind had not turned itself into the L O V E and R E S T of Christ, I would then show it you after the fashion of this present controversial world.

He must understand all the three principles with their figures; and then he hath power to open and reveal them, else his labour fall unto the *Turba*; I speak sincerely; if you please, read my book of the *Three-fold Life* aright, and there you shall find the *root* of the Magic; although there be *other* much deeper extant, yet I would you might but understand that, for it hath sufficient ground, else you will not be able to apprehend the other; if it please you then to search further you may *very well* obtain them, only there must be earnestness with all, otherwise they will remain dumb.

For the ground of it is deeply magical, as the illuminate mind shall find indeed, if it will but dive into it; therein the revelation is very easily to be understood, and in no other manner shall it at all be understood save from the mystery of God; he that is able to dive or sink himself into that, *he finds whatsoever he doth but search*.

Accordingly I would fain have you to prove your inflammation, that you might know the *guide* of the internal world, and then also the *guide* of the external world, that so the magical school of both worlds might be known to you, and then the noble mind would be freed from opinion and conjecture, for in conjecture there is *no perfection*.

The spirit must be capable of, and acceptable to the mystery, that God's spirit may be the guide in its seeing, else it only seeth in the outward mystery, viz. in the external heaven of the constellation, which oft-times doth vehemently enkindle and drive the mind of man; yet he hath not the divine magical school, which consists barely in a plain *childlike mind*.

The external guide laboureth and speculates only in the glass, but the internal speculates in the essence, which yet it is not able to do, unless God's spirit guide it; therefore God makes choice.

Whomsoever the heavenly school taketh, he is made a *Mage*, without his hard running, and albeit he must run hard, yet he is taken by God, and *driven of the Holy Spirit*.

Therefore man must try of *what guide* he is taken, if he finds that he hath the divine light shining in his seeing, that his guide doth bring him into the *heavenly school* upon the way of truth to *love and righteousness*, and that he is thereby assured and confirmed in his mind with divine certainty, then he may proceed in his work.

But if it be in conjecture and doubt, and yet in a fiery driving, then the guide is from this world, which ought to be tried by its will and purpose, whether he seeks *God's or his own honour and applause*; whether he willingly resigns himself to the *cross*, and only desires to labour in Christ's vineyard, and to seek the *good of his neighbour*, whether he *seeks God or bread*; and accordingly must his understanding judge, and give it leave, or reject, and tame it as need requires.

This I would not as a brother conceal from you in a Christian exhortation, and I entreat you, that you would accept of it no otherwise than as meant well unto you, as my due obligation requireth; for upon your desire I am your debtor in Christ, to your anxious seeking mind, as one *member* is *bound* to assist another.

Concerning your very Christian offer, I acknowledge and accept of it as done in love, as one member cometh to help the other in time of need; it shall be requited in *love*; be pleased to make me acquainted with what your mind doth further desire, and I shall not withhold anything from you, so far as God shall enable me; and so I commend you unto the love of Jesus Christ.—Your affectionate friend and servant,

J.B.

Dated Thursday se'n-night after Martin's day, 1620.
The name of the Lord is a strong tower,
the righteous runneth thither and is exalted.

Our salvation is in the life of Jesus Christ in us.

NOBLE and right honourable sir, The divine light, and the internal divine contemplation of the soul in itself, and all bodily welfare, with sincere good wishes, and co-operating desires of fellowship and member-like society in *our IMMANUEL*, premised.

Seeing I have observed that you are a lover of divine wisdom, and also a growing branch in the life-tree of God in Christ, in whom all the children of God are as members; and moreover perceived how the drawing of the Father hath brought you into a hungry desire after the true sap and divine power, and likewise, in some measure, hath enriched you with the knowledge of the same Tree of Life, thereupon I have taken occasion (in a Christian and member-like property and desire after the same life-tree of Christ) once more to salute you and mutually to exhort one another as labourers set in the vineyard of Christ, and called to do his work.

Especially that we look well to ourselves in this valley of darkness, and lift up our eyes and heads, in that we see the darkness and the very workings thereof before our eyes; and put ourselves in mind that Christ hath taught us that *our redemption draweth near*; and, indeed, *go out from Babel*, which hath a long time held us captive and imprisoned.

And not regard the loud cry, and pratings, where they promise to us golden mantles of grace, and put them about us, and comfort, tickle, and flatter us with a strange pretence as if we were received to be children of grace from without by a sundry *particular election*; also that we look *not* upon, or regard *our own merits*, or abilities.

All which avail nothing before God; but a new creature in Christ, born of God, availeth before God; for *Christ is only the grace*, which avails with God.

Now whosoever is born of Christ, and liveth and walketh in Him, and puts Him on (according to his inner man) in His *suffering, death, and resurrection*; he is a member of His body, from him only flow the streams of living water, through the powerful word of Christ, which as to the internal ground is become man in him, and doth speak forth itself out of him through the creature in the *cosmic spirit (in spiritu mundi)* of the external man.

For as God hath manifested the grand mystery (wherein the whole creation hath lain in an essential manner without formings) out of the power of His word, and through the grand mystery hath expressed the word of powers into the severation or variety of spiritual formings; in which spiritual forms the science of the powers have stood in the desire; that is, in the fiat; wherein every science in the desire to manifestation hath brought itself into a corporeal bodily being; *even so* likewise the same grand mystery, viz., the essential word of God's power lieth in man (the image and likeness of God) both according to eternity and time.

By which mystery the living word of God doth utter and express itself either in love or anger, or in fancy; according as the human mystery standeth in *a moveable desire to evil or good*; as it is written, *with the holy thou art holy, and with the perverse thou art perverse; also, such as the people is, such a God they also have.*

For in what property the mystery in man is excited and awakened, such a word uttereth itself from his powers, as we plainly see that nothing else but vanity is uttered by the wicked.

Now how should there be a good expression and will where the mystery to the speaking and willing is a false ground, and poisoned by the devil in the wrath of nature; which false mystery can neither will nor do any good that may be acceptable to God; unless it be first enkindled by God, that it obtain a godly will and desire; whence a divine expression and operation of good followeth.

For Christ said, *an evil tree cannot bring forth good fruit*; how then will he bring forth good fruit, where a false tree standeth, under a strange show? The purple mantle of Christ hath its fruits in it; but what is that to a false beast, that is full of poison, and will cover himself with that mantle and take it for his own, and yet bringeth forth nothing but hellish fruit? Or what hath the titular Christian to do to boast and glory that he is a Christian; whereas he liveth, walketh, and is, without Christ?

None is a Christian unless he be *tinctured anew* with the spirit of Christ, and sprung forth out of *God's love*; that the grace of

God in Christ be manifest in the mystery of his life, as to the soul; and co-operateth and willeth in the human life.

Now if he will become such a one, then he must turn from his imagining *in the cosmic spirit (in spirtu mundi)* wherewith the soul is covered and disguised, and enters into earthly workings, and must become as a child, that only inclineth itself with its whole affection to the mother, and draweth into itself the mother's *milk* of grace, whence a new *Ens* groweth, in which the life of grace ariseth; that is, the *imputed grace* must be born, and become a man in him as to the internal ground; without this, there is none *a Christian*, let him make never such devout shows; dissemble, flatter, and do what he will, his sins must be forgiven him only through the *divine inspiration in itself*.

For when Christ is conceived in the inspired word of grace, which the soul doth take and impress into itself from his promise, then the foundation is laid in the corrupt, or decayed mystery to a child of God; and then the divine impregnation beginneth and proceedeth, wherein the humanity of Christ is conceived and borne; which only is *the Temple of the Holy Ghost*, and from this new birth the fiery soul eateth God's bread, which cometh from heaven; and without this, man hath no life in him (*John 6*), which no hypocrite under the purple mantle of Christ can enjoy, but only that man who is not born of flesh and blood, nor of the will of man, but regenerate of God, in whom the word of God (whence the first man was created) speaketh, ruleth, liveth, and willeth.

For the life of man was in the beginning in the word (*John 1*) when the same was inspired or breathed into the created image; but when it turned itself from the speaking of the word into a peculiar self-willing and speaking in good and evil, that is, into its own lust and contrived imagination, the first goodwill in the creature to the re-expressing did perish; and now he must enter again into the *first speaking* word, and speak with God, or he is eternally *without God*.

Which this present world cannot nor will not understand, for it hath wholly and fully turned itself into a selfish speaking, to the *pleasure* of the *flesh*; and it speaketh forth in self-will mere earthliness and transitory things, as honour, might, power, and authority; moreover, pride, covetousness, envy, and malice; it utters nothing else but the cunning crafty serpent with its young, and when these, her young, cannot get and uphold that which the self-will willeth, then it speaketh forth from the cunning mischievous malice and iniquity, *with money*, through the selfish power and violence, *many thousand soldiers*, who must maintain it by force, that the self-will that is departed from God may be truly upheld, as we now see before our eyes, by which expression this self-will also is beaten down, and kills and *destroys itself*.

Therefore, beloved sir and fellow-member in the life-tree of Christ, I would entreat you in a Christian way, and stir you up (as one member is bound to do to another) in the present state of the world (where the *Turba Magna* doth also play and express itself, and a great contesting, pulling down, or degrading shall be) constantly and steadfastly to keep yourself in the internal speaking of God's mercy, and continually to enter into your internal ground, and in nowise to be persuaded and misled by the serpent, to the false speaking of *brother-slaughter*; but you (as a famous lord) continually behold yourself in the looking-glass of Christ's process and doctrine.

For this present speaking is spoken in the wrath of God through His awakened and enkindled anger; and it is very evil and dangerous to have a *hand and voice therein*, especially when the *Turba (punishment or severe execution)* must be spoken; it is altogether unfaithful, and it devours its father and mother that brings it forth, and it is a besom of God's anger.

Also there is great heed to be taken in respect of accepting and joining to any of the *supposed religions*, for which men contend and fight; and not to assent with the conscience of faith to one party that gets the victory; for there is no other true faith which saveth, but only CHRIST IN US, He only destroyeth sin in us, and bruiseth the head of the serpent's imagination in us; and ariseth in God's righteousness (which He with His blood hath fulfilled in us) from the *sleep of death*.

Christ must arise from death in our poor soul, namely, in a new humanity, which walketh and dwelleth with, and in, Christ in heaven, where heaven is in the new man; whereout *proceed the works of love*, as it is meet and requisite for the children of God.

And though the external man liveth in earthly weakness and infirmities, yet that taketh not away the temple of Jesus Christ, for Christ, in the internal ground, doth continually bruise the head of the serpent in the flesh; and Christ must be continually *stinged by the serpent in the heel* till we be *freed* of this *beast*.

Moreover, loving sir, I do entreat you, in a Christian brotherly way, seriously to take notice of this present time, in the true fear of God; if you be pleased to let my good meaning take place with you, it will never repent you; for I speak that which is made known to me from the *Most High*, out of His *grace*, be pleased diligently to consider of it, and let the spirit of God be your meditation.

For there shall shortly come a time where *good friends* shall be *sifted* and proved, that we might stand steadfast in Christ; of the which, in love, I would put you in mind; for the time of *refreshment* cometh *soon after*, where *faithful people shall entirely love one another*; after which love I continually hunger and thirst, and it is my sincere and constant wish that *Babel* may soon come to her end, and Christ may come into the *valley of Jehosophat*, that *all nations might see and praise Him*.

I entreat you to send my three Treatises (viz. 1. *of Repentance*; 2. *of the New Birth*; 3. *of Resignation*; some whereof I gave you myself, and the rest I sent by *Mr Rudolff*) to *Mr Rudolffus* of *Gersdorp*; for I have written to him that he should send them me to *Sagan*, to *Mr Christianus Bernhard*, from whom I shall have them by one or other; or if you yourself had any occasion toward *Sagan*, be pleased to send them to *Mr Christianus Berhhard*, dwelling upon the market place; a year since he was *customer*; he is a young companion of the *Theosophic school*; to him I have convenient opportunity every week. These treatises are very much desired of the lovers, and may do much good; I pray send them by the first opportunity, for it is of much concernment, and when you shall find convenient leisure to study, I will send you somewhat *more deep*, for I have written this *autumn* and *winter* without ceasing: And I commend you unto the love of Jesus Christ and His gracious protection.

Dated 19th Feb., 1623.

To Gottfried Freudenhammer, Medical Doctor von Freudenheim in Grossen-Glogau.

THE open Fountain of God in the heart of Jesus Christ be our refreshment and constant Light.

Worthy, much respected and very learned sir, I heartily wish unto you even that which my very soul desireth of God; namely, the real true *divine knowledge* in the love of Christ, that God would vouchsafe to open the *centre* of the soul, whereby the Paradisical lily-twig in Christ's rose-garden might spring forth, grow, blossom, and bear fruit, and the streams out of Christ's fountain might flow from you, and you might be taught of God that His Holy Spirit might drive and rule you: As it is written, *Those who are driven and moved by the Spirit of God, they are the children of God.*

I have received your letter, and thereby understand that you have read my writings, and that you do delight in them; and I wish from my very heart that the sense and right meaning of the same may be apprehended and understood; and then there would be *no need* of any further asking and searching.

For the book in which all mysteries lie is man himself; he himself is the book of the Being of all beings; seeing he is the likeness of God; the great *Arcanum* lieth *in* him, the revealing of it belongeth only unto God's spirit.

But if the lily in the humanity of Christ springeth forth in the new birth out of the soul; then out of the same lily the spirit of God proceedeth, as out of His own original and ground; and the same spirit seeketh and findeth *all mysteries* in the divine wisdom.

For the lily-branch which springeth forth in the new birth out of Christ's humanity (understand the *new born spirit*, out of the soul's essence, out of Christ's power) is the true real branch springing from and remaining in God's tree.

As a mother beareth a child, even so is the new man born in and out of God; and not otherwise at all is he God's child and heir, a child of Heaven and of Paradise.

No imputed righteousness availeth (a stranger cannot inherit God's kingdom), but an innate righteousness out of God's essentiality, out of the water and spirit of God, as Christ told us, that *We must become like unto children*, and be conceived in God's essence, and, like new children in God, we must spring forth and be born anew; as a fair flower springeth out of the wild earth, or as previous gold groweth in a rough stone or drossy ore; otherwise we cannot see nor inherit the kingdom of God.

For whatsoever will possess the internal spiritual world must be born out of the same; the earthly flesh from the four elements cannot inherit the kingdom of God.

But the *quintessence* (which is the one element, namely, *Paradise*), whence the four elements have their rise, birth, and proceeding, that same must be predominant and rule over the four elements in like manner as the light containeth the darkness as it were swallowed up, and yet the same is really in it; even so it must be with man.

Only it cannot be so with the outward man in this time of the *earthly life*; for the outward world ruleth over the outward man; seeing it was made manifest in man, which is his fall.

And therefore the external man must perish, as the external world perisheth and passeth away; and therefore man in this time cannot attain *perfection*; but the true man must continue in combat and strife against the earthly corrupt life, which is its own enemy, where eternity and time strive one against another.

For through strife, or mutual combat in Nature, the great *Arcanum* is opened, and the eternal wonders in God's wisdom are made manifest out of the soul's essence.

As the eternal God hath manifested Himself through the time, and bringeth His eternal wonders through the time, into combat and contest, that through the combat that which is hidden might open itself and be brought to light; even so in strife and combat, the great mystery must be revealed in man, where God's anger and love, as fire and light, are in combat and strife.

For in the soul (which ariseth out of the eternal fire out of the Father's property, that is out of the eternal uninchoative Nature, out of the darkness) that light (which did extinguish and disappear in Adam) must be renewed and born again in the incoming of Christ, and then the kingdom of Christ and of God is *freely* given him out of *grace*.

For none can take the same unto himself unless the love of

God doth again press out of grace into the centre of the soul, and bringeth the divine will out of the fire of the soul as a new sprout or new image into the heavenly essentiality, as the light shineth out of the fire.

Therefore all whatsoever *Babel* teacheth of the external imputed righteousness, and the external assumed adoption is without foundation and footing; Christ said, *You must be born again, else you cannot see the kingdom of God.*

The seeming holy flattering comfort with Christ's death availeth nothing, but to enter into Christ's death; and to spring up anew in Him; and to arise in Him and with Him and become Christ in the new man.

Like as Christ hath mortified, extinguished, and overcome the world, and also the anger of His Father (being the centre of the eternal nature), in the soul's property with His love (that is, with the new love-fire introduced into the soul's essence); into which the devil before had brought in and placed *his desire*; even so must we in and with Christ's spirit quell and quash the earthly *Adam* in God's anger, and mortify it through God's love, that the new man may spring forth, else there is no forgiveness of sin nor any adoption, nor any righteousness.

The kingdom of God must be inwardly innate and born within us, else we cannot see with the eyes of eternity into the angelical world.

All imaginations, inventions, and ways; all reading, studying, and teachings, is to no purpose, no art or reason can attain it; we must enter only through the gate which God hath opened to us in Christ, and spring forth in God's kingdom and die unto the earthly will, so that it neither hindereth nor sticketh on us and cloggeth us; *the seed of the woman must continually bruise the serpent's head in us.*

Self-reason cannot make a child of God, for it lieth not in our willing, running, and keeping a doing, as St Paul saith, *but on God's mercy and compassion.*

My selfhood cannot attain it; my selfhood must die in Christ's death, and fall or resign unto the nothing; and then my selfhood falleth into God's mercy; and is in the limit of the first man, and standeth again in the *world fiat*; where God's mercy in Christ's entrance into our humanity doth make the new man out of grace.

And therefore the corrupt earthly will must die in a real, true, upright repentance, and enter into the resignation, that is, into the nothing, and wholly surrender the will of reason unto death, and neither will or know himself any more, but enter into the mercy and compassion of God.

And then this saying hath its place and meaning, as God speaketh in the prophet, *My heart breaketh in me, that I must take pity on him. Can a mother forget her child that she should not have compassion on the son of her womb? And albeit she should forget, yet I will not forget thee; Behold, I have noted thee in My hands.*

In this (namely, in God's mercy), the new man doth arise, and springeth up in the kingdom of Heaven and Paradise, *though* the earthly body be in this world.

For *Saint Paul* saith, *Our conversation is in Heaven*: Thus the new man walketh in Heaven, and the old man in this world, for the heaven in which God dwelleth is in the new man.

Thus, beloved sir and brother, and in no other way and manner, have I found the mystery. I have not studied or learned the same, but if you or any other do thirst after it, I am engaged, as a brother in my affection and love, to show him the way how I met with it as I have set down at large in my writings, chiefly in the book of *the Threefold Life of Man*, and in the book of *the Three Principles of the Divine Being*.

Indeed, I did it for myself as a spiritual exercise in God's knowledge in the mystery of the great wonders of God, which, notwithstanding by God's providence and guidance, is come so far as to be published and read; and I would gladly that every one that earnestly desires to understand the same, might have it; and I wish from my heart that it may be really manifest and made known to the *reader of this Epistle*, and to every one *in himself*, and then there would be no need of any further searching and seeking.

But seeing God hath promised by the prophets (especially in *Joel*), that He will pour forth His spirit in the last days upon all flesh, therefore the time is to be considered and taken notice of.

I say as I have known it, that whosoever at present will die to himself, him shall the spirit of the Lord, according to *Joel's* prophecy, apprehend, and manifest His wonders by him; therefore if any be in earnest, he shall find it by experience.

Yet let every one be faithfully warned, that if God's light doth arise in him, that he continue steadfast in great humility in resignation, namely, in the death of Christ.

For heaven shall now at last evacuate the worldly void which the astral world has slowly built up in the very nature of man, so that it may not be overcome by the starry heaven, and may avoid ceasing to practise resignation by aiming at other than its appointed end.

As it may be seen in the *Metists* (the proselytes or disciples of Isaias Steefel and Ezekiel Metts, that held perfection in this outward flesh), who came even unto the gates of the *Deep*, and were again captivated by the starry heaven, and entered into themselves, and exalted themselves, and surceased the strife against the serpent, and entered into a singular Luciferian conceit of their own holiness, *supposing* that they were *changed into a deity*, and so they have confounded the external world with the internal.

Which is unsound, and void of ground, and of which we must take great heed, and see that we continue steadfast in deepest humility, that the seed that is sown may grown unto a tree, and may come to the blossoming, and the spirit of God get a form in us.

For out of the blossom ariseth *the morning star*, that man may learn to know himself what he is, and what God and time is.

I give you, sir, out of good affection, to understand that this present time is seriously to be taken into consideration, for the *seventh* angel in the *Revelation* have prepared his *trumpet*; the powers of heaven be in peculiar motion; moreover, both gates stand open, and light and darkness are in great desire; as everything is taken, so it shall go in.

At what the one shall exceedingly rejoice, the other shall mock at it; whereupon followeth the sore and severe judgement upon *Babel*.

And so I commit you and yours unto the pleasant and amiable *love* of Jesus Christ.

Dated Görlitz, 27th October, 1621.

A Letter written to one in Temptation and Trouble of mind, showing whence it ariseth.

DEAR Sir, my *fellow-member* and brother in Christ our Saviour; my cordial wish and co-operating desire of the divine love and grace premised: I desire to let you know in Christian love that I have considered your condition in a Christian sympathy and fellow-feeling, and have brought it before the gracious compassion of the Most High, to see what He would be pleased to let me know therein.

Whereupon, sir, I must tell you that I, in the same gracious compassion, obtained such an insight and *vision* of your condition and temptation, that the ground and cause of it is made known to me; and I will set it down in brief for a *memorandum*, that you may consider and ponder it seriously by yourself.

The *first* cause of such strong working temptation is the supernatural, superabundant, and unspeakable love of God (that is, the divine good will, and then the creature will of man struggling one against another); that the human will refuseth fully to resign and give itself up with total confidence unto such great grace of God, which is tendered unto it out of pure love, but seeketh itself and its *own love* of transitory things, and loveth itself and the *things* of this world more than God.

Therefore man's own nature (which in its centre without the love of God standeth in mere anguish, strife, enmity, and unquiet contrarity) tempteth him; into which also the devil shooteth his false desire, to lead man astray from such high grace and love of God.

This temptation is the greatest; and it is even the combat with Christ maintaineth with His love (shed forth into the nature of man) against such *selfness*, also against God's anger, sin, death, devil, and hell, in which combat the human dragon must be devoured by the love of Christ, and changed into an angelical image.

And if the love of God in Christ *had not its influence in you*, you should have none of this combat, but the dragon (viz., the false devilish will) would maintain his natural right and possession without *any such conflict* or disturbance.

Now, therefore, this perplexing and distressing temptation is wrought very sensibly in nature by the dragon, who is in travailing anguish with his own nature, when such great love of God cometh into him, and would change his natural right into a *divine will*.

For here Christ standeth in man, in hell, and stormeth or assaulteth the strong fortress of the devil, whence ariseth such strife; where Christ and Lucifer fight for the soul, as God hath given you to see, and know experimentally in the first temptation.

Thus *Christ bruiseth the head of the serpent, and the serpent stingeth Christ in the heel*, and the poor soul standeth in the midst in great trembling and sadness, and can do nothing, but only stand still in *hope*; it is not able also to lift up its face before God, and pour forth its effectual prayers, for the dragon turneth its face towards the vanity of this world, and shows it the beauty and glory of this world, and mocketh it, because it will become another creature; and represents unto it the kingdom in which it liveth, and its natural ground.

And here the soul standeth with Christ in the wilderness, in the *forty days' temptation*, where the might, glory, riches, and pleasure of this world is tendered unto it, alluring it to elevate itself and enter into its own self-will.

The *second* temptation of *Lucifer*, and the selfish dragon of nature, is this, that when the soul hath tasted the divine love, and hath been once illuminated, then the soul will have the same light for its own propriety, and work therein in its own power and ability, as in its own peculiar possession; understand, the nature of the soul, which being without God's light is a dragon as *Lucifer*, that I say will have it for its own propriety; but this dragon will not resign up his natural right; he will be a maker and disposer of the divine power, and live therein in great joy in his fiery nature; and this cannot be.

This dragon (viz., the fiery nature) must be changed with its own will into a love fire, and forego his natural right; but he is unwilling to do it; but he in such a change or transmutation looketh for an *own self-power*, and yet findeth none, and therefore he beginneth to doubt of grace, because he seeth that in such working he must forsake his natural desire and will; and hence he continually is afraid, and will not *die in the divine light from his own natural right*, but always *thinketh* that the light of *grace* (which worketh without such sharpness and fiery might) is a *false* light.

Whence it cometh, that the outward reason (which, however, is blind), continually thinketh: Oh! who knoweth how it is with thee, whether it be true or not that God hath illuminated thee, that He is in thee? It may likely proceed from such a *fancy*; thou seest not the like in other people, and yet they think to be saved as well as thou; thou makest thyself thereby only the fool of the world, and standest in fear and trembling at God's anger, more than those who comfort themselves only with the *promise* of grace upon the *future* revelation.

Thus it cometh to pass that then the internal ground doth sigh and pant after the inflammation and motion of the light, and fain would have it; but the nature is able to do nothing; it is as if it were wholly rejected of God, which is also true, as to the self-will; for *God* hath *planted* a new will *into it*; it must die to its own will, and be changed into God's will.

And because the will of nature must die and resign its own right to the will of God, therefore such grievous temptations are therein; for the devil will not have his fortress to fall or be demolished; for if Christ shall live in man, then the spirit of self-lust and imagination must die, and yet it doth *not wholly* die in the time of this life by reason of the flesh, but it *dieth daily, and yet liveth*; and therefore there is such contest, which no wicked man feeleth, but only those who have put on Christ, in whom Christ fighteth with *Lucifer*.

The *third* temptation is in the strongholds of the devil, namely, in the will and mind, as also in flesh and blood; where the false centres lie in man, as a peculiar self-will to the proud temporal life, to the lust of the flesh, to earthly things; also many curses of men which have been wished upon his body and soul through his temptation; all the sins which have grounded and concentred, and yet stand in the *astral* spirit, as a strong fort; in which Christ now fighteth, and will destroy it; which stronghold of might, pleasure, and beauty of this world the human will doth still esteem and hold for its propriety and best treasure, and will not resign it up and be obedient to Christ.

Therefore, beloved sir and Christian brother, I tell you, and give you to understand, what our loving Lord Jesus Christ hath shown me in my consideration; examine yourself, what your temptation is; our dear Lord said, *We must forsake all, and follow Him*; and so we should be right Christ-like poor (or *truly spiritually poor*).

Now if you yet stick with your mind in the self-lust, imagination, and love of earthly things, then therein (namely, in those centres which yet work in you) you have such temptation.

But if you will follow my child-like counsel, I tell you this, that when such temptation doth arise in you, you must then imagine nothing else to yourself save the bitter suffering and dying of our Lord, and consider His reproach and scorn, His contempt and poverty in this world, which He hath undergone and done for us poor men; and resign your *desire* and whole will thereinto, that you would very *fain be conformable to His image*, and with all unfeigned willingness follow him in his *way of life*, and patiently endure whatsoever is laid upon you to suffer, and that willingly, for His sake; and desire only to be conformable or like unto Him; and for His love sake will be content to be abject, despised, in contempt, and affliction, that you might be maintain and *keep this His love in you*, and will no longer to yourself, but only what Christ willeth through you.

Dear sir, I fear me there is yet *somewhat* in you that is *displeasing* to Christ by reason whereof there is such strife in you. Christ willeth that you should die with Him to your own will, in His death, and arise in His will, and live with Him; and *Christ is at present in your soul, and striveth for your soul*.

Let all earthly will go, and resign up yourself wholly and fully; let joy and sadness, comfort and conflict, be all one to you; and so you shall with Christ be *a conqueror* over the world, devil, death, and hell, and at last find by experience what Christ hath been in you, and wherefore this hath happened unto you, which hath been the process of all the children of Christ. I speak out of Christian affection.

J.B.

Dated on the day of Christ's going to His suffering
and dying, ANNO DOM., 1623.

A NOTE ON CORRESPONDENCES IN ALCHEMY AND ASTROLOGY

'Throughout the Alchemical Process' Knowledge of self and Knowledge of the World mutually interact until they become one. A wonderful event and the true aim of the Great Work, since inwardly and externally, as above so below, in the spirit and in nature and as in the human organism. The Three the Four, the Seven and the Twelve are all present.' (Jules Evola)

The Three Constituents: Sulphur, Mercury Salt.
The Four Elements: Earth, Air, Fire and Water (to which Hindu philosophy (Gita 13:6) adds a fifth: Aether)
The Four Humours: Phlegm, Blood, Choler, and Black Bile.
The Seven Planets: Sun, Moon, Mercury, Venus, Mars, Jupiter, Saturn.
The Twelve Signs of the Zodiac (ascending, north):
a) *Spring:* Aries, Taurus, Gemini; b) *Summer:* Cancer, Leo, Virgo; (descending, south): a) *Autumn:* Libra, Scorpio, Saggitarius; b) *Winter:* Capricorn, Aquarius, Pisces.

For Boehme, Sulphur, Salt, and Mercury, are the three most important elements and of these Mercury has the greatest number of implications. Sal is the *prima materia* astringency. Sulphur is a soul-spirit in the Inner Centre. Mercury is an astringent bitter fire but it is also Sound the vibration of the Word as it 'sounds and rings in the whole of the Father in all Powers' (Aurora 6:2)

Table of Correspondences according to Boehme

Virtues	Vices	Signs of the Zodiac	Metals	Boehme's 'Qualities'
1. Humility	Pride	Sun (Sol)	Gold	The Light of Nature
2. (Incarnation of Christ)	The Flesh	Moon (Luna)	Silver	Corporeity
3. Beneficence	Envy	Mercury	Quicksilver	Life, Sound, the Verbum Fiat
4. Chastity	Lewdness	Venus	Copper	The beginnings of substantiality
5. Meekness	Aggressiveness	Mars	Iron	The Fiery Strength
6. Wisdom	Cunning	Jupiter	Tin	The active desire in the astringency
7. Charity	Avarice	Saturn	Lead	Astringency, darkness

BIBLIOGRAPHY

Collected Works
Boehme, J. *Samtliche Schriften Faksimile—Neudruck der Ausgabe van 1730 begonnen von August Faust neu Herausgegeben von W. E. Peuckert* (Stuttgart-Bad Cannstatt, 1986).
11 vols. 8vo. Originally issued 1955–61.
——, *Die Urschriften* (Stuttgart-Bad Cannstatt, 1963–6).
2 vols. 4to. Edited by Werner Buddecke.
These two series represent the basic texts of all Boehme's writings and manuscript remains. A complete translation into English remains to be undertaken. The standard English text is the Law edition.
——, *The Works of Jacob Behmen . . . to which is prefixed the life of the author. With figures illustrating his principles, left by the Reverend William Law* (M. Richardson: London, 1764–81).
4 vols. This work was edited by G. Ward and T. Langcake—Law had no hand in it. It is based on the earlier translations of Sparrow, Blunden, and Ellistone.

ANTHOLOGIES
——, *The Confessions of Jacob Boehme*. Compiled and edited by W. Scott Palmer, with an introduction by Evelyn Underhill (London, 1920).
——, *Personal Christianity: The Doctrines of Jacob Boehme*. With an introduction and notes by Franz Hartmann (F. Ungar: New York).

Individual Works
——, *Aurora* (Watkins: London, 1914).
Edited by C. J. Barker. Reprinted, Cambridge, 1967.

——, *Concerning the Three Principles of the Divine Essence*. Translated by John Sparrow. Introduction by Paul Deussen. (Watkins: London, 1910).

——, *De Signatura Rerum:* The Signature of all Things with other writings (Dent. Everyman Library: London, 1912).
Introduction by Clifford Bax. Includes 'Of The Supersensual Life' and 'The Way from Darkness to True Illumination', all in Ellistone's translation.

——, *De Signatura Rerum* (Cambridge, 1969).
A later reprint of the above.

——, *The Epistles* (Glasgow, 1886).
A selection using Ellistone's translation, with a preface signed J. E.

——, *The Forty Questions of the Soul and the Clavis*. With Emendations by D. S. Hehner (Watkins: London, 1911).
Edited by C. J. Barker.

——, *Of the Incarnation of Jesus Christ*. Translated from the German by J. R. Earle (1934).

——, *The Key of Jacob Boehme*. Translated by William Law, with an explanation of the Deep Principles of Jacob Behmen in 13 Figures. Introduction by Adam McLean (Magnum Opus Hermetic Source Works: Edinburgh, 1981).

——, *Mysterium Magnum* (Watkins: London, 1924 and 1947).
2 vols. Edited by C. J. Barker.

——, *Mysterium Magnum*. Translation by N. Berdiaeff [into French] (Paris, 1945; reprinted 1978).
4 vols., with two long, valuable articles on Boehme by Berdiaeff.

——, *The Threefold Life of Man*. Englished by J. Sparrow, with an introduction by the Rev. G. W. Allen (Watkins: London, 1909).

——, *The Way to Christ*. Translation and introduction by Peter Erb (Paulist Press: New York, 1978).
An excellent edition with valuable notes.

Books about Boehme

Bailey, M. *Milton and Jakob Boehme: A Study of German Mysticism in the 17th century* (New York, 1914).

Benz, E. *The Mystical Sources of German Romantic Philosophy* (Allison Park: Pennsylvania, 1983).
Much on the influence of Boehme and his French disciple L. C. de St Martin.

Brinton, H. H. *The Mystic Will*. Based on a study of the Philosophy of J. Boehme (1931).

Buddecke, W. *Die Böhme-Ausgaben Ein beschreibendes Verzeichnis* (Göttingen, 1937 and 1957).
2 vols.

——, *Die Böhme Handschriften und ihr Schicksal* (New York, 1953).
From *The Jacob Boehme Society Quarterly* 1 (No. 4): 17–22.

Cahiers de l'Hermetisme. Jacob Böhme par Gerhard Wehr et Pierre Deghaye (Albin Michel: Paris, 1977).
With a life by Wehr and a very valuable article by Deghaye, 'Psychologia Sacra'. Full Bibliography.

Coleridge, S. T. *Marginalia I Abbt to Byfield*. Edited by George Whalley (Princeton University Press, 1980).
Collected Works, Vol. 12: 553–696. Would repay detailed study.

Deghaye, P. *La Doctrine Esoterique de Zinzendorf (1700–1760)* (Paris, 1969).
Throws light on the outworking of Boehme's teachings.

——, *La Naissance de Dieu ou la Dotrine de Jacob Boehme* (Paris, 1985).
By the leading French Boehme Scholar.

Freher, D. A. *The Paradoxical Emblems*. Edited from MS Add. 5789 in The British Library, with an introduction by Adam McLean (Magnum Opus Hermetic Source Works: Edinburgh, 1983).
By one of the earliest disciples and interpreters of Boehme.

Gichtel, J. G. *Theosophia Practica*. Traduite pour la première fois en Français (Sebastiani: Milano, 1973).

Gorceix, B. *Johann Georg Gichtel Théosophe d'Amsterdam* (Paris, 1975).
The only full life of Boehme's greatest disciple and editor.

——, *Flambée et Agonie. Mystiques du XVIIe siecle allemand* (Paris, 1977).

Grunsky, H. *Jacob Böhme* (Stuttgart, 1956).
The standard biography.

Harless, G. C. A. von. *Jacob Böhme und die Alchymisten* (Berlin, 1882).

Hirst, D. *Hidden Riches: Traditional Symbolism from The Renaissance to Blake* (1964).
Full of interest for the history of Boehme's influence.

Hobhouse, S., editor. *Selected Mystical Writings of William Law*. Edited with notes and twenty-four studies in the mystical theology of William Law and Jacob Boehme (1938).

——, Second edition. Foreword by Aldous Huxley (1948).

Hutin, Serge. *Les Disciples anglais de Jacob Boehme au 17e et 18e siècles* (Denoel: Paris, 1960).
Essential reading.

Jones, Rufus. *Spiritual Reformers in the 16th and 17th Centuries* (1914).

Jung, C. G. *Mysterium Coniunctionis* (1963).

Collected Works, Vol. 14. Many references to Boehme.

Koyré, A. *La Philosophie de Jacob Boehme* (Paris, 1929).
The most comprehensive analysis of Boehme's thought.

——, *Mystiques, spirituels, alchimistes du XVIe siecle allemand* (Paris, 1971).
Four long studies on Schwenkfeld, Franck, Paracelsus, and Weigel.

Leade, Jane. *The Revelation of Revelations*. Introduction by Adam McLean (Magnum Opus Hermetic Source Works: Edinburgh, 1981).
England's great Boehme disciple.

Martensen, Bishop H. L. *Jacob Boehme: Studies in his Life and Teaching*. New revised edition with Notes and Appendices by Stephen Hobhouse (1949).

Muses, C. A. *Illumination on Jacob Boehme: The Work of Dionysius Andreas Freher* (New York, 1951).

Nigg, W. *Heimliche Weisheit* (Zurich, 1987).
Second revised edition of this important series of studies of Schwenkfeld, Franck, Weigel, Arndt, Boehme, Gichtel.

Penny, Mrs A. J. *Studies in Jacob Böhme* (Watkins: London, 1912).
Preface by C. J. Barker. Very valuable series of articles reprinted from *Light*.

Sédir, P., (pseud. Yvon Le Loup), *Les Tempéraments et la Culture Psychique d'après J. Boehme* (Paris, 1894).

Stoudt, J. J. *Sunrise to Eternity: A Study in Jacob Boehme's life and thought*. Preface by Paul Tillich (Philadelphia, 1957).

Taylor, Edward. *Jacob Boehme's Theosophick Philosophy Unfolded* (1691).

Thune, N. *The Behmenists and the Philadelphians* (Uppsala, 1948).

Walton, Christopher. *Notes and Materials for an adequate biography of the celebrated Divine and Theosopher, William Law* (1854).
An inexhaustible mine of information on Boehme's disciples in England.

Wehr, G. *Jacob Böhme in Selbstzeugnissen und Bilddokumenten* (Berlin, 1971).
Rohwolts Monographien: 179.

Weiss, V. *Die Gnosis Jacob Böhmes* (Zurich, 1955).

FOUR
TABLES
OF
Divine Revelation

Signifying

What GOD in himfelf is, without Nature; and
how confidered in Nature; according to the
THREE PRINCIPLES.

ALSO

What HEAVEN, HELL, WORLD, TIME, and
ETERNITIE are; Together with all Creatures vifible and invifible: and out of what
all things had their Original.

Written in the *German* language by *JACOB
BEHM*, and Englifhed by *H. B.*

LONDON
Printed for H. *Blunden,* and fold at the Caftle
in Corn-Hill 1654.

APPENDIX

A Brief Explication of the first Table, of GOD revealed; how out of himself he continually begetteth, and breatheth forth himself: And how this Table is to be understood.

NUMBER I. Is the *Abyss*, the *Nothing*, and the *All*. There we begin to consider, what God in himself is, without [or besides] Nature and Creature; and this consideration of the hidden God, extendeth unto *Wisdom*, Numb. 7. Therein is understood how God dwelleth in all, and how all things from him have their existence; but, himself is to all *Incomprehensible*, and as a *Nothing*; yet through that *All*, he maketh himself visible, sensible, and (a) attainable.

Numb. 2. Is the *Will* of the *Abyss*. And by it, at the right side, FATHER, and on the other side, J.E. This signifieth the *Will* of the *Abyss*, which is the *Father* of all *Beings*. And the J.E. signifieth the Eternall *One*, as the *Name* JESUS from the Eternall *One*.

Numb. 3. Is the (b) *Delight* [Lubet] or Impression of the *Will*; by which (towards the right) standeth SON, and opposite to it, HO, signifying how the self will includeth it self in the place of its possession: The place is the procreation out of it self; where God begetteth God; according to the good pleasure of his propriety. The HO is the breathing of the will, through which the Delight passeth.

(a) Invenible **Findlich.**   (b) Good pleasure, *Beneplacitum*.

what God without Nature and Creature is, and what the Mysterium Magnum is: How God, by his breathing forth or speaking, hath introduced himself into Nature and Creature.		Abyss	
		1 *NOTHING & ALL*	
	Father 2	VVill of the Abyss.	JE
	Sonn 3	Delight or impression of the VVill.	HO
	Spirit 4	Science *or* Motion.	VA
		5 GOD in Trinitie.	*Thus is* GOD *without* Nature *and* Creature considered.
		6 VVORD in GOD.	
		7 VVisdom.	

Begining of Mysterii Magni *of the Eternal* NATURE

Here beginneth Mysterium Magnum as distinction in speaking the WORD; where the WORD by Wisdom is made distinct, Natural, Sensible, Comprehensible, and Invensible. The Eternal beginning of the Principles is here also understood, with Gods Love and Anger, in Light and Darkness.	GOD *in* LOVE		GOD *in* WRATH			
			9. The First principle			Spri-tual
	8 *The Second*	Principle	Dark,	Moving,	Thinking	
				Feeling,	Mind,	Nature
	11 V. Angel, Light, Love-fire.	10 Tincture or speaking of the Trinity.	1 Desire,	II. Prick or Science,	III Angush,	IV Five,
	Angelical World Root of the four Elements.	VI Sound or Distinction. VII Essence, or essential wisdom.	Austere	Cause of Enmity	Five root of heat	
			Hard,	Hellish-life,	Hell,	Sub-
	Growing or Greening in the Spiritual World.	12 Pure Element. 13 Paradise.	Sharpness cold fire	Root,	Devill,	stan-
			SAL,	MERCURIUS,	SULPHUR	tial.

14 *Begining of the external* World.

Here beginneth the external visible world, as the out-spoken visible WORD. 1 Is understood the good Life of the creature which stands in the Quint-Essence. 2 The poison and grossness of the Earth and Earthly Life. 3 The Reader understanding these, all Doubts and Queries cease in him: and Babel is left in Ignominie.	The third	Principle	
		15 Heaven.	
	Starrs	16 Quint-Essence	Good Powers.
	The	17 The 4 Elements.	Devill's Poyson introduced.
	Out spoken WORD.	18 Earthly Creatures.	

Numb. 4. Is *Science* or *Motion*: at the Right standeth SPIRIT, and over against it V A. *Science*, is the attraction of the *Will* to the place of God; where the *Will* comprehendeth the Delight which proceeded to the Son, or to the breathing; by which outbreathing is understood the Spirit of God. And here is understood the great Name JEHOVA, as the (*d*) Tri-une Being; how the Father of himself begetteth the Son; and how the Holy Spirit proceedeth from both, and yet they be but one Being, which hath nothing before it. For the *Science*, in the drawing in, is understood a Root of the Eternal knowledge, or motion.

Numb. 5. Is *God* in *Trinity*, signifying that the Tri-une Being, may be known, as a Similitude of the *Will*, *Mind*, and *Senses*; wherein lyeth the eternal understanding. Thus is the Ternarie, the one Eternal understanding, and cause of all things.

Numb. 6. Standeth WORD, signifying distinction in the understanding, as speaking, the (*e*) Perception of it self; which word abideth Eternally in God himself; and God as the Power of Perception, is the Eternal good.

Numb. 7. Standeth *Wisdom*, signifying the outspoken Word, as the power of the Divine Contemplation; wherein God to himself is Intelligible, Perceptible, and Revealed. And thus far is God to the Creature, Invisible, Incomprehensible, not Natural, nor Creatural.

Below the line standeth Beginning of the *Great Mysterie*, or of the *Eternal Nature*; As of the Separability, Perceptibilitie, and Sensibilitie of the Properties; wherein is understood, the Divine Extrication or Revelation, how God introduceth himself in the eternal Nature, in Love and Wrath; and not in himself, for himself is the one Eternal good, but without Distinction, were not perceptible or manifest.

Here is to be Noted, that the 7. *Capitall Forms of Nature*, are marked (to distinguish them from the other Numbers) with I, II. III. IV, V. VI. VII.

Numb. 8. The second *Principle*, standeth to the Right. And Numb. 9. The first *Principle*, to the left. Thus Numb. 9. sig-

----

(*d*) Three in one.   (*e*) Or sensibilitie   **Empfindligkeit.**

nifieth the Fathers Propertie, through the speaking of the Word in Wrath; And the second Numb. 8. signifieth the Sons propertie in Love; where the Love of God by the expressed Word is revealed. As that in Love, Numb. 8. sheweth the Angelicall power-world; and that in Wrath, Numb. 9. signifieth the Dark power-world of Painfulness, wherein God is an Angry God.

Numb. 10. Standeth *Tinctur*, signifying the Temperature of all powers, how there through speaking they go forth in Distinction and Formes; as first in the 7. Capital Forms, the Desire, *Science*, Anguish, Fire, Love-Fire, Sound, and Being. And further, there standeth by every Capital Form, what Properties are born and proceed out of themselves.

For, if there must be a speaking; then the power must first contract it self, that it may breath forth it self; then it begetteth that Comprehensive or Magnetick *Impression*, the something (which is the Beginning) wherein the *Fiat* which attracteth the powers is understood.

I. Is the *first Capital Form* of the spiritual Nature, and standeth with Numb. I. *Desire*, which Desire sharpneth it self, from whence existeth *Sour*, *Hard*, and the cause of *Cold*; and is the ground of all *Saltish* properties *Spiritual*, in the Spiritual world; and *Essential* in the External world. So also the Desire of *Impression* is cause of its own overshadowing, or Darkness in the Abyss; as all these Forms belong to Numb. I. To the desire of (*f*) Comprehensibility.

II. By the *Second Capital Form*, standeth (*g*) *Compunction* or *Science*; signifying the contraction of the Desire; where the first enmitie or contrary will ariseth; for hardness and motion, are not alike. Now in this *form* ariseth moving and feeling; as the root of pain; wherein is understood the Mercurial Poyson-life, both spiritual and (*h*) corporall; and in the *Darkness* the *paine* or Torment of the wicked life; Neither was the good life without the root of the Evill manifest unto him; and that is the root of Gods wrath, according to the Perception [sensibility] of the eternall Nature.

(*f*) **Jnfaßligkeit.**   (*g*) Pricking.   (*h*) Essential.

III. The *third Capitall Form* is *Anguish*; which ariseth from the desire of Impression, and from the Enmitie of Compunction, where the will standeth in (*i*) Torment, and is there the cause of feeling, and of the five *Senses*: for in the *Anguish* all Formes grow *Painfull*, and then are they sensible of one-another. And here is the *Word* become distinct; and is the root of *Sulphur*, both Spirituall and Essentiall, [Corporall] wherein is rightly understood the *Hellish Fire* in *Darkness*, in painfull life, as appears in the Table downward.

IV. The *fourth Capitall Form*, is call'd *Fire*; where is Understood the kindling of the *Fire*, from the painfull *Sulphurish root*; for the Will goeth out of Anguish again into Libertie; And the Libertie goeth to its Revelation in Anguish: In which Conjunction cometh that terrible [like a flash of lightning] Coruscation, where the *Abyss*, as the Eternall good, is revealed; And is in the *Forms of Nature*, the Understanding and Life, in the dark Enmitie; and in the *Libertie* is the root of *Joy*, or rouzing up the (*k*) Powers; and is the kindling of the Fire; in which kindling the *Abyss* becomes a shining Light, as Materiall.

V. The *fifth form*, is call'd the *Love-Fire*; where is understood how the Eternall good, through kindling the painfull Fire, introduceth it self into an elevating burning *Love-Fire*, which Love-Fire was first in God. But thus only it (*m*) windeth up it self that it becomes sensible and moving, where in the good Powers are operative.

VI. Standeth *Sound*, or *Distinction*, as the sixth Capitall *Form*; signifying, that the Naturall manifested Life, where the Eternall *Divine Word*, through the Formes of Nature, hath infolded it self; and where all the *Powers* of Wisdom stand *in* (*n*) *Sound*: therein standeth the Understanding Life; which in Light, is Angelicall and Divine; but in Darkness it is Diabolicall; As at the right, Numb. 11. standeth Angell.

VII. Standeth *Essence* or *Essentiall Wisdom*, of the out-breathed word; wherein all other Forms are revealed; and is even the *Essence of all Forms*; as good and Divine, in the Light; but in the

---

(*i*) *Cruciatus* 𝖣ual.   (*k*) Faculties 𝕶raffen.   (*m*) Infoldeth 𝖂ickelt.

(*n*) Noyse 𝕾challe.

Darkness Evill and Devillish: And therein is chiefly understood *Mysterium Magnum* [the great Mystery;] the *Angelicall* world is also therein understood; and likewise the Internall spirituall body of *Man*, which disappeared in *Adam*, when the Souls will departed from Gods will; but revived again in Christ, that giveth to him for the Essence of this Power-World, which is that *heavenly flesh. Joh.* 6. And it is the dry *Rod of Aaron*, which in the Spirit of Christ, again springeth up in Man.

Numb. 12. Standeth *Pure Element*, signifying *Motion* in the Angelicall world in Essence; and is the One, *Holy*, Pure Element; wherein the four Elements, in the Temperature, lay, and is a root of the 4. Elements.

Numb. 13. Standeth (*p*) *Paradise* signifying the Eternall springing, or spiritual growing, in the Spirituall world; from which the externall *visible world*, out of good and evill (as out of both Eternall Principles) is breathed forth: In which Source and Regimen, *Adam* in his Innocency stood; when the four Elements *harmoniously* existed in him, as in the holy pure Element.

Numb. 14. Standeth *Beginning of the External World*; signifying how God by his Word, hath breathed forth that spiritual *Mysterium Magnum*, as the Eternall Nature of all Spirituall Properties, into a visible externall formall Being; and through the *Fiat*, as the Divine Desire, hath fashioned it into Creatures; There standeth the third *Principle*, where 3. *Worlds* in one another, must be understood: as the dark world of Gods wrath; the Eternall light world of Divine Love; and this visible fading world.

Numb. 15. Standeth *Heaven*; signifying the (*q*) parting Mark, between the internall and externall world; as of the visible and invisible Essence; which Heaven standeth in the Essence of the spirituall firie water.

Numb. 16. Stands *Quintessence*; signifying the spirituall Powers, as the Paradise-Ground in the four Elements; as well the Afterall, breathed forth by internall powers at the beginning of

(*p*) Thus hath this place been before the fall of *Lucifer* and *Adam*; namely, in an equal temperature or Harmony, of the 7. Planets and 4. Elements.

(*q*) Heaven is the parting-mark out of the spiritual fire and water between the Heavenly and Earthly.

time; (and is that good in the four Elements wherein the light of
Nature shineth) as an outbreath'd (r) fulgor of the Eternall
light.

Numb. 17. Standeth four Elements, *viz. Fire, Air, Water*, and
Earth, as the created world, out of the dark and light world,
which is the framed word spoken out of the Eternall Natures
Essentiall power; therein did the Devill cast his poison, which
after the fall of Man, was accursed of God.

Numb 18. Stands (s) *Earthly Creatures*; signifying that out of
the Quintessence and the four Elements, were all Creatures of
this visible World created, and only from them have their life.
But the animated Man hath also in him both inward spirituall
worlds, according to the internall soul of man; therefore may
Gods love and wrath be manifested in him: for wherein the will
impresseth and kindleth it self, of that Essence it partaketh, and
the fame is manifest in him; as is seen in *Lucifer*.

Thus have you a brief Intimation of the first Table, and
[consequently] of all the Authors writings; faithfully imparted,
out of a good Christian affection to his loving friends; and [is] as
an ABC to beginners.

The Second Table Expounded

The word ADONAI signifieth an (a) opening, or free motion of
the bottomless Eternal Unity; how the Eternal generation, expansion, and effluence of the Trinity of God is in it self.

A, is a triple I, which comprehendeth it self Cross-wise, as in
a Beginning, Entrance, and Effluence.

D, is the motion of the triple I, as the opener.

O, is the Circumference of the triple I, as the birth of God's
place in it self.

N, is the triple Spirit, issuing forth of the Circumference out
of it self as a triple I.

(r) Or shine ⬥last.   (s) Man having a. Eternals in him; may be saved or damned.

(a) Or expansion.

AD	Father	Will	IE
O	Son	Delight	HO
N	Spirit	Science	VA
A	Power	Word	Life
I	Colours	Wisdom	Vertue

II. TABLE.

In this second Table, God is considered according to his Essence in Unity; what he is in Trinity without Nature and Creature, whereby he filleth all things, and yet needs no place.

TETRAGRAMMATON.

In this Table is considered the efflux of the Eternal Divine *WORD*; how the *WORD* through Wisedom brings it self from Unity into Separation and Multiplicity; as well in the Eternal Nature and Creature (according to which God calls himself angry jealous God, and a consuming fire ; as well as a mercifull God wherein is understood the foundation of Angels & Soules , and how they may receive salvation or damnation.)

In the *Septenary* without by it self , is understood the *Mysterium Magnum*, as the 7. properties of the Eternal Nature.

In the *Novenarie* downwards , are signifi'd the properties of Life.

In the fourth Form, as in Fire, 2. Principles separate themselves from each other, as Darkness and Light.

	Gods The	Wrath, first	or Dark Prin-ciple	World ciple	Gods The	Love, or Second	Light Prin-	World ciple.
	Simi-litude	1 T	2 I	3 N	4 C	5 T	6 V	7 R
E		Desire or Comprehending	Science or Drawing	Anguish	Fire	Light Love-fire	Sound	Essence
T		Dark	Feeling or Moving	Willing	Painful Life	Love-Life	Understanding	Working
ER		Austere Hardnes	Enmitie	Minde	Terror	Joy	Five Senses	Form
NAL		Sharpness	Elevating	Wheel of Life	Killing	Power	Love	Sperm
N		Furie	Pride	Despair	Hell	Glorie	Giving	Taking, or Coprehending
A		Greater Death	False will	Lesser Death	Souls ground Devill	Souls Spirit Angell	Praising	Increasing
T		Standing still	Breaking	From Original separating	Folly	Wisdom	Highnes	Humility
VR		Impotent	Self-will	Robbing	Fantasie	Knowledge	Strength	Throne

A. This lower A, is the object, or operation of the threefold I, or Spirit; from whence eternally spring Motion, Colours, and Vertue.

I, is the essential Effluence of the triple I, where the Trinity floweth forth into Unitie. And in this whole word ADONAI, is understood the Eternal life of Gods unity.

The word FATHER, is the Eternall beginning of operation and will in the threefold I of the Unitie.

The word SON, is that Operation of Power, as comprehension of the will into which the triple Spirit incloseth it self as a place of the divine (b) self-hood.

The word SPIRIT, is the living, issuing motion in the comprehended power; as by comparison may be understood in a Flower: where the opening or working of the growth, is the beginning; the power of the working, is the circumference and corporal comprehension of the growth; and the Scent [or smell] which proceedeth from the power, is the motion, or the growing issuing joy-life of the power, whereout the flower springeth; by which comparison may be seen, how the birth of divine power is typified.

The word *Power*, signifieth the breathing, going forth, understanding, and sensible life; as the foundation and fountain of the outflown knowledge of (c) distinction.

The word *Colours*, signifieth the subject, or object of Power, where the distinction and Original of the sensitive life and knowledge is understood; whence an Eternal contemplation existeth.

The word *Will*, signifieth the ebullition or motion in the opened Unitie; whereby the Unitie willeth it self into Trinitie, as the Nothing, into its proper something, wherein it hath its Motion and Action.

The word *Delight* [or *Lubet*] signifieth the effectual sensibility of the Will; as the highest ground of original love; where the will of the Abyss findeth its self in its (d) something, where it yields it self to something as to its sensibilitie, in which sensibility it worketh and willeth in its own Tast.

The word *Science*, signifieth the effectuall sensible knowledge and understanding in the love-tast; the root of the five Senses, and the ground of Eternal life: thence floweth the Understanding; and therein the Eternal Unitie (e) planteth it self.

The word, *Word*, signifieth how the Eternal love of the

(b) *Egoitas* Jchheit.   (c) Distinctness Unterscheiedligheit.   (d) *Aliquid* Etwas.

(e) Groundeth.

sensible unitie with knowledge speaketh forth it self eternally into an object: The *Word* is the speaking or breathing of the will out of the power by the understanding: It is the driving and forming of the eternal power into an infinitness of Multiplicitie; as the Creator of powers, out of the sole power in vertue.

The word *Wisedom*, is the outflown word, as an object of the divine knowledge of divine will; as essential power of the great love of God; from whence all things have received their motion and possibilitie: the ground of all the three *Principles*; A Revelation of the Unity of God; A passive essence of divine Operation; the foundation of all humility; the *Genetrix* of all knowledge of Creatures: An Eternal domicil of the active love of God, and a Ray and breath of the Omnipotent Spirit.

The word JEHOVAH, is the most holy Name of God, as the Divine sensual life, the only good; whereby the Holy Trinity, with Glory and Omnipotency, is understood; the life of the Abyss, as of the Unity; which chiefly standeth in the only love: And therein also is understood the most holy Name JESUS: as the egress'd I. is the ground and fountain of the breathing of Gods Unitie, and a forming of the understanding.

For the egress of the Unity, leadeth it self with the I into E, as in the fight or beholding of a *Chaos*; wherein the *Mysterium magnum* (according to the Divine manner) is understood; and is a triple breathing of the powers.

JE, is the breathing of the Unitie. HO, is the breathing of the JE. VA, is the breathing of the HO, and yet is only one breathing; but maketh a triple egress, of the 3. Centres or comprehensions. And therein is understood, how the triple I, at last closeth it self in A, as in a beginning to Nature.

Under [VA] standeth *Life*, signifying, that this threefold breathing, is a real life and power.

Under that, standeth *Vertue*, which signifieth, the immense *Vertue* of such a breathing life.

Now in this Table is rightly understood, what God, without Nature and Creature, is, in *Trinitie*; as in a triple breathing of the Unitie in it self; where nothing can be said of the place, or dimension of his habitation: for God is neither here, nor there, but every where alike; as the Abyss is consider'd, namely the

Eternall Unitie without Nature and Creature: and thus is he an active power and essence of Unity. But that really such power and vertue is therein, may well be understood, in the effluence of the world, and the Creatures therein, generated by the breath of God: and there is nothing in the being of this world, which beareth not witness thereof, if truly considered.

TETRAGRAMMATON

In this Table is also manifested how the holy Name of the Eternall power; with the knowledge hereof, from Eternity to Eternity; bringing it self into properties, in Nature to eternal light and darkness; and how the word of breathing forth, brings it self into a subject, and how self-will and acceptation of properties arise in the subject; wherein two Essences are always understood; as God's own effluence; and then the properties own acceptation in the free will; in which acceptation another ex-ternall kinde of subject is understood; whereby the Unity in its Effluence becomes more external; and thereby the Eternal love bringeth it self into a sensibleness, and like a fiery flame, as in the working of divine Power.

At the upper end of the Table standeth *Dark World*; and under, The first *Principle*: and over-against it standeth *Gods Love, Light World*, and below it, from the figure 4. to the figure 7. the second *Principle*; which signifieth how the outflown will doth inclose and overshadow it self, with acceptation of its own desire; and with the self desire bringeth it self into properties, and causeth Darkness; in which Darkness the egressed *one* by fire in the Light is revealed and made sensible; and is the cause of the Light; in which Light Gods love assumeth a fiery operation, from the fire of eternal Nature, and shineth in fire through the dark painful acceptation; even as the light from a Candle, or day in the Night; whence day and night have their names in Time; but in the (*f*) Eternal, there is also an Eternal light and darkness in one another: the Darkness is the ground of Nature; and the Light is the ground of the joyful Divine Revelation.

_____

(*f*) In the Eternal, is an Eternal light; but in the time here on Earth, darkness is the ground of Nature; and light the ground of the Kingdom of joy, the Revelation of God; that we may behold his works and our selves.

The Dark world, as the ground of the properties of self-desire and will, is called the first *Principle*; because it is the cause of Divine Revelation, according to sensibilitie; and also maketh a (*g*) proper Kingdom in it self, as namely painfull torment; according to which God calleth himself an Angry Jealous God, and a consuming fire.

And the Light which is revealed in the fire, wherein the unity of the divine effluence of Love is understood, is called the second *Principle*, as the divine Power-world wherein Gods love is a love-fire, and active life; as it is written, God dwelleth in a Light which no man can approach unto: for the power of the unity of God worketh in the Light, and is God; and the fiery quality in the Light is of the eternal Nature; wherein the Eternal love of the unity Perceiveth and loveth it self.

Below the first and second *Principles* (in the 7. spaces) stand seven numbers; which signifie the seven properties of the Eternal Nature; And under it standeth TINCTUR, distributed in the seven spaces; which signifieth the Divine Word in the (*h*) Temperature, or equality of the seven properties; wherein the divine powers lie in an equall will, action, and being; as the outflown name of God, wherein is understood the great Mysteries of Divine power and operation; with the characters of the letters [on the left side] divided into the seven Properties.

For the word *Tinctur*, is that separating word, from whence flow the seven properties.

T, is the *Tau*, or the opening of the Unitie [*monas*] the cross of the triple I a ground to the breathing.

I, is the effluence from *Tau*, or the egress of the Unity, as the cross-Angle of life.

N, is the effluence of the sounding Threefold spirit.

C, is the cutting of the sound; where the I as the effluence of Unitie, separateth it self again from Darkness, and where the (*i*) acceptation of the Eternal will breaketh.

T, under the figure 5. is that holy *Tau*, or the opening of Glory, in the fiery sensibility, openeth with (*j*) firing love, as with

---

(*g*) Own 𝔊𝔦𝔤𝔢𝔫.   (*h*) Moderation or mean.   (*i*) Or a willing receiving 𝔄𝔫𝔫𝔢𝔥𝔪𝔩𝔦𝔤𝔨𝔢𝔦𝔱.

(*j*) 𝔉𝔢𝔴𝔯𝔢𝔫𝔡𝔢𝔫 𝔏𝔦𝔢𝔟𝔢.

Gods Kingdom: and signifieth the great strength of the Light-Power.

V, is the true Character of the Holy Spirit with three points, the two upward signify the Fire and Light, and the third downward signifieth the Unity in love, as the meekness.

R, with this the holy fire and light, is comprehended in an active natural essence; for it signifieth the Kingdom, as the Throne; and hereby is intimated, how the holy Name with the outflown will introduceth it self in *Mysterium Magnum*, as into the Eternal mystery, whereout (*k*) existed the visible world.

The great Mysteries of the Tinctur, *or the highest ground of Gods Trinitie.*

T, is the triple I, the Father.

I, is that begotten I, JESUS.

N, is the threefold I, in Spirit.

C, signifieth CHRIST.

T, in the fifth Space, is the *Father in Christ.*

U, is the Spirit of Christ in the Word, which quickneth.

R, is the Royall Throne, about which Darkness and Light strive; there Satan and Christ stand against one another; namely according to the assumption of Satans self-will, as an Erronious Spirit, and according to the Unity, Christ; where is understood Love and Anger in one Ground; but in a two-fold Revelation. Here are understood those that belong to God; the other, (*l*) a Lock rather, at this place.

In this Table in the 7. Spaces is the ground of Angels and Soules; as that *Great Mystery* of the change, in which lyeth all Possibility. Sidewayes, after the seven figures, the efflux from (*m*) one into seven, is understood. The *first Principle* is to be understood, unto the *Fire*; out of which the *Light* is manifested: And from *Fire* to *Essence*, the *Second Principle*. And downward under every *Propertie*, is understood, what kind of Effluence, out of every property, in the cooperation of other properties, doth proceed; yet not so to be understood that *One* propertie alone, gives the efflux; but all seven afford it; though the *first Form* is

---

(*k*) *Originalis*, is outspoken.

(*l*) Ein Schlos darfer an diesem Dithe.

(*m*) Monas.

predominant therein, and retains the higher Regiment.

As under the figure I. standeth *Desire* or *Comprehending*, whereby is understood, that the *Desire* is *Magnetick*, and incloseth, and darkneth it self, which is also the ground of *Temporal* and *Eternal darkness*, and from that (*n*) attraction, cometh (under it) *Sharpness*, *Austereness* and *Hardness*; and is the Original of wrathfulness, whence ariseth the *Great Eternal Death*. For this *Magnet*, draweth the Powers into it self, and in it self incloseth them; so that the working *Standeth still*, and steps into *Impotency*; as under the Number 1. appeareth.

Under number 2. standeth *Science* or *Drawing*, which is the second Form to Nature; as the motion of the *Magnetick* attraction, from whence the sensibility of Nature existeth; and is the *ground of all Contraries*, for *Hardness* and *Motion* are Enemies; Motion breaketh the hardness again, and yet also begetteth Hardness by attraction. Thus two Essences have their existence in the desirous out-flown-will of God; as the drawing of the *Magnetick* power, giveth Motion and Sensibilitie; and the thing attracted affordeth Essence; wherein is understood the cause (*o*) of Spirit and Body; as in the attracting of Sensibilitie is caused the Spirit; and in the extracted, the body or cause to Corporietie. Now if this attraction and Effence be not able to reach the *Light* of Gods *Unity*, whereby it may be mollified; then in it self remaineth onely a Meer Enmitie, and is the cause of the torment of Fury and ambition: whence existeth self-pleasing, and Pride; for the will of self-pleasing is a false-will, a continuall corruptor of it self, and its Essence.

And in these two Forms, *Desire* and *In-drawing*, in their out-flown Properties, is understood Gods *Wrath*; and though they be the ground of the sensible life, Yet if the light shineth therein, then are they the ground of the Joy-Kingdom, as an inward motion of Gods Unitie; and a ground of the five Senses; whence also the creatural life hath taken its beginning; and therein standeth its (*p*) corruption, so farr as it loseth the light: for it is the *Spring* of Hellish Anguish, as the *cause* of painfulness; and is also the *Root* of Natural life.

In the *third space* standeth the *third Form* of Nature called *Anguish*, as a spiritual *Sulphur-source*, according to its *propertie*: This taketh its Ground from the first and Second Form; as from the *Magnetick Desire*, and from the Motion of Drawing; where the out-flown Eternal will, in that unquietness standeth in Anguish. This Anguish is the cause of Natural Will, Mind, and the Senses, and is the Wheel of Life, as the cause of the Firing-life: for when the out-flown-will of Gods Unitie standeth in *Anguish*, then it longeth again after Unity, as after Rest, and the Unity or Rest longeth after Motion and Revelation, for in the Unity there can be no Revelation without Motion; and therefore the Divine will freely floweth out of it self; and the Divine (*q*) good pleasure in the out-flown-will, bringeth it self into a Desire and Motion unto a sensibility; that it may perceive it self, and remain two in one Essence; as the sensible Divine delight, and the cause of sensibility; wherein God calleth himself a Loving God, according to the sensibilitie of Divine Love-delight; and an Angry God according to the cause of sensibility; as after the Eternal Nature. And thus, we understand by *Anguish* (when the divine Light is not revealed therein) the Hellish fire, and an Eternal despair and Terrour: where the Self-will of Nature continually standeth in a dying Torment; ever desiring to be released from such a condition, which I therefore call the (*r*) lesser Death; it is the Eternal dying Death; but in the Hardness, it is the great still-standing Death. This Form if it hath not Light, is the head-spring of the false minde; but if it perceiveth Light in it self, then is it the spring and ground of the sensible mind, and the right root of fire, as appeareth in number 3. downwards.

The fourth *Form*, numb. 4. is the *Fire* of the Eternal Nature; understand spiritual Life-fire: and that existeth from a continual conjunction or conjoyning of *Hardness* and *Motion*. Understand, that thence ariseth the *Painfulness*; but the *Splendor* existeth from the Delight of the *Free-will*; where the *Unity* of the *Delight* [*good pleasure*] is acuated in the properties; then like a flash [*of lightning*] it shineth through the continued Conjunction, of the great meekness of the Unity, and the *Fierceness* and *Motion* of the three first *Properties*; for then it is in the Essence of the Conjunction, as if Steel and Stone were rubb'd together; whence the flash ariseth. Such a *Flash*, is the true Natural *Life* of the *Eternal*; for it is the Revelation of Divine Motion, and hath the properties of Nature; and also the Revelation of the Unity of Gods effluence in it self. Now which of these two getteth predominancy, in that standeth the Life.

The splendor of the *Fire*, is the Light from the effluence of Gods Unity; and the Essence of the *Fire* is the out-flown will, which hath brought it self with the desire into such Properties. Thus in the out-flown fiery will, we understand *Angels* and *Souls*; and in the sensible sharpened Lights power from the Unitie, we understand the Spirit wherein God is revealed, and understood in the spiritual essence; and in the Fire two Kingdomes separate themselves, as the Kingdom of Glory from the efflux of Gods Unity, and the Kingdom of the properties of Nature; and yet [these two Kingdoms] dwell in one another as one. The Kingdom of Nature is in it self, that great *Eternal Darkness*, but the Light is the Kingdom of God; of which *S John* saith, *The Light shineth in darkness, but the darkness comprehendeth it not*. As day and night dwell in one another, and yet the one is not the other.

Thus from the Fires own propertie, comes the painful life, if it break it self off from the Eternal Light, and doth (as in the propertie of selfhood) enter the object; then is it only fantastick and foolish; even such as the Devills were, and the Souls of the Damned are; as appears Numb. 4. downwards.

In the *fifth Propertie of Nature*, is the second *Principle*, with its foundation understood; (as the Essence of the Unity in the Light-power) where in the out-flown Unity is a fire-flaming-love understood, whence existeth the true understanding-Spirit, with the five Senses.

The first three *Forms* are only the property to Life; and the fourth is the Life it self; but the fifth is the true Spirit. When the fifth property is revealed out of the Fire, then she dwelleth in all the rest, and changeth them all into her sweet love, that no more painfulness nor Enmity is discerned, but even as the day changeth the night.

In the first 4. *Properties*, is that life like the Devills; but when the Lights-power (as the second Principle) is revealed in the property, then is it an Angel, and liveth in divine power and holiness, as appeareth in the Num. 5. downwards.

The sixth Property, is the Understanding, as the *Sound*, where the properties in the Light stand all in an equality; then they rejoyce, and the power of the five Senses is manifest, and all the properties rejoyce in one another; and thus the love of the Unity leadeth it self into working, willing, sensibility, finding, and (s) certitude. Thus is there a contrary in the *Eternal Nature*; that the Properties existing therein, the love is known, and that there might be something, to be beloved, wherein the Eternal Love of Gods Unity may work, and God may be praised. For if the properties of life be penetrated with the Divine love-flame, then they praise the great love of God, and yield themselves all again into the Unity of God. Such rejoycing and knowledge could not be revealed in the Unity, did not the Eternal will bring it self into painfull moving properties.

The Seventh Property, is that Essence, wherein all the other are essential; wherein they all act, as the Soul doth in the Body: wherein the Natural, Essential, Eternal *Wisdom* of God (as the *Mysterium Magnum*) is understood; out of which the visible World, with its Essence and Creatures, did arise.

Thus by this Table is understood the hidden Spiritual world, as the Eternal manifestation of God; from whence the Angels and Souls of Men received their existence; therefore may they turn themselves to evill or good, for both lie in their Center.

This Spiritual world is no other than Gods revealed Word, and hath its being from Eternity to Eternity; for therein is Heaven and Hell understood.

(s) Highness **Hochkeit.**

III. TABLE. The seven Properties of the visible World, or external Nature. MACROCOSMUS In this Table is signified, how the hidden Spiritual, Eternal Word, (as the *Mysterium magnum*) by the motion of *Gods Word* issued forth, and became visible, manifest, and Material ; And how the inward Powers, through Gods working, have comprehended and fashioned themselves; how good and bad in every thing is to be understood ; and yet there was no evill in *Mysterium magnum*, but existed through the sensibility and assumption of self-desire. Here also is shewed what in the working issued forth from every property, and which have the predominancy; according to which every thing is formed and governed.	1 *Ground*	2 *of*	3 *Nature*	4 *Pure*	5 *Element*	6 *Para-*	7 *dise*
	Cold, Earth, Snow	Orig.nal of Air	Fire of Essence	Heaven	Light of Nature	Stars	Water
MACROCOSMUS	Saturn	Mercury the planet	Mars	Sol	Venus Soft	Jupiter	Luna
	Sal	Mercury thunder	Sulphur Flash	Sal-niter	Oyl	Power	Body
	Black, Gray	Mixt-colours	Red	Yellow	Green, and white within	Blew	white without within Red and Green
	Melancholy	Collerick		Sanguin		Phlegmatick	
	Grossness of Stone	Metal, Stone	Rust	Growing	Pearls	Jewels	Menstruum
	Lead	Quicksilver	Iron, Steel	Gold	Copper	Tinn	Silver
	Bone wood	Herbs	Resin	Tincture in the Earth	Sweet	Bitter	Grass
	Sour	Puyten	Woes	Opening	Healing	Strengthning	Flesh
	Stopping	Smelling	Feeling	Seeing	Tasting	Hearing	Loathing of Nature
	Dying	Lying	Wrath War	Richess	Noble	Reason	Own possession
	Lord	Craft	Force	Justice	Faithfull	Truth	Simplicitie
	Stealing	Deceiving	Losing	Finding	Earthly Love	being friendly	Light-minded
	Obstinate Sad	Confounded Senses	Careless	Constant	Pure	Joyfull	Ignorant
	Earthly	Beastly	Evill	Heavenly	Modest	Sensible	Low
	Wolfe	Fox	Dogg	Lyon	Bird	Ape	Great Beasts
	Worms	Venemous Wormes	Evill Beasts	Good Beasts	Flying Beasts	Tame Beasts	Fish.

An Explanation of the third Table

MACROCOSMUS

In this Table is understood, how the hidden spiritual world hath made it self visible; and with its own breathing forth, hath made it (*a*) an object where the Eternal *Principles* are out-flown; and the powers therein became co-material. For the External Nature is

(*a*) Gegenswurff.

no other than an efflux or object of the Eternal Nature. The 4.
Elements exist from the first 4 Properties of the Eternal Nature;
as the Earth and grossness of all Essences of the Dark desire,
where the other six Properties alwayes became co-material; as we
may conceive of Metals and Powers, good and bad. The Air
existeth from the motion of the *Magnetick* Impression; The Water
from the abruption [breaking off] of the Impression, where Heat
and Cold are in Strife; the Fire of the spiritual fire. The cold is
Perceived in the *Magnetick* sharpness, as in the right root to Fire.

Before the seven Properties, above the Table, standeth
Ground of Nature distributed in the three first Forms. And in the
fourth and fifth Form or propertie, is divided the word (*b*) *Pure
Element.*

With the word *Ground of Nature*, is understood the root of the
4. Elements, as the four causes of Motion and Sensibility. By the
word *Pure Element*, is understood the Temperature, or the equalitie of Nature, and the four Elements; where the Light also is
sensible, Moving, and Elemental. Thus is understood, how the
Eternal Element, as the motion of Divine Power is actuated by
the ground of Nature, and revealed in the Light; where the pure
Element is the motion of the inward Spiritual world; and at the
Creation of the world, went forth into a Being; and is understood
of the fifth *Effence.*

The word *Paradise* in the 6. and 7. Properties, signifieth the
spiritual work in the Lights Essence; as a springing up, or
spiritual growth, which at the beginning of the world, sprung up
through all the 4. Elements; and out of the Earth formed it self
into all manner of fruits, and changed all the properties of
wrathfulness into a Temperature. But when those fierce properties, with the 4. Elements, were awakened, by the alienated
desire, and false will in *Adam*, and attain'd the Dominion, then
the Greening [springing forth] retyr'd back; that is, it remayned
in the *Tincture* of the inward Ground, and is yet in the 4.
Elements, but, in the Inward *Pure* Element only; and may not be
attain'd but in the New birth of the inner man; and in the material

---

(*b*) The Pure Element is the equality in the Elements; and is called the *Quint-essence* of the
Element; as the *Tincture* of the equality of Nature: both are that occult *Arcannm* so much
fought for.

Tincture, wherein the Paradisical working is also fully manifest to our understanding.

This Table sheweth from whence all Essences [or Beings] in this world did arise; and what the Creator is; namely that the Creator hath been the divine power world; which the (*c*) Unity, as the Eternal will, hath moved, which will, is God himself, (*d*) But the Separator or Divider, was the owt flown will in the spiritual world; in such motion, he issued out of himself, and made him a subject for his working; in which motion, one subject issued out of another continually, untill the external matter of the Earth (through the divine motion) was drawn into a *Mass* or *Chaos*: and this drawing of the Motion standeth thus still: all things therefore fall in the deep towards the Earth; and that is the reason, that all Power of motion, even to this day, and to the end of Time, continueth so.

The seven Dayes, and seven Planets, signify the seven Properties of the spiritual world, The three Principle *in Spiritu Mundi* as *Sal*, *Sulphur*, and *Mercurius*, signifie the Trinity of the divine Revelation; as an everlasting Spring or Fountain, whereout all external Creatures are flown, do flow, and will flow, even to the end of this time; and therein the Separator, with the 7 *Properties*, is understood. In this Table we see what proceeded from the 7 *Properties*; and how the Spiritual power hath brought it self into a Material one (as in the *seven spaces* downwards appears) whereby we may understand whence Good and Evill sprung up in this World.

An Explanation of the fourth Table

MICROCOSMUS

In this Table, (*a*) *Man* is held forth as a similitude of the Three worlds, according to the Soul, Spirit, and Body; What he hath been in the beginning, according to his Creation; What he is

(*c*) Monas

(*d*) God made first the Angelical light world, which in this place (after the Devills Apostacie) separated into this external visible essence **Einheit.**

(*a*) What Man is in his Trinity; as first according to Paradise; Secondly, according to the Spirit of Error; Thirdly, according to the New-birth, which Christ teacheth and will have, *John 3*.

IV TABLE.

MICRO-COSMUS.

In this Table MAN is held forth; What he hath been in *Paradise*; as also how the *Properties* in him (without assuming Self-desire) equally stood in the Image of God: and what he is become through Satan's Deceits: what that Monster of the Serpent (whereby he is become earthly and mortal) is in him. And then how Gods Word and LOVE came in to help him again, new born in CHRIST, daily destroying that Serpentine Image: also in what danger & misery he standeth in such an Image, either on the ground of Hell or Heaven. Also a similitude of Divine Revelation and Knowledg in the seven *Properties* according to *Time* and *Eternity*, formed out of all the *Three Principles*; for a further understanding how he is wisely to regulate his Life; and unto what driving (impulsion) he should yield himself.

Humane Ground before and after the FALL	1 ℏ Saturday	2 ☿ Wednesday	3 ♂ Tuesday	4 ☉ Sunday	5 ♀ Friday	6 ♃ Thursday	7 ☽ Monday
	TINCTURE		**SOULE**		**SPIRIT**		**BODY**
Adam in Paradise	Desire	Motion	Sensibility	Seeing	Loving	Rejoycing	Peavenly flesh
Erring sp.	Sharpness	Anger	Pain	Bitter woe	Hating	Despair	Passion
Christ	Gods word	Life	Acceptance	Sweet	Glorie	Power	Divine Essence
Adam in Paradise	Similitude	Out going Spirit	Heating	High	Humble Will	Praising	Unity
Sathan	self-seeking	Self-knowl.	Self-will	Dominiering	Pride	Reproaching	Folly
Christ	Gods unity	Resignation	Suffering	Yielding	Desire	Equality of Power	Wisdom
Adam in Paradise	Tasting	Thinking	Mind	Understanding	Spirit	Speaking	Electrum of Nature
Sathan	Desire of division	Lying	Anguish	Doubting	Fall	Stinck	Extruding
Christ	Baptism	Law	Breaking	Hoping	Humility	Believing	Genius or Type
Adam in Paradise	Strength	Pentrating	Might	Holy	Modest	Powerfull	Throne
Sathan	Lord	Potent	Malice	Thirsty	Wanton	Mad	Self honor
Christ	Humility	Obedience	Mercy	Forgiving	Going	Generating	reverence
Adam in Paradise	Angel	Officious	Mild	Friendly	Beauty	Vertue	Diligent
Sathan	Devill	Perverse	Theevish mind	Murther	Belial's Whore	Poyson	Earthly flesh
Christ	Christ	returning	repentance	New life	Holy	Restoring	Sophia
Adam in Paradise	Heaven	Child like	Secret	Manifest	Singing	Sounding	Paradise
Sathan	Hell or Perdition	Strife	Torment	Ever falling	Fantasie	Changing	A Den of the Deep
Christ	Christs Calling,	Teaching,	Dissolving,	New-mind,	Rejoicing	Praying,	Springing.

become in the fall, by the Spirit of Error; and What he will be in the new birth through the Spirit of Christ; which is a true Essential Image, out of three Principles of the Divine Revelation; as from the outflown Word of the Divine will.

Man according to the Soul, is an Eternal Nature of the firing quality, as a spark out of the Centre, from whence the fire existeth: If this ground cannot reach into the divine Light; then is it a Darkness of the *Magnetick* attractive desiring power; but if he reacheth out of the fire, unto the light, that his *Magnetick* desire feeds on the out flown Unity of Gods Love; then ariseth from that fire the good true Spirit, even as light shineth out of a Candle. These are now two Principles, the *Soul*, in the fire of Eternal Nature; and the *Spirit* in the light of Divine Power. But the Body is the third Principle; as an Essence of the visible world, from the Starrs and Elements, formed into an Image, out of the seven Properties of Nature.

The Soul hath the seven Properties of the inward Spiritual world, according to Nature; But the Spirit of the Soul is without these Properties; (*b*) for it standeth out of Nature, in Gods unity but through the Souls firie Nature, is manifested in the Soul; for it is the true Image of God; as an *Idea*, in which God himself worketh and dwelleth; so far as the Soul brings her desire into God, and submits unto Gods Will: if that be not done, then is this *Idea*, or Spirit of the Soul, dumb and actless [not working], standing like an Image in a Looking-Glass, which soon vanisheth, and hath no being, as it befell *Adam* in the Fall. But if the Soul submits to God, and bringeth its Magnetick hunger into Gods Love, the Soul then attracteth divine Essence, namely, the Essential Wisedom of God; then her *Idea* or *Spirit* becometh Essential in the Lights power, and obtaineth a pious life; as being then the true Temple of God, wherein Gods Unity is revealed and operative.

But if the Soul herself with her desire, bring in self-love; and with her desire turn herself into the seven Properties, to try them; and feedeth on the vain delights of the seven Properties; then she extolls herself, and maketh to herself an (*c*) *Evestrum*, as an Astrall Object; which *Evestrum* presently hungreth after the vanity of the false delight; even as it befell *Lucifer* and *Adam*, where the

---

(*b*) N. B. The Difference between the Soul, and the Spirit of the Soul which without God, is but a dead Image.

(*c*) *Evestrum* is a continued Astral Influence in the 4. Elements, and likewise, an Astral Spirit in Man.

Evestrum of *Lucifer* imagined it self into a *Phantasie*; and the *Evestrum* of *Adams* Soul, into the Animalish Properties of the External world; whereby the Soul was poysoned, and the Body (out of the Earth's *Limus*) was suddenly infected; that the (*d*) Animalish properties awakened in him, and longed after Earthly, Beastly sustenance; as Heat, Cold, Sharp, Bitter, Sweet and Sour; and with these Properties introduced it self into a springing fountain of such delights; and so with the desire, *Fed* on *Good* and *Evill*; whereby the *Image of God*, as the *Idea*, became obscure and unactive. Thus the true Spirit (as the active *Idea*) became dumb and dead, even as an Image in a Looking-glass; and so was the Soul cut of from God, and stood in a Naturall will; but Gods will in the Spirit worked work'd no more; and the will of the *Evestrum* (as the Opposite Image of the dark eternal world began [to work], for the holy *Genius* was changed.

At the head of this Table standeth TINCTUR divided into the seven Properties; which signifieth the Equalitie of the seven Properties according to the Soul and Body that in the first man before the fall, the propertie [or inclination] to separation, (*e*) and Acceptation, stood in a like will; and all its desires were brought into Gods Unitie: thus were they the true Paradise; for the Essential Spirit with the Unity of God, was revealed in them, who were to work through Gods Love in all things. But the Devill envied them, and with his false Lust deceived the seven Properties of life, and perswaded them, it would be good for them, and they should become wise; if the Properties (each one according to its kinde) would introduce themselves into self-Acceptance, then should the Spirit tast and know what was Good and Evill: but then it could not subsist in Gods Unity, of that he told them nothing.

But no sooner had they brought themselves in their own lusts, than such a strife and contention awakned in them, that all the Properties began to be formed in their self-hood.

Thus the Unity, as the Element, was broken [or divided], and

_____

(*d*) How the holy similitude of God in Man became quenched, and a monstrous Image assumed.

(*e*) Acceptabilitie **Annehmligkeit.**

the four Elements strove for predominance, whereupon suddenly from without, fell in the Inequality, as *Heat* and *Cold*, and the *Astral* division working in the Body; and Gods wrath (according to the Dark worlds propertie) in the Soul; (*f*) which caused in them (according to the Soul), Horror, Anguish, Necessity, and Eternal despair; and in the Body, arose Heat, Cold, Woes, Sickness and a Mortal life. Thus Gods Image, the whole man, fell from his Ordinance; and became a disguised monster: and the awakened Properties presently began to set up their Government, with Envying, Murthering, Raging, Tearing and Tormenting. Love was changed into Pride and self-love; Desire, into Covetousness; Sensibility, into Envy; and the lifes fire, into wrath: Thus was the Hellish foundation, in the whole Man, revealed, and ruled both in Soul and Body.

Now this Hellish Foundation, is the Spirit of Errour; for which man must have been damned, had not the Divine mercy, the Serpent-treader (as the efflux of Gods love) after the fall, been presently (*g*) promised to the New birth, in the Holy Name Jesus. Which holy Name hath, in meer mercy, and great humility for mans soul and body, given it self forth, assumed humanity, broken the power of the diabolical Spirit of Error, killed the lives self-will, and brought again the Properties into Gods Unity. There the true Spirit (as the human *Idea* and Gods *Image*) is renewed again, and filled with the Divine Love-Essence. And thus the human Soul, through Christs Soul and Spirit in that love and divine Essence, hath again attain'd an open Gate unto God.

Thus in this Table is held forth [or drawn to the life] what *Adam* hath been; what, through the Fall, he is become; and how he is again Redeemed; (*h*) and what is his New birth out of Christ Spirit. And these are delineated in the seven Properties under the Word TINCTUR. In which Properties the Soul hath its *Center*, and in which the Spirit, and in which the Body [have their *Centers* also] of which the Reader may further consider; for under them

---

(*f*) Thus was our Nature first corrupted: which ground was never before so plainly discovered.

(*g*) *Origin is in-spoken.*

(*h*) Souls ground. 1, 2, 3. first Princip. Souls Spirit out of God 4, 5, 6. second Princip. the Body. 7. Heavenly, now earthly.

stand the seven Dayes of the week, intimating, that Man is even the fame.

This Table sheweth what Man is internally and externally; first according to the good *Adam*, and then according to the corrupted *Adam*; and also what he is again in Christ. Whereby, we may understand, how Evill and Good is man; and whence exist the Propertie of good and evill, both in the mind and senses.

By the word *Sathan* (signifying the Spirit of Errour) is not understood a Creaturely-Devill; but the Spring [or fountain] of the Spirit of Error.

And by the word *Christ*, is understood the New-Man (according to the internal) in the Spirit of Christ. The other spaces, are understood as in the other Tables; wherein is understood the cause of mutation.

FINIS

Of further interest . . .

RUDOLF STEINER
ESSENTIAL READINGS

Selected and Edited by Richard Seddon

Rudolf Steiner (1861-1925) was a supersensitive with a scientific education, a pairing which enabled him to combine both poles of life in a unique way. His spiritual research was as systematic as any science, and his rigorous path of self-development clearly mapped out for anyone to follow.

Anthroposophy, the path of wisdom and knowledge he initiated, is man-centred and holistic, and this volume plots its philosophy—man's struggle to attain full spiritual stature through the practical application of the forces brought by Christ. Steiner saw the spirit as the creative element in evolution, and his work is now being accepted as a practical vitalizing force for today's world.

EMANUEL SWEDENBORG
ESSENTIAL READINGS

Edited and Introduced by Michael Stanley

Emanuel Swedenborg was born in 1688, and three hundred years on he is remembered mainly for his visionary insight and his theological writings. He was, however, a man with interests both worldly and other-worldly—his studies in physics, mineralogy, anatomy, psychology, and spiritualism all anticipated major modern discoveries well before their time.

To anyone familiar with the teachings of the New Age, much of Swedenborg's spiritual work will seem familiar. By drawing on the intuitive source within, he discovered an essential key to wisdom, a key highly relevant to the now growing endeavour to grasp holistically the physical and spiritual dimensions of life. Arranged by subject and carefully explained, his ESSENTIAL READINGS finally make Swedenborg's seminal work accessible to the modern reader.